D0324014

Organizing for Transgender Rights

SUNY series in Queer Politics and Cultures

Cynthia Burack and Jyl J. Josephson, editors

Organizing for Transgender Rights

Collective Action, Group Development, and the Rise of a New Social Movement

ANTHONY J. NOWNES

Published by State University of New York Press, Albany

Printed in the United States of America

For information, contact State University of New York Press, Albany, NY
www.sunypress.edu

Library of Congress Cataloging-in-Publication Data

Names: Nownes, Anthony J., author.
Title: Organizing for transgender rights : collective action, group development, and the rise of a new social movement / Anthony J. Nownes.
Description: Albany : State University of New York Press, [2019] | Series: SUNY series in queer politics and cultures | Includes bibliographical references and index.
Identifiers: LCCN 2018014129 | ISBN 9781438473017 (hardcover : alk. paper) | ISBN 9781438473024 (ebook)
Subjects: LCSH: Transgender people—United States. | Pressure groups—United States. | Human rights—United States.
Classification: LCC HQ77.95.U6 N69 2019 | DDC 306.76/80973—dc23
LC record available at https://lccn.loc.gov/2018014129

10 9 8 7 6 5 4 3 2 1

Contents

Tables and Figures

Preface

If I have learned anything about transgender politics in the United States, it is due largely to my conversations with the transgender activists I interviewed for this book. And since this book is about them and not me, I will keep this preface short. Believe me when I say their words are more informative than mine ever could be. It is popular in some circles, especially in media, to assert that we are living in a "transgender moment." In some sense this may be true, as transgender rights issues are "front and center" in American politics in a way they never have been before. But talk of a "transgender moment" sometimes obscures the fact that transgender people have always existed in America, and always will. Moreover, for a transgender person, it goes without saying that every moment is a "transgender moment."

I started studying transgender rights interest groups several years ago primarily because I thought they could teach us a great deal about interest-group politics in general, especially about how oppressed and marginalized people organize to get a seat at the proverbial political table. But by the time I was done with this book, I had learned so much more. Specifically, I learned more than I ever could have imagined about things that America is supposed to be about—the freedom to be left alone, the ability to control your own body and your own destiny, and the ability to appeal to representative government if your rights are trampled. On the one hand, what I learned did not always make me feel good about my country. America, sadly, has not always lived up to its alleged ideals. On the other hand, the stories I heard from transgender rights activists—some transgender people themselves, others not—were transcendent. "Inspiring" is almost too banal a word to use here, which is why I chose the word "transcendent." I will not bore you with a list of clichés about the strength and resolve and impressiveness of these people. It must suffice at this point for me to say that virtually without exception, the people I describe in this book typically display more strength and radiate more dignity in one day than I've been able to muster over a period of years.

I want to acknowledge my limitless debt to the people who made this book possible, my respondents. Most of them are named in the pages that follow. Without demeaning the contribution of any of my respondents (they were, without exception, patient, gracious, and informative), I will single out a few for mention. First, thank you Dallas Denny, University of Tennessee graduate and transgender rights pioneer. You read everything I ever sent you, you tolerated a lot of dumb questions, and you even availed me of your formidable copy-editing skills (at no charge!). Your website is a treasure trove of information about the movement you helped develop, and you continue to fight the good fight, for which so many of us are grateful. Second, thank you Riki Wilchins, another transgender rights pioneer and gracious confidante. You too answered any and all of my questions, you responded to late night emails, and you even showed me some of your own work, which deserves a wider audience than mine does to be sure. Third, thank you Tony Barreto-Neto, transgender rights pioneer, musician, early LGB rights activist, peacemaker, and police officer. I am proud to call you my friend (do not worry, scholarly distance dissolved only *after* this project was complete); many of your words serve as advice to me every day even if you did not mean them that way.

Finally, thank you to the most important person in my life, Elsa M. Nownes. Yes, it is a cliché to thank your spouse. But how could I *not* thank someone who somewhat regularly during the course of my research for this book uttered phrases such as, "Well that's interesting," "Hmmm, tell me more," and "Really, that's amazing!"

1

Introduction

Organizing for Transgender Rights in the United States

In 2013, the American Psychiatric Association (APA) updated its *Diagnostic and Statistical Manual of Mental Disorders* (today known as *DSM-5*), replacing the term "gender identity disorder" with "gender dysphoria" (Beredjick 2012). This change did not receive as much attention as the APA's landmark reclassification of homosexuality in 1973, but it was significant nonetheless. A year later, the Department of Justice announced that discrimination on the basis of gender identity constituted sex discrimination under Title VII of the Civil Rights Act of 1964, and the Department of Health and Human Services announced that it would no longer stop Medicare from covering gender reassignment surgery (McLaughlin 2015). And, by the end of 2016, twenty states, the District of Columbia, and hundreds of local jurisdictions in states without statewide protections (including Atlanta, Miami, and New Orleans), had laws on the books banning employment discrimination on the grounds of gender identity (Transgender Law Center n.d.). In short, in recent years, gender-variant people—including those we now call transgender people—have won public policy victories that seemed unwinnable just a few short years ago.

What accounts for these victories? While the answer to this question is undeniably multifarious, one answer lies in *the rise of transgender rights interest groups in the United States*. Transgender rights interest groups and the other components of the larger movement have worked tirelessly over the years to advance the cause of transgender rights in the United States. And, in some cases, they have been successful. How did these groups manage to mobilize in the face of substantial barriers to formation and survival? And how did transgender rights advocacy groups go from virtually nonexistent in the 1950s, 1960s, and 1970s to more numerous in the 2000s and 2010s? These are the questions I address in this book. I hope that answering them can help us understand more about how other oppressed and marginalized people can overcome the barriers to collective action and form viable organizations to represent their interests.

The Rise of Transgender Rights Advocacy

A precursory look at the contemporary American political landscape shows that there are now twenty or so politically active organizations representing transgender people at the national level and hundreds more at the state and local levels. This is a relatively new state of affairs. As late as 1985, only a few national-level organizations dedicated even tangentially to transgender rights advocacy had managed to form and survive for any period of time. These included the pioneers of transgender organizing—the Erickson Educational Foundation (founded in 1964), the Harry Benjamin International Gender Dysphoria Association (now the World Professional Association for Transgender Health, 1979), the National Transsexual Counseling Unit (1968), Transsexual Action Organization (1970), and Tri-Ess (1976) (Beemyn 2014; Stryker 2008). In truth, calling any of these groups either "national-level" or "advocacy groups" at all is a stretch (I will have more to say about this later), and only two of them (the second and last) remained alive in 1985. But they were the proverbial only games in town for two decades. State, local, and regional transgender rights group numbers were quite low as well.

But weren't interest groups comprising the burgeoning gay and lesbian rights movement representing the rights of transgender people during this period? No. Despite the crucial role that transgender people played at Stonewall (1969) in particular and in the gay and lesbian rights movement in general in the late 1960s and early 1970s, nascent gay and lesbian rights organizations for the most part skirted the issue of transgender rights during these decades (Denny 2006, ch. 9). Indeed, throughout the 1960s, 1970s, and most of the 1980s, most LG and LGB groups resisted broadening their missions to include transgender rights (Rimmerman 2015). Not only were transgender people marginalized by many "mainstream" gay and lesbian rights organizations, but some gay and/or lesbian rights activists went as far as to openly criticize transgender people. In the dozen or so years after Stonewall, academic attacks, skepticism, and ostracization among gay and lesbian rights activists and organizations, as well as general societal marginalization, virtually banished transgender Americans and organizations from the political process.

All of this started to change in the late 1980s. Between 1986 and 2005, several nationally active, relatively well-funded transgender rights interest groups took root, including FTM International (founded in 1986), Gender Public Advocacy Coalition (GenderPAC 1995; now defunct), the National Center for Transgender Equality (2003), the National Transgender Advocacy Coalition (1999), the Sylvia Rivera Law Project (2002), the Transgender Law and Policy Institute (2000; now defunct), and the Transgender Legal Defense and Education Fund (2003). Moreover, during the same period, dozens of local and state transgender rights groups formed, including the Connecticut Transadvocacy Coalition (2002), the FTM Alliance of Los Angeles (2002), and the Massachusetts Transgender Coalition (2001), just to name a few. Since 2005, numerous additional state, local, and regional transgender rights groups have formed, including the Arkansas Transgender Equality Coalition (2014), the MetroTrans Umbrella Group (St. Louis, 2013), TransMaryland (2017), and countless others. By the end of 2016, a majority of states had some statewide and/or local group(s) working on behalf of transgender people. Today, virtually all of the country's largest and most influential LGB groups have "added the T"—that is, officially added transgender rights to their mission statements—including the Gay and Lesbian Victory Fund, Human Rights Campaign (HRC), Lambda Legal Defense and Education Fund, the National Center for Lesbian Rights, the National LGBTQ Task Force (formerly the National Gay and Lesbian Task Force), and PFLAG (formerly known as Parents, Families, and Friends of Lesbians and Gays).

In sum, transgender rights interest-group advocacy is now thriving in the United States (Taylor and Haider-Markel 2014). The proliferation of transgender rights interest groups has reshaped advocacy for both transgender individuals and gays and lesbians (Taylor and Lewis 2014). Indeed, not only are there numerous flourishing, influential organizations working on behalf of transgender people, but we now rarely think of LGB organizing without mentioning transgender people. It is my contention that all of this represents an important shift in contemporary American politics.

Transgender rights interest groups are important in their own right, as they have helped transform policy toward transgender people in America and raised awareness of transgender rights issues among the public. Thus, understanding the formation, survival, and proliferation of these groups can teach us a great deal about the determinants of policy change in an important policy area. But these groups are ideal for study for another reason as well—*they are exemplars of groups that represent historically marginalized and oppressed members of society*. Thus, by understanding the mobilization and proliferation of transgender rights interest groups, we can learn important general lessons about how organizations representing marginalized and oppressed people can form and maintain themselves in the face of widespread hate and misunderstanding, as well as the substantial barriers to collective action that all organizations face.

Overview of Major Findings

To address the research questions I pose above, I collected new quantitative and qualitative data on transgender rights interest groups in the United States. The quantitative data comprise an aggregation of the life histories of nationally active transgender rights interest groups in the United States founded between 1964 (the year that the first viable transgender rights advocacy group was formed) and 2016, as well as fragmentary (due to data limitations) data on the life histories of state, local, and regional groups during the same time period. I gathered this quantitative data primarily to "map" the population of groups I study and to discern the population's trajectory over time. The qualitative data comprise transcripts of extensive, original interviews with twenty-seven founders of transgender rights interest groups in the United States (see table 1.1). Twenty-four of the founders I interviewed spoke to me for attribution. I refer to the others as anonymous respondents. The quantitative and qualitative data allow me to undertake a comprehensive and detailed examination of the formation of transgender rights interest groups in the United States.

A Few Words about the Data and My Approach

While the quantitative data are useful, in the pages that follow, I rely primarily upon the qualitative data to reach conclusions. To examine this data, I engaged in *inductive* or *grounded qualitative analysis*. This entailed reading the interview transcripts iteratively, looking for dominant and significant themes, and bringing them to bear on my research questions. I coded seg-

Table 1.1. The interview subjects.

Name	*Group(s)*	*Jurisdictional Focus*	*Notes*
Melissa Alexander	TransOhio	State (Ohio)	
Anonymous #1	Anonymous Group #1	National	
Anonymous #2	Anonymous Group #2	National	
Anonymous #3	Anonymous Group #3	National	
Blake Alford	THEA+ (Transgender Health and Education Alliance)	State and local (Atlanta, Georgia)	
Anthony Barreto-Neto	Transgender Officers Protect and Serve (TOPS); Transexual Menace	National	Anthony was involved in the founding of two groups.
Thomi Clinton	Transgender Community Coalition	Local (Palm Springs, California)	
Loree Cook-Daniels	Transgender Aging Network	National	
Rachel Crandall	Transgender Michigan	State (Michigan)	
Masen Davis	FTM Alliance of Los Angeles	Local (Los Angeles)	
Dallas Denny	American Educational Gender Information Service (AEGIS)	National	Dallas was involved in the founding of several other organizations as well.
Justus Eisfeld	Global Action for Trans*Equality (GATE)	International, national	
Eli Erlick	Trans Student Educational Resources	National	
Brooke Cerda Guzman	TransWomen of Color Collective	National	

continued on next page

Table 1.1. *Continued.*

Name	*Group(s)*	*Jurisdictional Focus*	*Notes*
Mara Keisling	National Center for Transgender Equality; Transexual Menace	National	
Adrien Lawyer	Transgender Resource Center of New Mexico	State (New Mexico)	
Nancy Nangeroni	Boston Chapter, Transexual Menace; Gender Education and Media (GEM)	Local (Boston); National	Nancy was involved in the founding of two groups
Pauline Park	New York Association for Gender Rights Advocacy (NYAGRA)	State (New York)	
Jacqueline Patterson	Indiana Transgender Wellness Alliance	State (Indiana)	
Marisa Richmond	Tennessee Transgender Political Coalition	State (Tennessee)	
Joelle Ruby Ryan	Transgender New Hampshire	State (New Hampshire)	
Bamby Salcedo	TransLatin@ Coalition	National	
De Sube	Gender Expression Movement (GEM)	State and local (Hampton Roads, Virginia)	
Josephine Tittsworth	Texas Transgender Nondiscrimination Summit	State (Texas)	
Julie Walsh	GenderNexus	State (Indiana)	
Riki Wilchins	Transexual Menace; GenderPAC	National	Riki was involved in the founding of these two groups and others.
Andrea Zekis	Arkansas Transgender Equality Coalition	State (Arkansas)	

Source: Author's data.

ments of interview text on various aspects of interest-group formation (for example, "funding," "motivation"), and this allowed me to identify major themes (and a few minor ones). I read each interview transcript vertically (that is, from start to finish), but also horizontally, which means that I grouped segments of text across interviews by theme. Of course, my data analysis was not an entirely inductive exercise. To structure my interviews, I relied upon an interview protocol (see appendix A), which I developed after reading the extant scholarship on interest-group formation, and material on transgender history and politics. In this sense, my approach is also deductive.

It is important to note here that my approach—interviewing group founders about group formation—assumes that the group founder is a supremely important actor in the group-formation process. In fact, my approach assumes that without a founder—an identifiable individual who either alone or together with others puts the process of group formation into motion—an interest group will not form. Another way to put this is to say that each and every interest group mentioned in these pages had its origin with either one person or a group of people, and thus understanding what I call the group *founding decision*—the decision of the founder(s) to start the group—can help us understand group formation in general. I believe that extant theoretical and empirical work, much of which I review in subsequent chapters, makes my assumption that the founding decision is critical to group formation very reasonable. For more details about my approach and my methods, see appendix B.

How Transgender Rights Interest Groups Mobilized

The data paint a complicated but relatively clear picture of how transgender rights interest groups managed to mobilize in the face of substantial barriers. First, the data reveal that threats, grievances, and so-called disturbances—which are at the center of pluralist and relative deprivation theories of interest-group formation—were important spurs to transgender rights interest-group formation. It is fashionable to disparage theories of collective action and group formation that tab objective societal conditions as spurs to group formation as naïve and fatally flawed. But my data show that contrary to the most doctrinaire notions from rational choice and resource mobilization theories, threats, grievances, and disturbing events do indeed spur group formation. More specifically, my data show that they pushed individuals to form transgender rights groups. All of the groups I identify in this study began with the decision of one person or a small group of people to attempt to organize a group. And this decision was invariably spurred partially by the very real threats facing transgender people. In other words, in each and every case, a person saw a need for representation based on very real threats and decided to form a group to meet this need.

Second, the data reveal that while threats and grievances may push group founders *toward* the founding decision, they are not often *sufficient* to spur this decision. This leads to another major takeaway from the data analysis: threats and grievances spurred transgender rights interest-group formation only when they were coupled with extensive interaction between founders and other transgender people (in cases in which founders themselves were transgender people), transgender people (in cases in which founders were not transgender people), and to a lesser extent allies.Without exception, the founders of transgender rights groups I interviewed cited threats and grievances as important spurs to action. But they were also quick to note that the effects of threats and grievances were indirect. A clear understanding of the perils facing transgender people led group founders to seek out interaction with transgender people and allies, and it was this interaction that directly led to the founding decision. In short, interaction with other people, the data show, was the proverbial match that lit the fire for group founders. In the early days of transgender organizing (the 1950s, 1960s, and 1970s), founders physically looked for transgender people and, in some cases, nontransgender allies in places they heard were safe. Founders sent letters and made telephone calls, joined LGB groups and women's and feminist and civil rights groups, and went to transgender support-group meetings. In the 1970s and 1980s, transgender conferences became key forums for interaction. And, in the 1990s and beyond, founders turned to the Internet. What was it about interacting with others that spurred the founding decision? The data show that interactions had multiple effects. Specifically, interactions inspired founders, fueled their passion and excitement about transgender advocacy, raised their awareness of the multiple needs of transgender people, convinced them that extant LGB and (in some cases) other transgender rights groups were insufficient, persuaded them of the need for effective group representation, and even taught them skills that came in handy during the group-founding process.

Third, the evidence shows that the mobilization of other groups of oppressed and marginalized people (members of the LGB community, and women, for example) acted as a spur to transgender rights interest-group formation. The qualitative data support the conclusion that cross-movement effects and spin-off effects, which are often cited by sociologists as important spurs to group formation, are real and substantial. The data reveal that LGB groups, even when they were not particularly interested in transgender rights, served as training grounds for transgender rights activists. These groups, as well as some women's rights, civil rights, and transgender rights groups, played a vital, indirect role in the formation of many transgender rights groups by providing for founders forums for interaction, encouragement, inspiration, awareness, and learning.

Fourth, the evidence shows that it does not "take a village" to form a transgender rights interest group. The data show, just as some rational-choice theories of group formation imply, that the people who start transgender rights interest groups do a great deal of the work necessary for group formation themselves. And while rational-choice studies of group formation may endlessly debate where the money comes from, how group entrepreneurs manage to convince people to join their groups, what kinds of incentives and benefits do and do not attract members, what kinds of organizations patrons such as foundations and large donors do and do not support, and what sorts of people do and do not join organizations that represent their interests, the data show that in most cases these concerns are almost wholly irrelevant. Most transgender rights groups originate with people who work either alone or with a few friends and family members.

Fifth, the data show that forming a transgender rights interest group does not require enormous sums of money. Rational choice inspired incentive theory and resource-mobilization treatments of group formation imply that it takes substantial resources to start an interest group. Indeed, they imply that this is one of the reasons that we cannot take group formation for granted—it is costly. Yet despite the substantial attention paid to group formation by political scientists and sociologists, few studies actually attempt to discern the quantity of resources—financial or human—necessary to start an interest group. My data show that starting a transgender rights interest group takes time, money, and human resources; there is no such thing as automatic group formation. But group formation does not take *huge* amounts of money and/or human resources (time, yes). Indeed, most transgender rights groups were founded on "a shoestring" by (again) one person or a small group of people. This does not mean, however, that starting a group is easy or virtually costless. Rather, the data show that many of the resources seemingly necessary to form an interest group are not financial. The founders of transgender rights interest groups tend to be well-educated, reasonably affluent, resourceful, privileged people. These founders have a mix of traits and skills that are not easily bought, and that theories of group formation do not often consider. Most founders are intelligent, hard-charging, persistent, inspirational, well resourced, social, flexible, and empowered. Not just anyone can start an interest group.

Back to the issue of cost, my data also imply that the cost of starting an interest group is perhaps lower now than it ever has been. The Internet now does for free what previously cost large sums of money—it reaches huge numbers of people directly and instantly. Almost all of the founders who started groups after the advent of the Internet reported using it to promulgate their views, to get the word out that there was a new group in town, to raise money and other resources, and to interact with transgender people and supporters. It is simply not the case anymore (if it ever has been) that starting a group takes a great deal of money.

Sixth, the data show that the greater political environment did not play a large role in the formation of most transgender rights interest groups. There is some evidence, just as political opportunity structure (POS) theories of group mobilization would predict, that political factors matter in the formation of transgender rights interest groups. For example, the quantitative data show that the presence of Barack Obama in the White House, and a relatively liberal public, probably contributed to the formation of some transgender rights groups after 2005. But the qualitative data show that other factors loomed much larger than political factors in transgender rights interest-group formation. It is simply not the case, as some recent studies of group formation might predict, that transgender rights interest-group formation was spurred by government attention or activity and/or a favorable political environment. Indeed, the data reveal that for the most part, transgender rights interest-group formation preceded substantial government attention to transgender rights issues and favorable policy change.

Seventh, the data show that the rise of a transgender collective identity contributed somewhat to transgender rights interest-group formation and proliferation. I find some evidence that just as some new social movement (NSM) theories of group development aver, the rise of a transgender collective identity acted as a spur to group formation in some cases. The data imply that as transgender people began to interact with each other more extensively than ever starting in the mid-1980s, they began to get a sense that they indeed constituted a "we." This change in consciousness led several founders to more seriously contemplate forming an interest group. The data also reveal, however, that the rise of a transgender collective identity brought with it serious risks. Indeed, the data imply that as a group, after determining who they *were not*, transgender people had (and continue to have) a more difficult time determining who they *are*. This battle over collective identity has led to the founding in recent years of several "niche" groups—that is, groups that represent not the transgender population as a whole, but rather some identifiable subset of that population (e.g., black transgender people, Latina/o transgender people). It has also led to splintering, infighting, and conflict among actors within the larger transgender social movement.

Finally, the data reveal that density—that is, the size of the transgender rights interest-group population—helps explain transgender rights interest-group formation to some extent. The quantitative data show that the probability of new transgender rights interest-group formation started quite low (during the period 1964–1985), rose steadily from 1986 to about 2010, and has since fallen. This is in line with density-dependence theory, which posts that founding rates within an organizational population are affected by the size of the population. Specifically, the theory would predict that transgender rights interest-group formation is most likely after the organizational form, "transgender rights interest group" attains some substantial level of legitimation (which occurs after a few groups form and survive over some period of time), but before the population is crowded with too many groups. This is exactly what we see in the data. In short, the group founding decision is affected by density.

In all, the data paint a broad picture of how transgender rights groups have managed to form and survive in the face of substantial barriers. Some factors highlighted by extant theories of group formation—especially the existence of threats and grievances, extensive interactions between founders and others, the presence of privileged individuals willing and able to incur organizational costs, the cross-movement spread of ideas and skills and passion and awareness, and the legitimation of the organizational form "transgender rights interest group"—appear to have been essential in the rise and proliferation of transgender rights interest groups. Other factors, including the rise of a transgender collective identity, and openings in the political opportunity structure, played less of a role, but were important nonetheless. And still other factors, including government attention to transgender rights and the existence of entrepreneurs willing to start new transgender rights groups for personal gain, appear not to have been important at all.

Definitions and Terms

Before I lay out my plan for the rest of this book, I will take a few moments to define some important and recurring terms.

Transgender

There are numerous definitions of the term "transgender," but the following definition appears to be widely accepted and is the one I adopt here:

> [Transgender is] [a]n umbrella term for people whose gender identity and/or gender expression differs from what is typically associated with the sex they were assigned at birth. People under the transgender umbrella may describe themselves using one or more of a wide variety of terms—including *transgender.* (Gay and Lesbian Alliance against Defamation, n.d.)

Most transgender organizations hold that even defining the term "transgender" is somewhat limiting, as many people who view themselves as transgender may not fit a specific definition, and many people who fit a specific definition may not identify as transgender (see, for example, Sylvia Rivera Law Project n.d.). Moreover, there are ongoing debates within the transgender community (and without) about what the term really means. I do not intend to wade into this debate, as my interest here is primarily in organizations representing transgender Americans, no matter how that term is precisely defined.

Transgender Rights Interest Group

I define a transgender rights interest group as "an interest group whose primary political purpose is to advocate on behalf of transgender people." My definition excludes groups that advocate for transgender rights but have other concerns as well, including broad-based gay and/or lesbian and/or bisexual rights groups such as HRC, the National LGBTQ Task Force, and PFLAG. It also excludes broad-based civil liberties and civil rights groups such as the ACLU that work on transgender rights issues in addition to other issues, as well as organizations such as business firms, churches, charities, labor unions, and religious groups, that periodically weigh in on transgender rights issues. In short, I assume here that stand-alone, autonomous, transgender-focused organizations are integral parts of the larger transgender movement for equality.

My definition encompasses only groups that engage in *political activity*, which I define as "any attempt to influence government policy on transgender rights." I define political activity very broadly to include direct lobbying efforts (such as meeting with government officials), indirect lobbying efforts (for example, mounting grassroots lobbying activities or engaging in public protests or demonstrations), electoral lobbying efforts (such as working for or against a candidate for public office), and public education efforts (such as publicizing the effects of an existing or proposed piece of legislation or educating people about the rights or lack thereof of transgender people). I do not limit myself to the study of groups that are primarily or even substantially political. Thus, some of the organizations I study here are/were primarily political, such as It's Time America, GenderPAC, and the National Center for Transgender Equality. But others, such as the pioneering organizations Erickson Educational Foundation and Tri-Ess, are/were *not* primarily political, but rather exist(ed) primarily to do nonpolitical things but do/did politics "on the side." In fact, some of the groups I study here, including the relatively early groups Tri-Ess and Renaissance Transgender, deny publically that they are political. But since I adopt a broad definition of political activity, I consider groups like these political groups even though, clearly, they exist for nonpolitical purposes and engage in very low levels of political activity.

Finally, my definition includes groups that operate anywhere in the United States. I will have more to say about this later, but for now it will suffice to say that to be included in this study, a group need not be national in scope.

Transgender Rights Social Movement

Third, there is the term "transgender rights social movement." Defining this term is not easy, because there are numerous widely used definitions of the term "social movement" (Della Porta and Diani 2016, ch. 1). Here, I adopt the following definition of social movement: a "set of constituents pursuing a common political agenda of change through collective action" (Batliwala 2012, 3). I adopt this definition for two primary reasons. First, it is concise and parsimonious. Second, it encompasses aspects of other, more complicated definitions.

As this definition makes clear, a social movement is not just *one thing*, but rather is a set of many things. I assume here that among these many things are interest groups—formal organizations that work on behalf of movement goals. It is fair to say that many scholars are not exactly sure where interest groups fit into social movements, and do not share the view that interest groups are constituent parts of social movements (Smith 2014, xix-xx; Tarrow 2011, 9).

Nonetheless, within political science and increasingly within sociology, interest groups are generally considered participants in these broader things called social movements (Skocpol 2004, 135; Soule 2013, 108).

Based on this understanding of social movement, I define the transgender rights social movement as "the set of constituents pursuing a common interest in affecting policy on transgender rights in the United States." I assume that the transgender rights social movement comprises a large variety of movement actors, among them transgender rights interest groups. I do not assume, however, that transgender rights interest groups *are* the transgender rights social movement or even that they comprise the most important parts of this movement.

Interest-Group Formation

Finally, there is the term "interest-group formation." While the generic term seems straightforward, it is not. First of all, it means different things for different types of groups. For business firms, charities, churches, and other types of organizations that are formed for nonpolitical purposes, forming as an interest group means becoming "politically active"; it does not mean "coming into existence." In contrast, for an organization that is formed partially or fully for political purposes, forming as an interest group simply means coming into existence. Most, though certainly not all, of the organizations I write about in this book formed at least partially for political reasons, and thus "formed" as interest groups when they came into existence. But there is the occasional group that started as something other than an interest group (a support group, for example) and then became an interest group later.

The second reason that defining interest-group formation is not straightforward is that there is a fine line between group formation and group maintenance, and discerning the former from the latter is difficult if not impossible. Here, I define interest-group formation as "the process by which a group comes into existence." My definition assumes that the *process* here is successful. To say that a group has come into existence is to say that it has obtained at least several of the trappings of an extant and continuing organization, such as a budget, a professional website, a staff, a board of directors, an organizational chart, recognition from some governmental body (for tax purposes, for example), sufficient resources to disseminate information to the public or the media or the government (via, for example, newsletters or press releases or brochures), media recognition, a physical location, or a lobbying presence.

Outline of the Book

In chapter 2, I trace the history and development of transgender rights interest groups in the United States. I also address a number of questions that inform the analyses that follow: Which specific people and organizations have been and are at the forefront of transgender organizational advocacy? How has the universe of transgender rights interest groups in the United States evolved over time?

In chapter 3, I begin to address the primary question at hand: How did transgender rights interest groups manage to form and survive in the face of substantial barriers to group formation? I bring the qualitative data to bear on this question and demonstrate that threats and grievances played a vital role in the formation of transgender rights groups. From here, I explain how these threats and grievances led to interactions between transgender rights group founders and transgender people (and allies), and eventually spurred group formation.

In chapter 4, I continue my analysis of group formation by presenting data showing that interactions, some of which occurred in non-transgender rights groups and movements, led to learning by group founders—learning that convinced founders there was a need for new transgender rights groups, inspired them to become activists, and even taught them some of the "nuts and bolts" of group formation.

In chapter 5, I delve into the actual processes by which transgender rights interest-group founders got their groups off the ground and made them going concerns. The data in this chapter show that contrary to many rational choice treatments, group formation is largely an individual or small-group exercise; it does not take members or large numbers of supporters or patrons. It also shows that group formation is not particularly costly. It does, however, take skilled people with some resources—both human and financial—at their disposal.

In chapter 6, I examine the social and political context of group formation. In this chapter, I seek to discern the role of the larger political and social context in which transgender rights groups and activists operate in group formation. While I uncover some evidence that political factors contributed to the formation of some new groups, I also find that such factors were not particularly important for most groups. One feature of the environment in which transgender rights groups operate, however, is crucially important in group formation—other transgender rights groups. The quantitative data confirm that the development of the transgender rights interest-group population displays density dependence in the founding rate, just as many population ecology studies would predict.

In chapter 7, I examine the role of collective identity in transgender rights interest-group formation. I find that while collective identity did in some sense contribute to group formation, it also caused problems within the larger transgender movement. It also led to the formation of several "niche groups."

Finally, in chapter 8, I attempt to wrap things up by summarizing my major findings and attempting to answer the questions I pose at the beginning of this chapter. I also comment on the generalizability of my findings.

2

A Brief History of Transgender Rights Organizing in the United States

Reed Erickson was born in El Paso, Texas, on October 13, 1917. Not long after his birth, Reed moved with his parents to Philadelphia, where he eventually attended the Philadelphia High School for Girls. Historical accounts indicate that Reed "became involved with a circle of lesbian women" while in high school and started referring to himself as Eric in their company (Devor 2002, 384). After high school, Reed moved with his family to Baton Rouge, Louisiana, where his father relocated the family smelting business. In 1946, Reed graduated from Louisiana State University with a degree in mechanical engineering and soon thereafter moved back to Philadelphia to work as an engineer. He returned to Baton Rouge in the early 1950s to work for his father. There, he started his own company, one that manufactured stadium bleacher seats. Reportedly, by the late 1950s, Reed began to wear male attire regularly (Bello n.d.). While Reed was successful financially during this period, he became truly wealthy in 1962 when his father died and left him the family business, Schuylkill Lead Corporation.

In 1963, Reed starting seeing Dr. Harry Benjamin, a pioneering "sexologist" perhaps most famous for his work with Christine Jorgensen (of "Ex-GI Becomes Blonde Beauty" fame) in the 1950s (New York Daily News 1952). Between 1963 and 1965, Reed transitioned. Despite his chaotic personal life, which featured three marriages, extensive drug use, and eventual self-exile to Mexico to avoid drug charges, Reed Erickson remained a wise investor and eventually amassed a fortune of more than $40 million (Shibuyama 2011). In 1964, Erickson used some of this money to start what is generally considered the first nationally viable organization dedicated to "transsexualism" (a term not used today) in the United States—the Erickson Educational Foundation (EEF). The foundation was not primarily political but was crucial in getting "transsexualism" and its attendant issues recognized by media, the public, and policy makers at a time when the word "transgender" did not exist and attention to issues of gender identity was very limited. The EEF's undertakings are legendary. Among other activities, the organization sponsored groundbreaking conferences on gender identity (including the First, Second, and Third International Symposia on Gender Identity); funded research by many of the earliest physicians and social scientists interested in transgender issues, including Harry Benjamin, Milton Diamond, and June Reinisch; provided direct services including "one-on-one emotional support and informal counseling" and referrals to transgender people (Devor and Matte 2007, 51); worked to develop support groups throughout the country; engaged in public outreach (through the publication of educational materials, public speaking engagements, and numerous media appearances); provided early financial support for pioneering organizations including the National Transsexual Counseling Unit; and funded the Johns Hopkins Gender Identity Clinic. Despite its successes, the EEF had run its course by the late 1970s. The mercurial Erickson, clearly affected by the zeitgeist, turned his attention to psychoactive drugs, animal communication, and various new age concerns, and the EEF essentially disbanded in 1977.

The EEF, however, was just the beginning. While the number of transgender rights interest groups in the United States has never been large, it is larger now than ever. In this chapter, I trace the evolution of the population of nationally active transgender rights interest groups in the United States. The story starts with the EEF, proceeds through the lean organizing decades of the 1950s, 1960s, 1970s, and culminates with two-and-a-half decades of more substantial transgender rights group organizing. In what follows, I also say a few words about the evolution of the population of sub-national transgender rights interest groups. But because data on state and local transgender organizing are fragmentary and difficult to come by (see appendix B for details), I say much less about this population of groups. I should caution that this chapter is not meant to be a definitive history of transgender rights organizing in the United States; I will leave this to historians. My goal here is to provide a general sense of what the population of transgender rights organizations looks like today and how it has evolved over the past fifty years. This chapter sets the stage for the analyses that follow.

The Early Days of Transgender Organizing

Historians note that at least one transgender organization predated the EEF—a small group of crossdressers in Los Angeles which began meeting in 1952 (Ekins and King 2006). The group, founded by Virginia Prince, called itself the Hose and Heels Club. It later changed its name to the Foundation for Personality Expression (FPE), then merged in 1976 with another group to form the still-extant national organization for "heterosexual crossdressers," Tri-Ess (The Society for the Second Self) (Tri-Ess n.d.). The group is probably most famous for its trailblazing publication, *Transvestia* (Ekins and King 2006). While in some quarters Virginia Prince is today considered a transgender hero, in others she is criticized for her organization's exclusion of gay and bisexual male crossdressers and transgender women.

The Stirrings of a Movement

Throughout the 1950s and 1960s, a lot of what we now call transgender activism comprised efforts by drag queens and crossdressers. For example, in May 1959, two Los Angeles police officers entered Cooper's Donuts, an all-night establishment popular with drag queens and hustlers, many of them black and/or Latina, and/or poor, and/or gay, and crossdressers, and proceeded to harass and detain customers. A melee resulted, during which patrons tossed donuts, utensils, and coffee at the police officers, who then called for backup (Faderman and Timmons 2006). In another noteworthy incident, in August 1966, police in San Francisco showed up at Compton's Cafeteria in the Tenderloin district of the city after an employee called and reported that a group of customers was causing a disturbance. When a police officer tried to arrest a drag queen, she threw coffee in his face. Accounts of the incident suggest that several other drag queens and transgender women responded to police harassment by throwing dishes, furniture, and purses, and the "crowd trashed a cop car and set a newsstand on fire" (Pasulka 2015). Police reinforcements arrived, and several transgender people fought back as police attempted to detain them. Historian Susan Stryker has labeled the Compton's Cafeteria riot, "the first known instance of collective militant queer resistance to police harassment in United States history" (Dignan 2006).

While the Cooper's Donuts incident apparently did not lead to much organizational activity, the Compton's Cafeteria riot did. Members of incipient local organizations, including the Street Orphans (a group of lesbian "street people") and Vanguard (an LG youth organization), were active participants in the melee and in its immediate aftermath, a group called Conversion, Our Goal, morphed into the pioneering San Francisco–based National Transsexual Counseling Unit (NTCU) in 1968 (Beemyn 2014, 515). Some sources call the NTCU the first transgender organization in the United States, even though it got off the ground with funding from the EEF. The NTCU employed peer counselors to help transgender people, answered inquiries from across the country, and acted as a liaison between transgender people and local police. One of the founders of NTCU has stated that she started the group "to help ourselves and our peers get through the process of changing sex." The group educated transgender people on "how to get ID [and] who to see to get hormones," and how to approach and interact with health care professionals. The group also provided referrals to "lawyers and friendly bail bonds offices" (Suzan 2012). Meanwhile, across the country in New York City, nurse Mario Martino and his wife founded the Labyrinth Foundation Counseling Service, which was designed to help transgender men transition (Martino and Harriet 1977). Labyrinth is widely considered the first transmasculine organization in the United States.

Stonewall

By the end of 1968, three relatively high-profile transgender organizations—the EEF, the NTCU, and Labyrinth—had formed and begun working on behalf of transgender people. These groups were not advocacy groups per se, but two of them—the EEF and the NTCU—engaged in public education efforts designed at least partially to affect public policy.

On June 28, 1969, a series of violent demonstrations took place at the Stonewall Inn in New York City. A great deal has been written about Stonewall, and there is no need to discuss the incident at length here. For the purposes of understanding transgender organizational activity in the United States, however, two things about Stonewall are important. First, Stonewall stimulated some, but not a great deal of, transgender rights interest-group mobilization. Stonewall is widely considered the birthplace of the broad gay and lesbian liberation movement in the United States (though this may overstate things a bit, as historian Genny Beemyn [2014, 515] notes) primarily due to its considerable consequences, including increased public visibility for LGBT people, the formation of numerous new LGB organizations including hundreds of campus chapters of the Student Homophile League, and increased politicization of LGBT people. But, although Stonewall led to *some* transgender organizing, it did not stimulate a vast proliferation of transgender rights interest groups. Second, Stonewall—or more accurately the aftermath of Stonewall—revealed a rift between lesbian and gay people and organizations on the one hand, and transgender people and organizations on the other hand.

Organizing Immediately after Stonewall: Real but Limited

Historical accounts suggest that in the year or two after Stonewall, transgender people were integral in the formation of Gay Liberation Front groups in cities across the nation (Beemyn 2014). More important for our purposes, however, Stonewall stimulated the formation of three pioneering transgender rights groups in 1970—the Street Transvestite Action Revolutionaries (STAR, New York City), the Queens Liberation Front (New York City), and the Transsexual Action Organization (TAO, Los Angeles). STAR was formed by Stonewall veterans and transgender women Sylvia Rivera and Marsha P. Johnson, self-described economically disadvantaged, multiracial transvestites who made their living through sex work (Nothing 1996). STAR focused primarily upon the practical needs of gay and transgender people—"the immediate concerns of life"—as one essayist has called them, but archival materials indicate that the group had wide-ranging public policy goals as well (Nothing 1996, 9). Around the same time, self-described transvestites Lee Brewster and Bunny Eisenhower founded the Queens Liberation Front, an overtly political organization formed to decriminalize public crossdressing (Beemyn 2014, 518). The Queens Liberation Front published *Drag*, a magazine with political content, which described itself as "The Magazine about the Transvestite." The group was a pioneering user of the courts to change policy, and Lee Brewster bragged in the first anniversary issue of *Drag* that the group had successfully challenged a city law that required any organization seeking a dance permit from the city to agree that attendees would not include "men dressed in the female attire" (Brewster 1972, 12). Finally, TAO was formed by Angela Keyes Douglas in Los Angeles. Archival sources indicate that TAO made some noise in 1970 when it reportedly convinced the Peace and Freedom Party to include in its platform the right to undergo gender-reassignment surgery (Brewster 1973). The group, which moved to Miami with Douglas in 1972, is well known for its multiracial character and its pioneering newsletter, *Moonshadow*, which was published partially in Spanish (Peña 2010).

In short, Stonewall appears to have stimulated a modicum of transgender organizing. And the effects of Stonewall on LGBT people cannot be underestimated. But Stonewall did *not* lead to large-scale transgender rights interest-group mobilization. Figure 2.1 graphs the population of nationally active, viable transgender rights interest groups in the United States over time.[1] Table 2.1 lists the groups that comprise and have comprised this population over time. As figure 2.1 shows, there was a slight rise in the number of transgender rights interest groups in the few years after Stonewall. But the real growth in the population did not occur until almost twenty years later. Figure 2.1 also plots the number of nationally active, viable LG and LGB groups in the United States for some of the same period (unfortunately, data were not available for the entire period).[2] The pattern here is quite different. As the figure shows, there was explosive growth in the number of LG groups in the United States in the 1970s. While there were fewer than ten nationally active, viable transgender rights interest groups as late as 1995, the population of LG groups surpassed this milestone by late 1970. In sum, the number of transgender rights interest groups in the United States, in contrast to the number of LG groups, did not grow tremendously in the immediate and not so immediate aftermath of Stonewall.

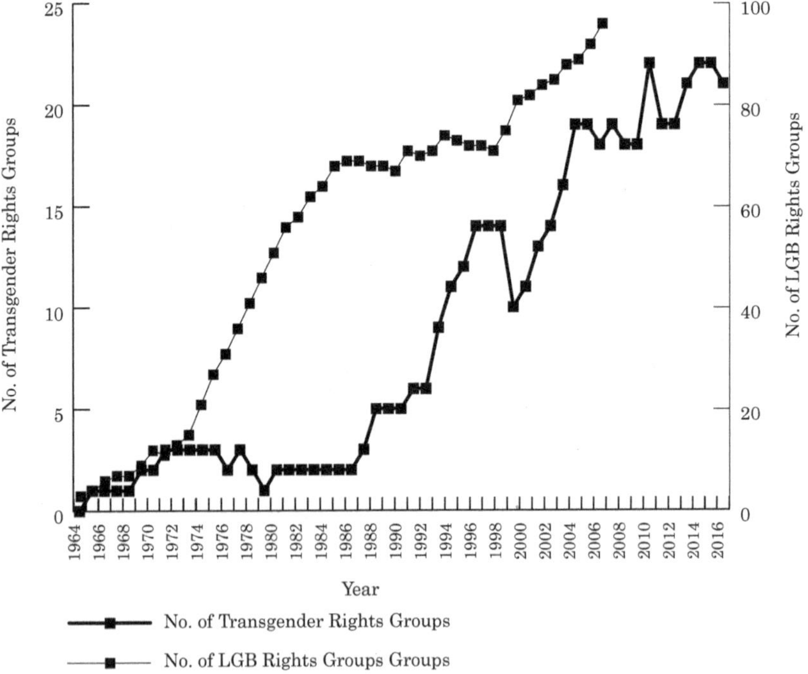

Figure 2.1. The number of nationally active transgender rights interest groups (1964–2016) and LG/LGB/LGBT rights groups (1964–2007) in the United States. *Source:* Author's data.

Table 2.1. List of nationally active transgender rights advocacy groups in the United States, 1964–2016.

Organization	*Year Founded–Year Died*
Erickson Educational Foundation (EEF)	1964–1977
National Transsexual Counseling Unit (NTCU)	1968–1975
Transsexual Action Organization (TAO)	1970–1978
Tri-Ess	1976–
Harry Benjamin International Gender Dysphoria Association (HBIGDA; now The World Professional Association for Transgender Health [WPATH])	1979–
FTM International	1986–
The Renaissance Transgender Association	1987–
The International Foundation for Gender Education (IFGE)	1987–2013
American Educational Gender Information Service (AEGIS)	1990–1998
Transgender Nation	1992–1994
International Conference on Transgender Law and Employment Policy (ICTLEP)	1992–1997
Congress of Transgender Organizations (CTO)	1992–1998
Intersex Society of North America	1993–2010
Transexual Menace	1993–2010
It's Time, America!!	1994–1998
Transgender Alliance for Community	1994–1998
Transgender Officers Protect and Serve (TOPS)	1995–2001
Gender Public Advocacy Coalition (GenderPAC)	1995–2009
Survivor Project	1997–2010
National Transgender Advocacy Coalition (NTAC)	1999–2010
Gender Education and Advocacy (GEA)	2000–2005
Transgender Law and Policy Institute (TLPI)	2000–2010
Transgender Community of Police and Sheriffs (TCOPS)	2001–2007
Gender Education and Media (GEM)	2001–2010
Sylvia Rivera Law Project	2002–
Transgender Law Center	2002–

continued on next page

Table 2.1. *Continued.*

Organization	*Year Founded–Year Died*
National Center for Transgender Equality (NCTE)	2003–
Transgender American Veterans Association (TAVA)	2003–
Transgender Legal Defense and Education Fund (TLDEF)	2003–
TransYouth Family Allies	2006–2014
Black Trans Advocacy (Black Transmen and Black Transwomen are affiliates)	2009–
Trans People of Color Coalition	2009–
TransLatin@ Coalition	2009–
Global Action for Trans*Equality	2009–
FORGE (originally founded in 1994)	2009–
Brown Boi Project	2010–
National Coalition of Transgender Advocacy Groups	2010–2011
Trans Advocacy Network	2010–2015
Trans Student Educational Resources	2011–
Trans Justice Funding Project	2012–
United States Transgender Advocacy	2012–
Trans Athlete	2013–
Trans Women of Color Collective	2013–
Gender Proud	2014–
Trans United Fund	2016–

Source: Author's data.

The Rift

Historian Susan Stryker calls the 1970s a "difficult decade" for transgender people and organizing (Stryker 2008, ch. 4). Despite the incidents at Cooper's and Compton's, as well as the prominent role of transgender people at Stonewall and in many early homophile organizations (it is worth noting that the EEF provided early financial support for the pioneering, early homophile group ONE, Inc.) (Devor 2002), transgender people were more or less abandoned by the larger gay and lesbian rights movement in the months and years after Stonewall. For example, the ground-breaking New York group Gay Activists Alliance (GAA), founded in late 1969 by gay men, vowed to work "completely and solely" for gay rights, pushing aside the political interests of transgender people (Duberman 1993, 232). In an interview in 1972, STAR's Marsha Johnson noted:

> Well, I went to GAA one time and everybody turned around and looked. All these people that spoke to me there were people that I had known from when I had worked in the Gay Liberation Front community center, but they weren't friendly at all. It's just typical. (quoted in Kay and Young 1972, 118)

Sylvia Rivera had similar thoughts about GAA. She said: "And I was happy at GAA for a while. But it wasn't my calling. I found out later on that they only believed in acquiring civil rights for the gay community as a whole. Which is fine. They did a lot of good just concentrating on the gay issue. But they left the queens behind" (quoted in Fouratt 2015). And on a similar note, in a 1973 interview for QLF's *Drag*, Angela Douglas said:

> Seriously, let's see. Gay Lib, to me, was and is a very beautiful and needed concept. I became involved for many reasons. I don't mind being considered gay. I do mind being oppressed as a gay: when I got into Gay Lib I encountered a tremendous amount of prejudice on the part of the male gays because I am TS, so I stayed with it basically to confront anti-TS prejudices on the part of homosexuals. Some of the scenes were very brutal ones. (Brewster 1973, 30)

In perhaps the most widely known episode of shunning, in late 1972, the germinal lesbian rights group Daughters of Bilitis, founded in 1955 in San Francisco, expelled former vice-president Beth Elliott on the grounds that she was not "woman-born" (Meyerowitz 2004, 259). In another infamous incident, in early 1973, Elliott was scheduled to perform as a singer-songwriter at the West Coast Lesbian Conference in Los Angeles but received a rude reception. In her keynote address to the conference, feminist poet and activist Robin Morgan called Elliott "an opportunist, an infiltrator, and a destroyer, with the mentality of a rapist" (1973, 32). Elliott's supporters at the conference, however, beat back efforts to expel her entirely. As if to top off a difficult decade for transgender people and activists, in 1979, feminist Janice Raymond wrote *The Transsexual Empire: The Making of the She-Male*, in which she said that female "transsexuals rape women's bodies by reducing the real female form to an artifact, appropriating this body for themselves" (Beemyn 2014, 519).

The Stonewall Legacy: A Dream Deferred

In the end, Stonewall did not do a great deal to increase transgender organizational strength in the United States. Few organizations formed in the incident's wake, and transgender activists who might have made the larger LG movement transinclusive were for the most part shunted aside. Moreover, Stonewall laid bare a rift between LG groups and transgender rights groups that remains to some degree to this day (though clearly a great deal of peace has been made in recent years). Nothing demonstrates this rift more than the so-called TERF (transexclusive radical feminist) Wars[3]—in which some lesbian feminists launch pointed attacks at the very idea of "transgenderism"—which in some quarters continue to this day.

Ironically, however, it appears that the gay liberation movement helped lead to the creation of the category of "transgender." Ethnographer David Valentine has noted that prior to the rise of the gay rights movement, many transgender people, as well as many drag queens and crossdressers, identified as gay because they lived in the same communities, frequented the same bars and clubs, and were subject to the same police harassment that gay people were. He also has argued that as the gay rights movement honed its focus on sexual orientation, "transgender" arose as a separate and distinct category (Valentine 2007). I will have more to say about this later.

The 1970s and 1980s: "The Contemporary Nadir"

The two decades after Stonewall were not good for transgender rights organizations. Historian Genny Beemyn writes that the 1970s to the early 1980s are often viewed as a contemporary low point for transgender people (2014). The same can be said of transgender organizing. As figure 2.1 shows, the number of new transgender interest groups founded during the 1970s and 1980s was pitifully low. In addition, the NTCU was gone by the mid-1970s (a casualty of police harassment; Stryker 2008, 92), the EEF shut its doors in 1977 (Devor and Matte 2007), and TAO was defunct by 1978. My best estimate is that by the beginning of the 1980s, there were only *two* nationally active, viable organizations representing in any way the interests of transgender people—Tri-Ess (which remained small and for the most part eschewed advocacy) and the Harry Benjamin International Gender Dysphoria Association (HBIGDA; today called The World Professional Association for Transgender Health or WPATH). The latter was founded in 1979 by "physicians, therapists, and researchers who worked with transsexuals" (Meyerowitz 2002, 255) and was designed primarily as a professional association that issued recommended "standards of care" for transgender people. Though the group can hardly be considered political by most standards, I mention it here because at the time, it was one of the proverbial "only games in town" for transgender people. As Meyerowitz notes, with the passing of almost all groups run by transgender people and for transgender people during this period, no one else but the medical professionals in HBIGDA spoke in any way for transgender Americans (2002, 255). This was problematic, of course, as HBIGDA for years was not particularly keen on having transgender people as members, often seemed to put the interests of its professionals ahead those of transgender people, and did not have a transgender-identified person as its leader until the mid-2000s. In addition, many transgender activists have since lamented HBIGDA's medical model of transsexualism (Denny 2001). But as transgender activist Dallas Denny has pointed out, most transgender people themselves accepted the medical model at the time the group was formed and thus shared at least some of HBIGDA's goals (2001).

While the 1970s were quiet on the organizing front, there were at least some stirrings in the mid-1980s. First, in 1986, author Lou Sullivan founded the still-extant FTM International, "the largest and oldest continuously running organization serving Female-to-Male community and their [*sic*] allies" (Online Archive of California 2006; see also Lou Sullivan Society n.d.). Sullivan, originally from Milwaukee, began writing about his gender identity in the early 1970s and started to identify as a "female transvestite" in 1973 (Stryker n.d.). He moved to San Francisco in 1975 and unsuccessfully (partially because homosexuality was considered a "counter indicator" for surgery at the time) began seeking gender-reassignment surgery shortly thereafter (Stryker n.d.). For the next decade, Sullivan worked on behalf of himself and other transgender men to change discriminatory medical practices. He also became a grassroots activist, printing instructional booklets for transgender men. In 1979, Sullivan found professionals willing to help him transition (Highleyman 2008). In the same year, Sullivan formed a peer support group for transgender men, which later morphed into FTM International (O'Brien 2009, 848). Though the group started as a peer support group, it has always been involved in public education to some extent.

Second, in 1987, Merissa Sherrill Lynn founded the International Foundation for Gender Education (IFGE) in Boston. The group grew out of the seventh Fantasia Fair (an annual transgender conference and social gathering) in 1981, after which several activists (many of whom were cross-dressers) decided that a new national organization was needed to sponsor events at which transgender leaders and activists could come together (Ness 2015, 1381). The group was a success. At one point, IFGE had a budget of several hundred thousand dollars, issued a periodic journal called *Transgender Tapestry*, and held an annual conference that was a touchstone for transgender rights activists across the country (Denny 2009). Largely due to its conferences and public education efforts, the group became a crucial national organizational actor at a time when few transgender organizations existed. While the group has apparently fallen on hard times lately, it was one of the transgender organizational success stories of the 1980s.

Third, in 1987, Renaissance Transgender Association was founded by Angela Gardner, Alison Laing, Trudy Henry, JoAnn Roberts, and Melanie Bryan in Philadelphia (Roberts 2012). The group, which still exists, describes itself as a nonpolitical support and education organization (Renaissance Transgender Association n.d.). Again, however, because the group has considered public education a part of its mission from the start, I consider it at least somewhat political. Moreover, one of its founders, JoAnn Roberts, was crucial in the formulation of a "Gender Bill of Rights," an overtly political project (Bolich 2007, 264).

Thus, by the late 1980s, there were signs (albeit faint) that transgender organizing was on the upswing. The three groups I mention here managed to do enough to make it into retrospective histories of transgender politics and are considered national organizations, if modest ones.[4] Ephemera from the era indicate that during the same time period, groups were mobilizing in states and localities across the country. Among such groups operating in the mid-1980s were the Black Alliance of Transexuals in Detroit, California Dreaming, the Empathy Club in Seattle, the Gender Activists League in California, Hidden Life in Honolulu, the Jorgensen Society in San Diego, the Texas T-Party, the Transvestite Information Service in North Carolina, Trans-People in Houston, the United Transsexual/Trans-Gender Rap Group in Los Angeles, and the United Transvestite and Transsexual Society in New

Jersey (Meyerowitz 2002, 237; D'Emilio, Turner, and Vaid 2000). There were undoubtedly many more local, state, and regional transgender organizations founded in the 1980s whose names have been lost to history.

The 1990s: Transgender Organizing Comes of Age

Figure 2.1 demonstrates graphically what many histories of transgender politics describe narratively—a meaningful proliferation of transgender rights interest groups in the 1990s. The decade started with the founding of Dallas Denny's American Educational Gender Information Service (AEGIS; later reconfigured as Gender Education and Advocacy), an organization dedicated to educating the public about transgender issues. The group published the groundbreaking magazine *Chrysalis*, sponsored numerous influential conferences, and went on to start the National Transgender Library and Archive (in 1993) (Denny 2013). The prolific Denny continues to write, speak, and blog on transgender issues to this day.

The Early and Mid-1990s

AEGIS was just the beginning. Between 1991 and 1995, several new national transgender rights organizations were formed, some of which remain active. In 1992, for example, Kansas native Anne Ogborn, who had earlier founded the Kansas City Gender Society, formed the fugacious Transgender Nation, a direct-action group not unlike the direct-action AIDS groups of the time (Califia 2003, 226). It is also worth mentioning that one year earlier, transgender activists received national attention when they started Camp Trans—an educational event held at the Michigan Womyn's Music Festival. The latter, which started in 1976, became infamous among transgender activists in 1991 when an attendee asked transgender woman Nancy Burkholder if she was indeed transgender, and she refused to answer (Taormino 2000). Burkholder was ejected from the festival by security (Califia 2003, 227). The festival owner retroactively enunciated a "womyn born womyn" policy to justify its actions. The 1991 incident led to the Camp Trans demonstrations, in which protestors decried the festival's antitransgender policies. The Camp Trans demonstrations took place annually between 1991 and 2011.

Also in 1992, the first International Conference on Transgender Law and Employment Policy was held in Houston (ICTLEP). The conference was the brainchild of longtime transgender activist and lawyer Phyllis Frye, who described it as "an annual meeting devoted solely to developing strategies for progressive change in the law as it effected [*sic*] transgenders" (2001). By the end of 1993, the conference had turned into a nonprofit organization, and Phyllis Frye began to crisscross the country speaking on transgender issues (Frye 2001). The group's conferences featured a veritable "who's who" of transgender activists and organizers, and its transcripts became required reading for lawyers and advocates interested in transgender issues. The ICTLEP held its last conference in 1997. Phyllis Randolph Frye has since stated that the conference ended primarily because other effective groups, many incubated at ICTLEP conferences, formed in its wake (2001).[5] And in 1993, Cheryl Chase founded the Intersex Society of North America (ISNA), after her harrowing childhood experience as an intersex person. She formed the group, she said, to "end shame, secrecy, and unwanted genital surgeries for people born with an anatomy that someone decided is not standard for male or female" (Intersex Society of North America n.d.). While there is little doubt that intersex and transgender are not the same thing, I include the group here because, at least at its inception, the group clearly was part of the larger transgender movement.

Two noteworthy coalitions of transgender organizations got off the ground for a short time in the early 1990s. First, the Congress of Transgender Organizations, which operated for a time as a part of IFGE, went independent in 1992. The group, essentially a coalition of transgender rights organizations throughout the country, published *TransAction*, a newsletter mainly designed to keep transgender political leaders talking to one another (Denny 1996). Second, the Transgender Alliance for Community formed in 1994, dedicating itself to "educating helping professionals" by setting "up tables in the vendor areas of a number of conferences, including the American Psychiatric Association, the National Association of Social Workers, and the American Association of Sexuality Educators, Counselors, and Therapists" (Denny 2016). The group met for several years in the mid-1990s at the IFGE's annual convention, acting essentially as an information-exchange device for other transgender rights organizations. A number of regional organizations also popped up in the 1990s, including the Greater New York Gender Alliance, the Garden State Alliance, the Mid-America Gender Group Information Exchange (MAGGIE) in St. Louis, the Southern Association for Gender Education in Atlanta, and the Magnolia Alliance in Asheville, North Carolina.

My best estimate is that by the end of 1993, there were nine viable, nationally focused transgender rights interest groups active in the United

States. Again, there were undoubtedly many dozens of state and local organizations as well. Group proliferation continued throughout the rest of the 1990s. For example, in 1994, Jessica Xavier, Karen Kerin, Jane Fee, and Sarah DePalma, founded It's Time, America!, a national coalition of state and local transgender rights organizations (Xavier 1996, 2). The group formed primarily to advocate for laws against discrimination based on gender identity, and eventually bore numerous state and local chapters including chapters in Connecticut, Illinois, Maryland, Massachusetts, Minnesota, and Texas. It's Time, America! was a crucial player in the first Washington Gender Lobbying Day in 1995, at which archival materials indicate the group "coordinated a largely successful effort to have each and every one of the over 500 Senate and House officeholders lobbied by transgender activists" (Transexual Menace 1995, 1–2). It's Time, America! is perhaps best known as an early critic of leading gay rights organization Human Rights Campaign (HRC), which the group (and many other transgender groups and activists) accused (seemingly correctly) of cutting transgender people out of its lobbying efforts for federal employment nondiscrimination legislation throughout the 1990s and early 2000s (TransGriot 2007). At the national level, some version of the Employment Non-Discrimination Act (ENDA), which would prohibit employment discrimination on the basis of sexual orientation, has been introduced in every Congress since 1994, and for many years, HRC supported a nontransgender-inclusive version of the bill. This, of course, infuriated transgender activists, many of whom were active in It's Time, America!. A group called FORGE was also founded in 1994. The group began in Milwaukee as an effort "to connect trans-masculine folks who were living in the Midwest" (FORGE n.d). In the early 2000s, however, the group shifted its focus to sexual violence, and by 2009 it had become a national, federally funded, antiviolence organization with a large budget. I will say more about FORGE later.

Also in 1994, Riki Wilchins and Denise Norris founded the Transexual Menace. The group started, Wilchins has written, with the printing of "Transexual Menace" t-shirts, and was "modelled on a combination of the Lavender Menace (who confronted NOW over its exclusion of lesbians) and the genderfuck of *Rocky Horror Picture Show*" (2014, 525). A direct-action group somewhat like Transgender Nation, Transexual Menace began informally with Wilchins and others including transgender activist Nancy Nangeroni passing out T-shirts at gatherings of activists (Wilchins 2014, 526). As the group started to gain traction, *The Village Voice* published a story about the murder of Brandon Teena in Falls City, Nebraska (Minkowitz 1994). The story was horrifying enough—Brandon Teena was raped and murdered by two men who were allegedly his friends. But Transexual Menace was also troubled by the way the *Village Voice* article rubbed "salt in the wound by positioning Brandon as a 'hot butch,' a lesbian dreamboat, and [kept] referring to him as 'Teena' and 'she' and 'her' throughout" (Wilchins 2014, 526). Transexual Menace jumped into action, picketing *The Village Voice* and the piece's author shortly after publication. "The Menace" also received nationwide attention when it sent emissaries to the trial of Brandon's murderers in Falls City, Nebraska. The group held a vigil outside the courthouse the first day of the trial, walked the streets of Falls City in Transexual Menace t-shirts, and confronted neo-Nazis on the streets of the small town (Wilchins 2014, 526). Historian Susan Stryker notes that Transexual Menace "garnered unprecedented media attention by sponsoring vigils outside of courthouses where cases involving anti-transgender crimes were being tried" (2008, 141).

Riki Wilchins has noted that after a short time coordinating memorial vigils and shining a light on anti-transgender violence, she and several other activists realized that a more overtly national strategy was necessary. "All our actions had been local," Wilchins has written, "one event, one city" (2014, 527). In 1995, representatives from several extant transgender groups gathered at a conference in Philadelphia sponsored by Renaissance, and started the group GenderPAC, naming Wilchins the inaugural executive director. The group was founded as "a national advocacy organization that focuses on eliminating gender stereotypes and ending discrimination and violence on the basis of how individuals look, act, or dress in terms of gender or sexual orientation." The organization, which one source has noted formed also in response to "the lack of inclusion of transgender and broader issues in the agendas of national lesbian and gay organizations" (Smith and Haider-Markel 2002, 121), managed to grow a sizable budget relatively quickly and became well-known in Washington in the late 1990s as an organizational sponsor of National Gender Lobbying Day.

GenderPAC can be viewed as the organizational spawn of Transexual Menace, and so perhaps can another group—Anthony Barreto-Neto's Florida-based Transgender Officers Protect and Serve (TOPS), a group formed to represent transgender police and fire officers. Riki Wilchins has written that Anthony Barreto-Neto served as "security" for Transexual Menace at some of its vigils, and he famously liasoned with police officers in Falls City during the Brandon Teena trial (Wilchins 2014, 526). TOPS was the first association of transgender professionals in the United States. Its founder, Anthony Barreto-Neto, became well known among transgender activists for his ability to negotiate with local police forces before transgender events. There is no question that his efforts were crucial in keeping transgender events and demonstrations free of violence at a time when support for transgender causes was very low (Califia 2003, 265). TOPS appeared at the 1996 protest of the American Psychiatric Association's annual conference in Washington, DC, and Barreto-Neto made numerous media appearances to speak on transgender issues. He also testified at the 1996 trial of Sean O'Neill, a Colorado transgender man who was arrested for "having sex with teenage girls who believed he was a young man" (Califia 2003, 234). Barreto-Neto is perhaps most famous, however, for his successful lawsuit against the Hardwick, Vermont Municipal Police Department. Barreto-Neto was hired by the department in 2002, but shortly after his arrival, town officials learned that he was a transgender man and passed this information along to the police department. What followed was a "pattern of harassment and inferior work conditions that became so severe [that Barreto-Neto] had to leave his job." Barreto-Neto sued, and the town settled out of court for a small cash settlement and a promise to "train its employees on transgender issues" (GLAD 2014).

The Late 1990s and early 2000s

Archival materials indicate that by the end of 1996, transgender activists were openly optimistic (if cautious) about the prospects for transgender organizations to make real progress in the battle for transgender rights. For example, It's Time, America! co-founder Jessica Xavier wrote in 1996: "As recently as five years ago, the very notion of transgendered people becoming actively and openly involved in our American political process was looked upon as fantasy." She continued: "But . . . this transgendered 'movement' of ours has reached a certain level where there are enough activists out in varying degrees to begin the difficult work of liberation" (1). Similarly, activist Dallas Denny wrote in the same year: "In addition to the seven national organizations, a number of transgender groups and organizations exist on local, regional, and national levels. One or more groups can be found in most major cities and many smaller ones" (1).

In the late 1990s, the groups kept coming. In 1997, the Survivor Project was formed in Portland, Oregon, to address "the needs of intersex and trans survivors of domestic and sexual violence through caring action, education and expanding access to resources and to opportunities for action" (Survivor Project n.d.). The group, which was a pioneer of Internet education for transgender people, lasted for over a decade (it was seemingly defunct by 2010). The group's "Guide to Intersex and Trans Terminologies" was reproduced in numerous books and articles in the late 1990s and early 2000s (Koyama n.d.). Some people rely on this resource to this day. And in 1999, a "group of experienced lobbyists" founded the National Transgender Advocacy Coalition (NTAC), which specialized in publicizing crimes against transgender people in an effort to convince the public that anti-discrimination laws were necessary (Allen 2015). The group appeared in media quite regularly for a few years in the early 2000s but appears to have lost steam by 2010.

2000 and Beyond

The early 2000s were also good for transgender organizing. In 2000, two new national groups were formed—Gender Education and Advocacy (GEA), and the Transgender Law and Policy Institute (TLPI). GEA came from a merger of AEGIS and It's Time, America!. The group was founded by veteran activists Jamison Green, Dallas Denny, Jessica Xavier, Gwen Smith, Penni Ashe Matz, and Sandra Cole. The group continued AEGIS's focus on education and information but aspired to become an "effective national organization focusing on the many areas of 'non-political' advocacy" (Gender Education and Advocacy 1999). Also in 2000, Paisely Currah, Shannon Minter, and others founded the Transgender Law and Policy Institute. The group was formed to engage "in effective advocacy for transgender people" and specialized in tracking "current developments in legal and public policy issues affecting transgender people and their families" and writing summaries of these developments and posting them on their website (Transgender Law and Policy Institute n.d.). The group also served as a clearinghouse for "litigation, legislative, and education advocacy materials for use by other advocates" (Transgender Law and Policy Institute n.d.).

In 2001, two additional groups were formed—Gender Education and Media (GEM), and Transgender Community of Police and Sheriffs (TCOPS). GEM was formed by Nancy Nangeroni (a founding member of the Boston chapter of Transexual Menace) and Gordene MacKenzie "to educate, inform, and inspire positive social change by presenting quality written, spoken, audio, and video programming about gender diversity and social justice issues" (Gender Education and Media n.d.). The group is probably best known for its Gender Talk radio program, which ran for eleven years and produced more than four hundred episodes. The edifying radio programs, which are still available on-line, contain interviews with transgender activists and much, much more educational material. Also in 2001, TCOPS was formed by Julie Marin to represent transgender law enforcement officials. The group's goal was to serve as a "peer support network" and to "advance the cause of transgender employee's [*sic*] right to be employed and/ or retain employment, through advocacy, support, and education" (Transgender Community of Police and Sheriffs n.d.). Both GEA and TCOPS attracted media attention, spread the word about important transgender rights issues, and provided valuable information to people interested in transgender issues.

In the early 2000s, transgender organizing hit its high-water mark, with the birth of five national organizations: the National Center for Transgender Equality (NCTE, 2003), the Sylvia Rivera Law Project (2002), the Transgender Law Center (2002), the Transgender Legal Defense and Education Fund (TLDEF 2003), and the Transgender American Veterans Association (TAVA 2003). The National Center for Transgender Equality was formed by activists, including Mara Keisling, a marketing consultant and veteran of LGB rights activism (Dahir 2002, 38). The group is a truly national organization, complete with headquarters in Washington DC and a double-digit staff. It is arguably the biggest and most prominent transgender rights organization in the history of the United States. The Sylvia Rivera Law Project was formed by lawyer and law professor Dean Spade as a "non-profit law collective that provides free legal services to transgender, intersex and gender non-conforming people who are low-income and/or people of color" (Spade 2016). The organization, named for GAA, Gay Liberation Front, and STAR founder Sylvia Rivera, also engages in litigation and public education. Today, the group is regularly involved in high-profile legal cases concerning transgender rights and has helped thousands of transgender people obtain legal services. Also in 2002, the Transgender Law Center was formed in Oakland, California. The group—originally a project of the National Center for Lesbian Rights—was founded as a statewide organization, but not long after its inception became a truly national organization. The organization, as the name implies, provides direct legal services to transgender people, but it also engages in advocacy and education. The group has an annual budget of $2.5 million, employs over 15 people, and is as of this writing the largest stand-alone transgender advocacy organization in the United States. The Transgender Legal Defense and Education Fund was founded in 2003, focusing on test-case litigation in cases concerning transgender rights, but also providing direct services, and engaging in policy advocacy (Transgender Legal Defense and Education Fund n.d.). The group was founded by lawyer and LGB rights activist Michael Silverman, and now regularly engages in high-profile legal actions that make national news. Finally, in 2003 the Transgender American Veterans Association was founded by Angela Brightfeather and Monica Helms, who sought to help transgender veterans "who had to deal with the VA medical facilities and for other health-related issues" (TAVA n.d.). The group was active in the battle over "Don't Ask, Don't Tell," surveyed transgender veterans on their needs and experiences with the VA, and takes partial credit for the federal government's decision in January 2016 to allow transgender people to serve in the military. The group is not large, but it still exists today.

The mid-2000s were a relatively quiet time for transgender rights group formation. However, one notable group was formed in 2006: TransYouth Family Allies. The group was designed to be an organization not of transgender people so much as family members of transgender people, especially parents. The group's stated mission is "to bring the issues facing gender variant and gender questioning children and their families into greater public awareness" (TransYouth Family Allies 2017).

The late 2000s were better for transgender organizing. In 2009, FORGE, which was founded in 1994 in Milwaukee as an education, support, and service delivery organization, morphed into a nationally active, federally funded support, education, and advocacy organization focusing on antiviolence education. Two other groups were formed in 2010: the National Coalition of Transgender Advocacy Groups (NCTAG) and the Trans Advocacy Network (TAN). NCTAG was designed to be a coalition of local transgender rights groups, while TAN was designed to be a coalition of local, state, and campus transgender rights groups. Neither organization lasted long or made much of a splash.

Many of the new groups founded in the late 2000s represented people in the transgender community who felt that extant groups did not represent their needs as well as new, more narrowly focused groups could. For example, in 2009, long-time transgender, AIDS, and LGB activist Bamby Salcedo (the subject of a documentary called *Transvisible* released in 2014) founded the TransLatin@ Coalition in Los Angeles. The group works on issues important to transgender immigrants who reside in the United States, a group of people that its founder believed was not well-represented in other organizations (BambySalcedo.com n.d.). Also in 2009, Kylar Broadus founded the Trans People of Color Coalition, "as a response to people of color (POC) that felt unheard and underrepresented in the trans equality movement" (Trans People of Color Coalition, n.d.). Like Salcedo, Broadus felt that the unique needs of transgender people of color were not being adequately addressed by extant organizations (Lilly 2016).

In 2010, Carter and Espy Brown founded Black Trans Advocacy in Dallas, Texas (with its affiliated organizations Black Transmen and Black Transwomen). The group explicitly focuses upon the interests of African-American transgender people. Also in 2010, Malachi Larrabee-Garza co-founded the Brown Boi Project, another group based on the premise that certain groups of transgender people—in this case the young and the brown—were not well represented by extant transgender advocacy groups. The group's website says it works "to build leadership, economic self sufficiency, and health of young masculine of center womyn, trans men, and queer/straight men of color—pipelining them into the social justice movement" (Brown Boi Project n.d.). The eclectic Oakland, California-based group focuses on training young men of color for social activism. The group holds training seminars aimed at preparing participants for work in transgender and LGBT organizing.

Yet another group formed to represent underserved transgender people is Trans Student Educational Resources, founded in 2011 by teenage high school students Eli Erlick and Alex Sennello. The group focuses on the needs of transgender students, working to change policies toward transgender youth in schools across the country. The group engages in a wide range of activities, including training youth leaders, providing scholarships, and responding to (and taking action on) complaints from transgender students (Trans Student Educational Resources n.d.). In 2013, Lourdes Ashley Hunter and Vanessa Victoria founded the Washington, DC–based Trans Women of Color Collective (TransWomen of Color Collective n.d.). The group, still in its incipient stages, seeks to be a grassroots group that empowers transgender people to help themselves socially, politically, and economically.

Some newer groups are broader in focus. For example, in 2009, Global Action for Trans*Equality (GATE) was formed by activist Justus Eisfeld (formerly of Transgender Europe). The group is unique in its international focus, has achieved enormous notoriety throughout the world during its brief existence, and currently has an annual budget of over $1 million. The group has put considerable effort into building an international transgender movement (by, for example, surveying transgender groups across the globe to learn about their challenges and needs) and has also worked hard to improve health care for transgender people across the globe. In 2012, Karen Pittelman and Gabriel Foster co-founded the New York–based Trans Justice Funding Project, an ambitious new organization that provides small grants to transgender groups of all kinds across the country. To date, the group has dispersed close to half a million dollars to grassroots organizations, including some of those listed in table 2.2. The group raised almost $200,000 in 2015, and currently has a budget larger than this. And in 2014, model and transgender woman Geena Rocero and antipoverty activist Allie Hoffman founded Gender Proud, which has a top-flight website and a large media presence. Its international focus is unusual among transgender groups, and its high-profile founder makes numerous media appearances and has spoken throughout the nation since her group's inception. Gender Proud also operates as a media production company, however, so it is difficult to tell at this point whether or not the group will maintain much of an advocacy focus moving forward.

Finally, in 2016 a group of transgender activists formed a new national group, Trans United (together with its sister organization Trans United Fund), with the expressed goal of being a national advocacy organization that aggressively seeks to build "the political power of the trans and gender expansive communities and our allies to advocate for trans equality" (Trans United n.d.). The group endorsed Hillary Clinton for president in 2016 and promises to ramp up its activities during the Trump years.

The years 2009–2015 were not kind to some older groups, which seem to have either gone by the wayside or changed considerably. First, the lodestar GenderPAC morphed into TrueChild in 2009, essentially following the lead of its leader Riki Wilchins. TrueChild is not a transgender rights group per se, but rather is an organization that conducts trainings and briefings designed to help "donors, policy-makers and practitioners reconnect race, class *and* gender through 'gender transformative' approaches that challenge rigid gender norms and inequities" (TrueChild n.d.). Second, two legendary groups—the IFGE and Transexual Menace—appear moribund. The IFGE's website has not been updated since 2012, and Transexual Menace has no web presence at all (at least in the United States). Third, while determining the precise years in which groups cease to exist is difficult, based on extensive research it appears that in 2010 (or at least by 2010), several additional older transgender rights groups disappeared. Among these are Gender Education and Media (which has had little but a website for several years), The Intersex Society of North America (which determined that it had accomplished what it set out to accomplish and transferred its money and copyrights to a new group called the Accord Alliance), the National Transgender Advocacy Coalition (once considered one of the most important national groups in the country), Survivor Project (which seems to have shut down, but whose zombie website exists), and the Transgender Law and

Policy Institute (whose website has not been updated since 2010). In addition, as I mention above, the National Coalition of Transgender Advocacy Groups and the Trans Advocacy Network, both founded in 2010, seem to have never really gotten off the ground.

The news is not all bad, of course. As I mention above, the new-ish groups FORGE, GATE, the Trans Justice Funding Project, and Trans United, are going strong and growing. In addition, several groups that have been formed within the last few years are seeking traction and may well get it. Among them are United States Transgender Advocacy (an Illinois-based group with a web presence), Trans Athlete (founded by transgender Ironman athlete Chris Mosier in 2013), and the Institute for Transgender Economic Advancement (a New York–based group that for now seems to comprise just a website).

Nationally Active Transgender Interest Groups Today

By necessity, my treatment here is expansive rather than fine-grained and detailed. But I believe this brief history allows a basic understanding of the contours of national transgender organizing in the United States since 1950. To summarize, as figure 2.1 and table 2.1 show, the data reveal that the population of transgender rights interest groups in the United States was born in 1964. It remained very small for the next twenty-two years. There was a steady increase in transgender organizing between 1986 and 2002, and there was even more organizing between 2003 and 2009. Since 2009, a few new groups have formed and a few have perished. The population is now larger than it has ever been, and today there is a solid set of relatively well-funded, professional organizations at the national level.

For descriptive purposes, I will characterize the population of extant nationally active transgender rights organizations as follows. The categories and categorizations I use here are strictly mine, and I use them because I think they provide insights into the contours and qualities of national transgender organizing today. First, there is what I call "The Big Six"—six relatively well-resourced, relatively visible, highly professionalized organizations, which form the core of the national transgender advocacy community. In this category are the National Center for Transgender Equality (NCTE, founded in 2003), the Sylvia Rivera Law Project (founded in 2002), the Transgender Law Center (founded in 2002), the Transgender Legal Defense and Education Fund (TLDEF, founded in 2003), FORGE (founded in 1994, gone national in

2009), and Global Action for Trans*Equality (GATE, founded 2009). The NCTE arguably is the dean of transgender rights organizations, with annual revenues of approximately $1 million, a dozen staffers, and a Washington DC office. The group's leaders and staff advocate on behalf of transgender people before Congress and other parts of the federal government, work at the state level (when state governments consider antitrans legislation or regulations), and make regular media appearances.[6] The group also works extensively with national LGBT organizations, and the group's leader, Mara Keisling, is one of the most visible proponents of transgender rights in the country today. The Transgender Law Center has an annual budget of $2.5 million, employs more than fifteen people, and as of this writing appears to be the largest stand-alone transgender advocacy organization in the United States. The Sylvia Rivera Law Project is also well resourced, with an annual budget of nearly $1 million, a New York City office, and a staff of nine. The group provides legal services for low-income transgender people—but also engages in more traditional advocacy activities including direct lobbying and grassroots organizing. Its founder, law professor Dean Spade, makes regular media appearances, and his group often works with other transgender groups and LGBT organizations on nonlegal advocacy activities. The New York City–based, nonprofit law firm TLDEF has an annual budget of approximately $500,000, and six employees. The group, led by professor and attorney Jillian Weiss, who took over for longtime activist Michael Silverman in 2016, provides legal services for transgender people and engages in advocacy in the courts and other branches of government. It is probably best known for its Name Change Project, through which it matches transgender people with lawyers who help them change their names free of charge (Lee 2016). As I mention above, FORGE has morphed into a national transgender rights powerhouse. And finally, the relatively new, New York–based GATE has assets of over $250,000 and is making waves both in the United States and internationally. It has a solid foothold and seems to be growing.

Second, there is a group I will call "The Stalwarts"—older, well-established groups that are less overtly political than the Big Six are and serve primarily support and informational roles. This group comprises some of the pioneers of transgender organizing—FTM International, the Renaissance Transgender Association, and Tri-Ess. All three groups appear to be hanging on if not going strong, though none is particularly well resourced. Probably the most visible of the three—FTM International—is a long-lived group founded by transgender rights pioneer Lou Sullivan and modernized and grown by activist Jamison Green (the author of *Becoming a Visible Man* [2004], a touchstone for gender studies). The group remains the largest and oldest group for transgender men in the United States. Now led by Rabbi Levi Alter, the group has a less overtly political profile than any of the Big Six but acts as a clearinghouse for information on transgender issues and a resource for transgender people seeking support and education. The group does not have a large annual budget (probably under $200,000) but is a regular participant in transgender political events across the nation and makes regular media appearances. The pioneering Renaissance Transgender Association is still around, primarily offering support for transgender people in local and regional groups. It appears to operate on a shoestring budget (of around $20,000), but still has over four hundred members. The group does not appear to engage in direct advocacy, but it engages in public education designed ultimately to affect policy. Finally, the decades-old Tri-Ess still exists, providing support and education for cross-dressers through local and regional chapters. Tri-Ess, like the others in this category, has a small budget (probably around $40,000) and does not engage in direct advocacy, but does have a speaker's bureau for public education.

Third, there is a group of what I call "Up and Comers"—relatively new groups that seem at this early stage to be off to a reasonably fast start. Each of the groups in this category has raised some money and received widespread publicity and seems to have what it takes to survive in the long term. In this group I put Gender Proud, Transgender American Veterans Association (TAVA), Trans Student Educational Resources, the TransLatin@ Coalition, the Trans Justice Funding Project, and Trans United. Gender Proud has a highly professional website and a large media presence, though its budget remains quite small. Its leader, Geena Rocero, is a well-known media spokesperson on transgender issues. TAVA is not new, but, after some rough years, appears to be rebounding somewhat. Under the leadership of retired army major Evan Young, the group has updated its website and now claims to have more than two thousand members. Trans Student Educational Resources is gaining strength, and its leader, Eli Erlick, is a "go-to" spokesperson for issues involving transgender youth. The TransLatin@ Coalition has a similarly impressive leader in Bamby Salcedo, whom I describe above. The Trans Justice Funding Project, the new organization that has provided microgrants to scores of transgender organizations across the country, seems to be going strong. Finally, Trans United seems to be off to a very good start.

Fourth, there are six relatively new, primarily niche, groups that are still attempting to get their footing. I will call these groups "The Potentials."

They are Black Trans Advocacy, Brown Boi Project, Trans People of Color Coalition, United States Transgender Advocacy, Trans Athlete, and the Trans Women of Color Collective. All six of these groups seem to be getting some traction, though none has a particularly large budget or staff.

Finally, as a primarily professional organization, WPATH is in a category of its own. The group is a professional organization with an active membership and an annual budget of over $500,000. WPATH continues to provide information for health care professionals by way of its Standards of Care and Ethical Guidelines for the treatment of transgender people and includes advocacy among its stated purposes. The group sponsors courses for health care professionals, appears regularly at conferences, and sponsors a biennial scientific symposium. It continues to be one of the best-resourced organizations working on transgender issues in the world, though there is still controversy about whether or not the group is too focused on the needs of its health care professional members rather than transgender people.

State and Local Transgender Rights Advocacy Today

Historical data on transgender rights advocacy groups operating at the state and/or local levels in the United States are hard to come by. As such, I do not attempt to trace the trajectory of this population here. I have mentioned a handful of state and local groups already, but any attempt to put together a truly comprehensive historical treatment of local and state transgender rights groups is bound to fail given the lack of systematic information on such groups. Nonetheless, I will survey the landscape of subnational groups to get a general idea of what this population looks like today. To do this I attempted to compile a list of extant, active groups. This list is found in table 2.2 below. The list contains only groups that I believe engage in at least some political activity, even if it is not much. This list is probably not comprehensive and definitive, but it is, I believe, the most comprehensive list of sub-national transgender groups in the United States in existence. Based on this list and archival research, I believe that three general observations about the evolution of state and local transgender rights advocacy in the United States are in order.

First, there is now a thriving population of state and local transgender advocacy groups in the United States. As table 2.2 shows, there are active transgender rights interest groups in thirty-eight of the fifty states and the District of Columbia. In addition, many of the biggest cities in the United States, including New York, Los Angeles, Chicago, Houston, Philadelphia,

Table 2.2. List of extant state and local transgender rights interest groups in the United States (and their founding dates), 2016.

State	*Group(s)*
Alabama	Alabama Gender Alliance (2005–2011)
Arizona	Arizona Trans Alliance (2008–) Southern Arizona Gender Alliance (1998–)
Arkansas	Arkansas Transgender Equality Coalition (2014–) Transgender Equality Network (Fayetteville, 2014–)
California	FTM Alliance of LA (Los Angeles, 1999–) Gender Health Center (Sacramento, 2010–) Gender Justice (Los Angeles, 2011–) Gender Spectrum (East Bay, Northern California, 1997–) The Lou Sullivan Society (San Francisco, 2007–) Transgender Community Coalition (Palm Springs, 2014–) The Transgender, Gender Variant and Intersex Justice Project (San Francisco, 2004–) Trans E-Motion (Fresno, 2005–)
Colorado	Gender Identity Center of Colorado (1978–)
Connecticut	Connecticut Transadvocacy Coalition (2002–) CT Equality (2010–)
Florida	Florida Transgender Alliance (2015–) Jacksonville Transgender Action Committee (2013–) Trans Miami (Miami, 2011–) Transgender FORGE (2003–)
Georgia	LaGender (2001–) Transgender Health and Education Alliance, Inc. (2015–)
Hawaii	TransSpectrum (2012–)
Illinois	Chicago Gender Society (1987–) Transformative Justice Law Project (2008–)
Indiana	GenderNexus (Indianapolis, 2011–) Indiana Transgender Network (2015–) Indiana Transgender Wellness Alliance (2014–) Transgender Fort Wayne (2011–) Transgender Resource Education and Enrichment Services (2012–)
Kansas	Kansas Statewide Transgender Education Project (2010–) Wichita Transgender Community Network (2015–)
Kentucky	Trans and Sexuality Teaching, Advocacy, and Research, TSTAR (2012–)

continued on next page

Table 2.2. *Continued.*

State	*Group(s)*
Louisiana	Louisiana Trans Advocates (2011–)
Maine	Maine Transgender Network (2009–) Maine Transgender Political Coalition (2001–) Trans Youth Equality Foundation (2007–)
Maryland	Baltimore Transgender Alliance (2015–) Gender Rights Maryland (2011–) Maryland Coalition for Trans Equality (2011–) TransMaryland (2007–)
Massachusetts	Freedom Massachusetts (2015–) Massachusetts Trans Political Coalition (2001–) Translate Mass (2004–)
Michigan	Transgender Detroit/Gender Identity Network Alliance (2005–) Transgender Michigan (1997–) TransYouth Family Allies (2006–)
Minnesota	Gender Education Center (1994–) Minnesota Transgender Health Coalition (2002–)
Missouri	Metro Trans Umbrella Group (2013–) Trans People of Color (Columbia, 2010–)
Montana	Gender Expansion Project (2008–) Montana Two Spirit Society (1996–)
Nevada	Gender Justice Nevada (2011–)
New Hampshire	Transgender New Hampshire (2009–)
New Jersey	Black TransMedia (2013–) Gender Rights Advocacy Association of New Jersey (2002–)
New Mexico	National Native Transgender Network (2013–) Transgender Resource Center of New Mexico (2009–)
New York	Greater New York Gender Alliance (1993–) Lorena Borjas Community Fund (Jackson Heights, 2012–) New York Association for Gender Rights Advocacy (NYAGRA, 1998–) Organization for Transgender Health Empowerment Resources (New York City, 2013–) Transgender Advocates of the Capitol Region (Albany, 2012–) TransLatin@ Coalition (2007–)
North Carolina	Kindred Spirits (Asheville, 1993–) Tranzmission (2001–)

State	Group(s)
Ohio	Heartland Trans Wellness Group (2007–) TransOhio (2005–)
Oregon	Northwest Gender Alliance (Portland, 1980–) TransActive Gender Center (Portland, 2007–)
Pennsylvania	Hearts on a Wire (Philadelphia, 2007–) Transgender Education Association of Central Pennsylvania (Harrisburg, 2006–)
Rhode Island	Transgender Intersex Network of Rhode Island (2011–)
South Carolina	Gender Benders (Greenville, 2011–)
Tennessee	Tennessee Trans Journey Project (Nashville, 2014–) Tennessee Transgender Political Coalition (2003–)
Texas	Black Transmen Inc. (2011–) Gender Infinity (Houston, 2011–) Fort Worth Transgender.org (Fort Worth, 2012–) Texas Transgender Nondiscrimination Summit (2009–) Trans Pride Initiative (Dallas, 2011–) Transgender Education Network of Texas (2009–) Transgender Foundation of America (Houston, 1998–)
Utah	Transgender Education Advocates of Utah (2003–)
Virginia	Gender Expression Movement of Hampton Roads (Hampton Roads, 2004–)
Washington	Transgender Educational Association of Greater Washington (1982–) Transgender Parents of Washington (2015–)
Washington, DC	DC Trans Coalition (2005–) Organization for Transgender Health and Employment Resources (2013–) Transgender Health Empowerment (1996–) Transgender Legal Advocates of Washington (2012) Trans People of Color Coalition (2010–)
Wisconsin	Transgender Aging Network (part of FORGE, 1994–) Transgender Health Coalition (2013–)

Source: Author's data.

Dallas, Jacksonville, San Francisco, Indianapolis, Fort Worth, Detroit, Washington DC, and Boston are home to at least one active transgender rights interest group. Further, some state and/or local transgender groups are as big, as well-resourced, and as active as the largest and most active national groups. The Transgender Law Center, for example, was founded as a state group but achieved national notoriety almost immediately. Based in the California Bay Area, the group engages in extensive advocacy and provides a variety of services for transgender people. Similarly, the Transgender Resource Center of New Mexico in Albuquerque, founded in 2009 by Adrien Lawyer and Zane Stephens, is one of the five largest transgender organizations in the United States, with an annual budget of $500,000 and a huge variety of programs and services for transgender and nontransgender people alike. A number of other subnational groups are relatively large (with budgets in the hundreds of thousands of dollars) and active, including Transgender Health Empowerment in Washington DC and the FTM Alliance of Los Angeles.

Second, as table 2.2 shows, state and local transgender rights organizations thrive in exactly the sorts of places one would expect—liberal, diverse jurisdictions. Thus, the states of California, Maryland, Massachusetts, Minnesota, New York, and the cities of New York, Los Angeles, San Francisco, and Portland have many transgender rights groups. This said, it is not the case that transgender groups are absent from less liberal, less diverse jurisdictions. Several seemingly unlikely places have active transgender groups. For example, the Alabama Gender Alliance, Arkansas Transgender Equality Coalition, Louisiana Trans Advocates, and Transgender Education Advocates of Utah prove that transgender rights groups can and do exist in decidedly conservative places as well as liberal ones. Nonetheless, the states with a dearth of transgender advocacy organizations are those that are generally quite conservative, including Mississippi, Nebraska, North Dakota, South Dakota, and Wyoming.

Third, in general, the population of state and local transgender advocacy groups in the United States evolved much like the population of national transgender rights advocacy groups did. Figure 2.2 plots the founding dates of the groups listed in table 2.2. Figure 2.2 must be viewed with caution, as it does not contain the founding dates of groups that no longer exist, as data on such groups are impossible to find and verify. Still, figure 2.2 and archival research allow us to piece together a general picture of transgender organizing in states and localities. As I mention above, the first local and state transgender organizing took place in the late 1950s and early 1960s, primarily in New York City and San Francisco. The number of state and

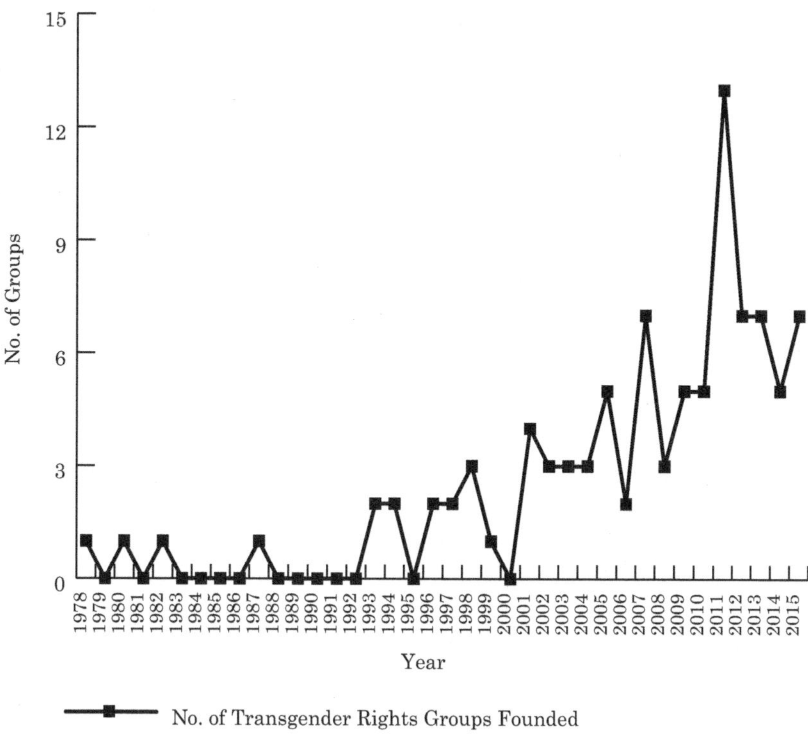

Figure 2.2. The founding dates of extant state and local transgender rights interest groups in the United States, 1978–2015. *Source:* Author's data.

local groups remained relatively small throughout the 1960s, 1970s, and 1980s. But since 1993, as figure 2.2 shows and historical accounts suggest, state and/or local groups have steadily proliferated. One, two, or three extant groups were founded every year between 1993 and 1999 (except for 1995), and then after 2000 the number of new groups steadily increased, picking up even more steam in 2007, when seven extant groups were formed. Group proliferation has continued since 2007, and thirty-nine extant groups have been founded since 2011. Interestingly, figure 2.2 suggests that while the size of the population of nationally active groups has remained approximately the same for the last decade, the size of the population of subnational groups has not. If we consider 2011 an outlier, the number of group foundings per year has remained between five and seven every year since 2009.

Summary and Conclusion

In this chapter, relying on archival materials, original research, and historical accounts including those by Susan Stryker and Genny Beemyn, I have attempted to provide a thumbnail sketch of the history of national transgender rights organizing in the United States. Figure 2.1 graphically represents the evolution of the population of nationally active transgender rights groups in the United States, and I have attempted to provide some historical background on the groups listed in table 2.1 by discussing their founders and origins.

My simple descriptive treatment is just the beginning. Indeed, the purpose of this chapter is to provide context for the primary question that animates this study: How did the groups listed in tables 2.1 and 2.2 manage to mobilize in the face of substantial barriers to formation and survival? The data also beg several additional questions, which they will help us answer along the way, including the following: What explains the pattern we see in figure 2.1, which shows that transgender rights advocacy groups went from virtually nonexistent in the 1950s, 1960s, and 1970s, to more numerous in the 2000s and 2010s? How did pioneers of transgender advocacy manage to form credible and effective organizations in the decades before widespread attention to transgender issues and in the face of opposition from not just "ordinary" Americans, but also putative allies in the LGB and women's rights movements? In the next five chapters, I will examine the data for answers to these questions.

3

The Crucial Role of Grievances and Interactions

WITH JAMI K. TAYLOR

In the midtwentieth century, political scientist and classical pluralist David Truman surveyed "accounts of American legislative sessions" and politics and concluded that interest groups were at the center of many of them (Truman 1951, 3). He noted, however, that students and scholars of American politics more or less ignored interest groups, focusing instead on other ostensibly more important parts of the political system such as Congress and voters (vii). One of the questions Truman asked in his foundational study of interest-group politics in America, *The Governmental Process*, was the following: What is the process by which unorganized constituencies become organized groups that pursue their interests before government? This is the primary question, albeit slightly modified, that I ask in this book. Truman was one of the first political scientists to take this question seriously, and his answers were at the center of political science treatments of interest-group formation for many years. Truman's work fell into disrepute in the 1970s as rational-choice theory came to dominate political science. But in more recent years, Truman's brand of pluralism has made a comeback, and it is clear that his flaws and elisions aside, Truman was on to something. In fact, as this chapter shows, my data provide strong support for the following notion, which is at the center of Truman's pluralist theory of interest-group formation—*threats, grievances, and disturbances (events that throw society or some of its segments into "disequilibrium") act as spurs to group formation.*

The data reveal, however, that threats, grievances, and disturbances are not *sufficient* to spur group formation. Rather, they tend to increase interaction among individuals who are subject to them, and it is this interaction that ultimately leads to group formation.

Pluralism: Threats, Grievances, Disturbances, and Group Formation

"Simple societies," Truman wrote in *The Governmental Process*, "have no associations" (1951, 57). New interests and thus new interest groups, Truman argued, emerge naturally as societies evolve and become more complex. From time to time, the process of natural societal evolution is vastly accelerated by specific disturbances such as recessions, depressions, or wars that lead to substantial grievances among certain groups of people and that drive individuals who share interests under threat to join groups to address these threats and grievances to make their lives better. To demonstrate his theory in action, Truman sketched a portrait of the history of major farm interest groups in the United States. He argued that the American Farm Bureau, the Farmers Alliance, the Farmers Union, and the National Grange all emerged between 1867 and 1900 "out of the increased interactions of farmers in response to intense disturbances of their accustomed behavior" (87). These disturbances, including the growth of corporate power, chronically low commodity prices, industrialization, technological change, and westward expansion, threatened the livelihoods of farmers, and spawned a wave of farm organizing, as aggrieved and financially stressed farmers gathered together and formed interest groups to represent their interests before government. In short, threats and grievances born of disturbances led to group formation.

At the center of Truman's theory is the appealing assumption that a self-interested individual will engage in collective action when the interests he/she shares with others are threatened, or when his/her grievances become substantial enough to cause serious discomfort. Robert Dahl, the other "classical pluralist" of the immediate postwar period, proceeded from the same assumption. His *homo civicus*—the common person who generally evinced little interest in or participation in politics—would eschew his/her customary lethargy and act collectively when his/her interests were threatened by societal forces (Dahl 1961). The basic pluralist theory of group formation—often referred to short-handedly as "disturbance theory"—is a decidedly demand-side theory, as it focuses on the environmental conditions under which we can expect citizens to join together in interest groups. It more or less assumes that demand (i.e., the demands of people who share an interest under threat) will lead to supply (i.e., the creation of an interest group). Thus, to explain when groups form, who forms them, who joins them, and what they do, pluralists look primarily to the larger context in which citizens live and interact.

Some sociologists adopted a similar demand-side approach to explaining collective action, positing that frustrations and grievances and threats to well-being give rise to collective action, as discontented people can be expected to lash out, often aggressively and sometimes in organized groups, to improve their lives (Davies 1962; Kornhauser 1959; Smelser 1962). A sophisticated version of this approach appears in Ted Gurr's classic *Why Men Rebel* (1970), in which relative deprivation is tabbed as a crucial determinant of individual decisions to engage in collective political violence.

For reasons I discuss in more detail later, many contemporary treatments of interest-group formation dismiss pluralist notions of interest-group formation out of hand. They do so because it is *de rigueur* to question the assumption that aggrieved individuals will naturally engage in collective action to protect their interests. After all, critics of pluralism note, throughout American history, large groups of Americans (for example, slaves and their descendants) have faced substantial threats to their well-being and did not act collectively on a large scale for various reasons (including the fact that they were not allowed legally to do so). Moreover, these critics note that forming and maintaining organizations require resources, which groups of aggrieved and destitute and persecuted people often do not have.

Yet my data suggest that dismissing pluralist theories out of hand is ill-advised. In the rest of this chapter, I address the role of threats, grievances, and disturbances in transgender rights interest-group formation, showing that just as David Truman and other demand-side, pluralist theorists might have predicted, threats, grievances, and disturbances were important spurs to the formation of transgender rights interest groups.

Reasons and Motives: Pluralism and Grievances and Connections

To address the role of threats and grievances and disturbances in transgender rights interest-group formation, and to test pluralist notions of interest-group formation, I asked all of my respondents the following open-ended, multi-part question. "Please tell me about the founding of [your group]? Can you briefly describe the origins of this organization? In other words, how did your group come about? Can you tell me what motivated you to start the group?"

There Are Always Grievances and Threats

Answers to these questions were multifaceted and various. But one theme clearly stood out in respondents' answers: threats to, and grievances among, transgender people played a role in *all* respondents' decisions to start transgender rights interest groups. In sum, each of my twenty-seven respondents mentioned threats to the well-being of transgender people and the existence of substantial grievances among transgender people as motivating factors in his/her decision to start a transgender rights interest group.

The accounts of my respondents concerning the threats facing transgender people and their grievances about a political and economic and health care system that historically has brutalized and oppressed them are harrowing, and they could fill an entire book. This comment from Thomi Clinton was quite typical:

> [Before I started my group], I was seeing a lot of suffering, and I was seeing these people that were allegedly leading [the movement], and our people [i.e., transgender people] were in the suicide ward, where they were getting beat up, where they were facing domestic violence, or they were losing their jobs. These people—[other activists]—were doing nothing about it. I just couldn't sit back and just deal with it anymore.

On a similar note, Adrien Lawyer told me: "Trans people experience discrimination and physical violence every day and across all class and race [lines]. We're dying by suicide at a rate that should just have everybody completely alarmed." Mara Keisling also cited violence and suffering as an important impetus for starting her groups. She told me that she traveled to Washington DC in the early 2000s to speak at a conference on LGBT rights. She went on to say,

> [I saw all] these young women who were really just trying to get by in DC without having proper ID because they were trans, without having family support because they were trans. [And they were] always facing violence because they were trans, and [all of that] just really, really bothered me.

Joelle Ryan told me that she could not simply stand by and do nothing while transgender Americans suffered so much:

> There was a fundamental inner voice that said, "What's happening to transgender people, the oppression, the discrimination, the prejudice, is wrong. It's morally unjust, and we have to stand up and be counted. We have to get out there front and center. We have to come out and be visible."

Blake Alford, the Georgian and transgender man who started THEA+, told me that while transgender people everywhere face obstacles and threats of various kinds, the threat of violence is pervasive in his deep red, southern state:

> People being transgender has been around since dirt. [But] . . . especially the world the way it is today, [they] find [all of this] extremely hard. Especially Bubba, [he] finds it real hard to accept a man in a dress, to be blunt. Bubba don't like guys like myself, once he finds out who we are. He likes me as I am right now . . . but once he finds out I am trans, God help me when the sun goes down . . . if he catches me after dark.

Tony Barreto-Neto, the early activist who founded TOPS, told me that he was pushed toward activism because of "all the murders happening [at the time]" and he founded his group. For Julie Walsh, it was the HIV epidemic—an epidemic that disproportionately affects transgender Americans. She told me: "There was a need there. I worked in the HIV field [in my regular job], and I [learned] there are a disproportionate number of transgender people who are HIV positive. I wanted to develop a hub [for these people]." Masen Davis, a co-founder of FTM Alliance of Los Angeles, told me that he co-founded his group partially because of the substantial obstacles virtually all transgender people face in their quest for quality health care:

> So a lot of the work that happened early on with the FTM Alliance was around access to health care . . . [just] getting primary care here in Los Angeles, as a trans man . . . at that time [was very difficult]. And [there were] significant barriers to getting access to hormones specifically . . . and especially since people were not insured who were low income.

Anonymous Respondent No. 1 relayed an awful story about the day he learned that transgender people were under threat in the United States. The incident, he told me, did not lead him to start a group (he was in high school at the time), but it opened his eyes to the dangers that transgender people faced, and he never forgot it:

> [I was in high school]. [A classmate of mine], she came out to me [and told me she was going to transition]. She goes, "What do I do? I have to do this. I have to transition." Not being all too knowledgeable at the time, I was as supportive as I possibly could be. Long story short, she came out to her parents; her dad totally rejected her [and] beat the living crap out of her. [Then] she found a .45 caliber handgun and put a bullet in her head.

Anonymous Respondent No. 1 told me this incident spurred him to learn more about transgender issues at an early age and to remain involved in transgender politics for his entire life. Learning about the agony of his friend was the proverbial first step in the process by which he started his group.

Eleven respondents told me that they had been aware for many years that transgender people faced obstacles and threats but that coming out or transitioning made them even more aware of these problems. Adrien Lawyer, for example, told me he decided to start the group because his experience of coming out was dark and isolated, and he did not know another trans person. Adrien told me that after he started getting testosterone, he underwent some serious changes: "I had really biblical acne in the first two or three years of T, and I was like, 'Oh my God, I'm just always going to look like this!'" From here, Adrien said he decided he needed to do something. In other words, Adrien's decision followed years of bad experiences as a transgender person. De Sube told a similar story, one about coming out and then gradually realizing over time that she wanted and needed to start a group: "When I came out, there were no resources." She continued:

> I thought I was alone. The term "transgender" had just been pretty much invented and entered into use, the Internet was in its infancy, [and] I found . . . some chat rooms for transgender people. [After spending some time in these chat rooms] and connecting with [other transgender people], I made up my mind that if I could do anything about it, I would not let people be alone and feel alone, because that's how I felt.

Josephine Tittsworth described the gradual process by which she came to the decision that she would start her group:

> In the beginning [after coming out], I tried contacting all the national organizations that I knew of, and not one single national organization even acknowledged that they got my email or request or anything. I felt all alone, and I wasn't getting any help from anywhere from anybody.

And Andrea Zekis, who did not cite any specific danger to herself in explaining her decision to start a group, told me that after coming out she learned that many others were not as lucky as she was. She said that she could not sit still while so many transgender people were suffering. She started her group, she told me, because "there is a need for these trans organizations . . . [Transgender people] were not free to live their lives freely and openly to be themselves."

Coming out was not always a bad experience for founders. And, in one case, it was the positive experience of coming out that spurred the founding decision. The early activist Nancy Nangeroni told me that coming out was such a positive experience that she felt compelled to become more active in the transgender movement. When I asked her about her motives to start her group, she told me:

> Yeah. I had a terrible motorcycle accident that nearly killed me. I had a pretty badly damaged leg. And other damage. And I mourned the loss of the beautiful pristine body that I had once inhabited. And I attribute that directly to my gender dysphoria, my discontent with the gender roles that were imposed on me. There was this deep kernel of anger that definitely drove me. I feel like it was more than just the accident. It was my life. I lived with terrible shame and guilt, very privately. And that impacted every aspect of my life for decades. And it was completely unnecessary. The motorcycle accident pushed me out of the closet. When I came out, in healing from the accident and coming out, which happened simultaneously, I was surprised at the amount of caring that was shown to me by so many people . . . the caring and acceptance. So for a long time I was motivated by this gratitude . . . that I had found this place of loving acceptance with the people in my life that I had not had

[before] because I was so immersed in my own fears and guilt and so forth.

Nancy was very positive about her experience coming out. But she, like all the other respondents, was well aware of the serious and constant threats to the well-being of transgender people in the United States. The data point to this general conclusion: *Transgender people, including the founders themselves, face/have faced substantial barriers and threats in many, many aspects of their lives, and these barriers and threats were crucial to the founding decisions of all my sample founders.* The political system historically has not protected transgender people from discrimination, the legal system has allowed criminals to brutalize transgender people with relative impunity, and the health care system historically has been unresponsive to the needs of transgender people. Words such as "danger," "discrimination," "oppression," "threats," and "violence" recurred in my interviews. Perhaps no one was as straightforward about all this as Joelle Ryan was when she gave me her general assessment of the conditions facing transgender people: "I knew that what had happened to me and all the transgender people I knew was not fair."

The Role of Disturbances

So where do disturbances fit in here? So-called disturbance theory is often mistakenly characterized as positing that the types of disturbances that lead to group formation are specific, discrete events. In reality, David Truman defined the term "disturbance" quite broadly as virtually any phenomenon—either discrete or prolonged (lasting, for example, several years)—that upsets the established equilibrium in society or threatens the interests of some unorganized group of people. Thus, if we take Truman's authentic conception of disturbance seriously, the data show that *all* of my respondents cited disturbances as important factors in group formation, as all of my respondents cited the overall conditions threatening the well-being of transgender people as factors in their group-formation decisions. The disturbances that motivated my respondents were prolonged, ongoing disturbances.

After establishing that all of my respondents cited prolonged, ongoing disturbances in the form of enduring threats to transgender people's well-being as important motivating factors in their decisions to found groups, I combed the data for answers to another question concerning disturbances: Did any of my respondents also mention a specific, discrete event as a motivating factor? The answer to this question is "yes." In all, ten of my twenty-seven respondents mentioned a specific, discrete event or occurrence as a primary factor in the decision to start a transgender rights interest group. It is important to reiterate here that all ten respondents also mentioned long-standing threats to the transgender community as motivating factors. What makes these founders different is that in addition to ongoing threats, they mentioned a specific occurrence or event as a motivating factor.

The specific incidents that my respondents mentioned fit into two categories: (1) *personal incidents*—that is, things that happened directly to them; and (2) *societal incidents*—things that did not happen directly to them. Five respondents mentioned incidents that fit into the first category. The incidents are as follows: (1) an instance of job discrimination; (2) relocating (after falling in love); (3) having a bad experience at a funeral for a transgender murder victim; (4) getting in a motorcycle accident; and (5) meeting a new spouse. Respondents who mentioned personal incidents used quite similar language in describing the role of these incidents in their decisions to start interest groups. Melissa Alexander told me that job discrimination led her to start her group:

> I had always been politically active and have always been interested in the law. I have been involved in many, many issue campaigns . . . and I work on youth sports [in my town]—youth soccer, baseball. I [started this group, however, when] I faced discrimination. I realized that this would happen, of course, [when I transitioned]. I faced discrimination many times, at work as well as in organizations and other places. And I knew [that lots] of other transgender people faced discrimination too.

Brooke Cerda Guzman told me that before starting her group, she had long been active on LGBT issues but decided to start the TransWomen of Color Collective directly as a result of a disturbing incident:

> We had a horrible experience. [It was at the] vigil for [murdered transgender woman] Islan Nettles [in 2003]. The founders of [a local LGBT group in charge of running the vigil] . . . blocked us from participating in the organization of the vigil for her! They lied to us. They said that it was only going to be family allowed to participate. We told them she was our trans sister, and why can't we participate? . . . I keep asking [the person in charge of the group], "Why don't [you] put black or brown trans women on [the] board of directors?" [I] never got an answer.

Brooke added: "It started from there." And Justus Eisfeld told me that he started his group when and where he did because he "fell in love with a New Yorker," moved to New York, and realized shortly thereafter that no extant group did what he wanted to do.

Five respondents mentioned what I call societal incidents: (1) the murder of Brandon Teena and the subsequent media coverage; (2) the consideration by a government entity of a non-discrimination bill (three respondents cited this kind of incident); and (3) the murder of a transgender person. Riki Wilchins, one of the driving forces behind the pioneering Transexual Menace (and later, GenderPAC), told me that for most of her early life she eschewed politics. "I completely avoided it," she told me. "I was your typical self-hating transsexual for years." Then something happened. "We started Transexual Menace mainly as a [response to that] horrible *Village Voice* piece about Brandon Teena." (I talk about this tragedy and the *Village Voice* piece in chapter 2). After that, Riki continued, "there was the murder trial. [Transexual Menace] became a name to organize under." The rest, as they say, is history, as Riki went on to co-found GenderPAC, another pioneer of transgender rights interest-group representation. Mara Keisling also cited a specific incident of violence as crucial in her decision to start a group. She told me:

> I was sitting in my office, and I got word via email that two young transgender people had been murdered in DC. It just broke my heart and I couldn't continue [what I was doing]. It was August 12th, 2002. I couldn't wrap my head around it. That was the moment my work was in the way of my activism.

Marisa Richmond described the event that pushed her to found the Tennessee Transgender Political Coalition:

> We were formed in May of 2003. The impetus came from those of us in Nashville. In the early part of 2003, there was a nondiscrimination ordinance introduced in our council here in Nashville, which had left out transgender people. [Then] transgender people were attacked by members of the council. The advocates and supporters of that ordinance basically turned their backs on us and said, "We left them out. Don't worry about that." Transgender people were insulted and angry, so a bunch of us got together and said, "What can we do?" We realized this

was a national problem, not a Nashville problem, and that we needed to organize statewide. That's how we got going.

In sum, when queried about why they started their groups, all twenty-seven of my respondents mentioned threats, and/or grievances, and/or disturbances. The data show that just as David Truman and other pluralists argued, sometimes when bad things happen to people, they respond by forming interest groups.

Pluralism and Threats: The Role of Interaction

One underappreciated aspect of pluralist theories of group formation, especially disturbance theory, is that they do not, as some critics maintain, aver that group formation is automatic in the face of threats and grievances. In other words, Truman and other pluralists did *not* argue that threats and grievances *inevitably* lead to group formation. Instead, pluralists argued that threats, grievances, and disturbances lead to increased *interactions* among individuals affected by them, and it is these interactions that ultimately give rise to new organized groups. In one telling passage of *The Governmental Process*, for example, Truman notes that the American Medical Association was not borne directly of threats to the well-being of doctors but resulted from these threats coupled with "improved means of transportation and communication [which] permitted a great frequency of contact" among physicians (1951, 94). In a more general passage, Truman writes of an unorganized group of people who share an interest and how this group becomes organized; again, interactions are crucial: "Their [the individuals'] interaction is increased in frequency as a consequence of sufficiently prolonged and intense disturbances" (97). And in an even more telling passage, Truman concludes: "A minimum frequency of interaction is, of course, necessary before a group . . . can be said to exist" (24).

Pluralist theories of group formation look better when we consider Truman's argument *in toto*. Threats, grievances, and disturbances lead to group formation, but not automatically or directly. Rather, in some cases they lead to increased *interaction*, which is the proximate cause of group formation. Of course, this begs two questions: (1) Under what conditions do threats, grievances, and disturbances lead to interaction? and (2) What is it about interactions that lead to group formation? Pluralists did not address either of these two questions satisfactorily. I will attempt to address them in subsequent chapters, but for now it will suffice to say that by tabbing interactions as proximate causes of group formation, pluralists provided invaluable insights into the group-formation process.

In what follows, I describe data showing that indeed, interactions were crucial in transgender rights interest-group formation. My respondents were unanimous in the sentiment that transgender people have always had it tough in America and that threats, grievances, and disturbances were important spurs to group formation in general and the founding decision in particular. But what pushed founders over the edge to start a group was interacting with transgender people and/or supporters of transgender rights, which they did after becoming acutely aware of the threats to the well-being of transgender people in America.

When Grievances and Threats Meet Interaction

When my respondents talked about how interactions sparked group formation, they mentioned three general forums in which interactions took place: (1) other organizations; (2) conferences; and (3) the Internet.

Other Organizations

The data suggest that other organizations were the most important forums in which founders interacted with others as a result of the realization that transgender people were under threat and in danger. Of my twenty-seven respondents, all but two told me that other organizations were important forums in which they interacted with transgender people and allies before starting their own groups. By other organizations, I mean LGB groups, LGBT groups, other transgender advocacy groups, women's rights/feminist groups, and transgender support groups.

Support groups loomed especially large, as twenty-two respondents said they were involved in such groups before the founding decision. Marisa Richmond, for example, told me that a support group was the crucible in which she formed her group. She told me that she had "been involved in political campaigns and various issues over the years that had nothing to do with trans," and eventually began attending "a support group for people coming out of the closet." This is when she made a great deal of contact with other transgender people, and it started her on her road to group formation. Melissa Alexander also reported being heavily involved in support groups before her founding decision: "Early on, I was involved in a lot of support groups." Not only did these support-group interactions help Melissa get through a difficult time in her life, but they also helped her stay connected to transgender issues.

Transgender support groups were not the only kinds of groups in which founders engaged in extensive interaction with transgender people and allies. In all, twenty-five of twenty-seven founders told me that they were involved in LGB, LGBT, or transgender organizing before the founding decision, and six told me that they were active in women's rights/feminist groups before the founding decision. Brooke Cerda Guzman, for example, told me that early in her career as an advocate, she did a two-year internship at the LGBT center in Manhattan. In addition, she told me that she worked as an intern in Spanish groups in Jackson Heights. Only after these experiences did she go on to start her own group. This was a common refrain among respondents. I will say much more about my respondents' experiences in other organizations in the chapters that follow.

Conferences

Conferences were also important forums in which respondents interacted with transgender people and allies. Eighteen respondents cited transgender conferences as important stimuli in the founding decision. Riki Wilchins told me that conferences were "the backbone of the transgender movement" early on and that almost everything flowed from there. Another pioneer of transgender organizing, Dallas Denny, emphasized the importance of conferences in helping her organize: "These conferences started popping up. I can't tell you how high energy some of those early conferences were, and the politicking that was done in the halls." She later added:

> We were having these discussions nationally through pages of newsletters and at conferences. We were talking about what we were going to call ourselves and asking who are we as people, and we were all communicating. And it just took off. I was happy to start a new organization.

Tony Barreto-Neto talked about the early days of Transexual Menace, and then his law enforcement group, TOPS:

> TOPS [was really] a result of my getting together with, I think it was [Nancy Nangeroni] and also Riki [Wilchins], and a few of us from the Southern [Comfort] Conference [an annual transgender conference that started in 1991 and ended in 2016]. That was in 1994. [We] decided to go national . . . [to work on] the murders [of Brandon, Teena, and others]. I started TOPS because I was in law enforcement, and there were no support groups or any groups, really, that were looking out for the rights of transgender cops and firefighters. From [these conferences], that is where the whole thing [came together]. I was meeting the other activists, because [before then] we were all isolated in different groups all around the country. We just had never come together before.

Bamby Salcedo told me that in her position as a health educator for the state of California, she went to numerous professional conferences. At one of them in 2009, she met with several other activists, and they discussed the scourge of HIV and AIDS in the transgender community. She told me: "We called a meeting, and we all came together and started talking about this. 'What are we going to do [about this]?' We decided that we wanted to form a group, and we formed it." Later in the same year, at the United States Conference on AIDS, Bamby says that she "took the opportunity to call out a meeting, and at this meeting . . . there were people from different places across the country, and thirty-three people came to the meeting that I called." That is how her group went national.

Stories like these were very common. When discussing conferences, respondents used words such as "interaction" and "communication," as well as phrases such as "came together" and "met up with." Conferences, it appears, were vehicles for huge amounts of interaction which led to group formation. Anonymous Respondent No. 3 told me the following:

> It is impossible to overstate how important these conferences were [in the early and mid-1990s]. There was a conference culture. That is where we got together. It was the only place we could really get together with other people like us. I learned I wasn't alone. I wasn't ashamed anymore. I dressed the way I wanted to and acted the way I wanted to. And I learned so much [about the issues]. It was really inspiring, and it inspired me to start [my group].

The Internet

Finally, in addition to conferences and other organizations, the Internet was cited by fourteen respondents as a direct facilitator of interaction that contributed to group formation. Mara Keisling, for example, told me that she is convinced that the Internet is what led to the surge in new transgender rights groups in the mid-1990s:

> Yes, the Internet [is what really led to group proliferation during that period]. I say this for two reasons. One, for the obvious process reasons. But it also made us all safer. It made us able to build communities faster and better. And it made everybody in rural areas understand that there were other people like them. The Internet was the most important part of all of this [in the 1990s].

Thomi Clinton told me that she remembers well what a difference the arrival of high-speed Internet made:

> Back in the old days, if we didn't have the Internet, we would not be able to connect with one another. Basically, the Internet got [us] around that [attitude that existed at the time that], "We don't talk about that. We don't talk about Uncle Johnny being a woman now or dressing as a woman." The Internet was a pivotal moment [for us] in the LGBT community, not just the trans community. I remember in the 1980s, you used to have dial-up with AOL. I actually worked for AOL Canada when I lived in Oklahoma City. Boing, boing. Yeah, twenty-five megabytes. I had fourteen megabytes per second. I was pimping it.

The Internet, respondent after respondent told me, allowed transgender people to connect with other transgender people, and this provided a spark for interacting and then organizing. Dallas Denny told me that even when it was slow and clunky, the Internet revolutionized group formation:

> The Internet facilitated communication, and people that I had brought into the community were bringing other people into the community, and it just got bigger and bigger until suddenly

> you have Laverne Cox on the cover of *Time*. For years I used what I call "the brick-and-mortar model" of group formation. Then I got my Internet account, in '92 maybe. Then I started what I believe was the first online mail reposting service on trans issues. I think it had possibly been done on bulletin boards where you had to call in, and only one person could be on at a time. I was sending information out several times a month of every mention in any media that I could find, any news around the world about trans issues. It was funny because there would be four or five items twice a month. And things evolved, and it eventually became the Transgender News Yahoo Group.

Dallas told me that by 1995 she had realized that she could reach an almost unlimited audience on the Internet. On a similar note, Marisa Richmond emphasized the ability of the Internet to facilitate interaction among transgender people. She told me that for the first time, people could learn that there were people just like them.

Joelle Ryan told me that garnering support for the cause became much easier with the advent of the Internet. She told me:

> I think certainly it's probably many different reasons, but our visibility has just skyrocketed, our presence in the media, the amount of support groups around the country that exist, but also the development of the Internet. That's just been gargantuan. When I first started, there was no Internet. Now, including in rural places like New Hampshire, you can pop online and get support immediately through different Internet venues. [For my group] Transgender New Hampshire, a lot of what happens there now is through the Facebook group. The Facebook group now has over 1,000 members. When we started, I don't remember what it was, but it was very few.

It is important to note that in their earliest stages, some transgender rights groups are/were Internet-only groups. For these groups, the Internet is not just an important spark to group formation; it is the very platform for group activity.

Conclusion: Do Threats, Disturbances, and Grievances Matter?

Did threats, disturbances, and grievances, which feature prominently in pluralist and relative deprivation theories of group formation, matter in transgender rights interest-group formation? The data show that the answer to this question is a resounding "yes." Each of my 27 respondents cited the very real and very significant threats to the well-being of transgender people as spurs to group formation. Threats, grievances, and disturbances may not have been the only factors that spurred transgender rights interest-group formation, but my data show that they were unquestionably important in the group-formation process in virtually all of the cases I examine.

But the data reveal that threats, disturbances, and grievances alone do not *necessarily* lead to group formation. After all, if threats to the well-being of transgender people and the existence of grievances among transgender people were *sufficient* to cause group formation, there would have been transgender rights groups on the scene in the United States well before the 1960s. The data reveal that for the groups under study, the relationship between the existence of threats, grievances, and disturbances on the one hand, and group formation on the other, was not direct. Rather, threats, grievances, and disturbances led directly to extensive interactions between founders and others, which then led to group formation. Another way to put this is as follows: extensive interaction between founders and others was the spark that lit the fuse of group formation, which was smoldering but not burning due to longstanding threats to the well-being of transgender people. My respondents' accounts of the founding decision indicate that transgender rights interest-group formation was helped along by interactions that took place in forums including other organizations (especially transgender support groups, and LGB and LGBT groups), conferences (especially transgender issues conferences), and the Internet. In fact, the data suggest that without these extensive interactions, group formation probably would not have taken place; it was interactions that pushed sample founders over the proverbial edge.

~

I will have more to say about interactions in the next chapter, but for now it will suffice to say that just as pluralist thinkers might have predicted over fifty years ago, interactions borne of threats, grievances, and disturbances were the proximate causes of transgender rights interest-group formation. The importance of interactions borne of grievances and threats and disturbances begs the following question: What exactly is it about interaction that spawns group formation? It is to this question I turn next.

4

Interactions, Learning, and Connections

The data I present in chapter 3 lead to two clear conclusions. First, threats, disturbances, and grievances are important in the process by which transgender groups mobilize. Second, threats, disturbances, and grievances *alone* do *not* lead to group formation. Instead, they lead to group formation when they are combined with interaction. It is impossible to conclude that threats, grievances, and disturbances coupled with interaction *will* lead to group formation, but the data suggest that threats, disturbances, and grievances combined with interaction *increase the probability* of interest-group formation.

Theory: Interactions, Cross-Movement Effects, and Spillover Effects

Perhaps it is not surprising that group founders tabbed interactions at conferences, via the Internet, and in other organizations as absolutely crucial in the group-formation process. I say this because though political scientists (at least since Truman) have not said a great deal about how interactions spur interest-group formation, sociologists have for years focused upon how connections between people lead to collective action. Recently, for example, Heaney and Strickland have shown that "interest group emergence could be better understood by modeling new organizations as the networked product of prior interest groups or other strategic actors" (2018, 435). In addition, numerous studies tab "spillover" or "cross-movement" effects as important determinants of group formation. Studies in this vein assert that ideas about how to organize and whom to organize are transmitted via interpersonal linkages between sets of individuals. Meyer and Whittier, for example, identify concrete ways that networks and inter-connections among individuals affect group formation across movements (1994). In their empirical study of how the women's movement affected the nuclear freeze movement of the 1980s, they conclude that activists working in the women's movement interacted with other activists in the movement in a variety of ways, and this interaction sparked the nuclear freeze movement. The new movement borrowed tactics, mobilization strategies, and personnel from the old movement. Perhaps most importantly, many of the leaders of the nuclear freeze movement gained experience and knowledge and connections with supporters within the women's movement that subsequently helped them found nuclear freeze organizations. Moreover, women's groups had an indirect effect on the freeze movement. Specifically, the women's movement

> won relaxation of both formal and informal restrictions on women's entrance into professional, scientific, and technical careers, and this allowed women to become recognized experts in nuclear weapons issue, arms control, or Washington politics. (Meyer and Whittier 1994, 292)

Elisabeth Clemens also recognized the role of social networks and connections in group formation (Clemens 1997). In her book *The People's Lobby*, Clemens concluded that many citizen groups founded around the turn of the twentieth century morphed from other successful organizational forms, including nonpolitical women's groups, churches, and fraternal organizations. Similarly, Jennifer Hadden demonstrates that many new environmental groups formed out of already extant organizations (Hadden 2015). And finally, and most importantly, sociologist Debra Minkoff tabs social networks and connections as crucial to group formation (Minkoff 1994). In her examination of the founding of women's and ethnic minority interest groups, she shows that in the 1950s and 1960s, many such organizations succeeded in legitimizing the grievances of the people they represented by engaging in service provision and shying away from advocacy. Once these groups establish "baseline legitimacy," Minkoff argues, "the field of activity becomes open for groups that directly challenge social and political institutions" (1994, 947). In short, new interest groups essentially followed in the footsteps of preceding organizations that had done a great deal of the legitimizing work necessary for successful group formation.

One noteworthy study of how social networks and connections might lead to group formation is particularly relevant here—a 2004 study by Schrock, Holden, and Reid of how transgender support groups gave rise to transgender rights interest groups. Schrock and his colleagues argue that membership in support groups led to interpersonal emotion work that primed transgender people for group motivational framing and led to the formation of transgender rights groups.

What Interactions Do

In sum, many studies support the conclusion suggested by my data that connections and interactions between individuals, often in other groups and movements, are important to group mobilization and survival. So what is it about interaction that spurs group formation?

I discovered four general themes in respondents' statements about how interactions affected them and pushed them toward group founding. They are as follows. First, interactions spurred the founding decision by *raising awareness among founders about the needs of transgender people*. Second, interactions spurred the founding decision by *providing founders with emotional benefits*. Third, for some founders, *interactions provided practical information about the nuts and bolts of group formation*. And finally, for some founders, interactions spurred the founding decision by *linking founders up with other people who directly encouraged them to form a group*. In this section, I will describe what respondents told me about how interactions affected the founding decision. I will pay particular attention to how interactions within other groups and movements affected the founding decision, as these sorts of interactions appear to be the most important for my respondents.

Interactions Raise Awareness

Twenty-five of twenty-seven respondents told me in one way or another that interactions at conferences, via the Internet, and in other organizations raised their awareness of the difficulties and threats facing transgender people and nudged them toward group founding. Of course, all of my founders were aware of the problems and dangers affecting transgender people in America well before they started extensively interacting with other people (especially transgender people). Moreover, many respondents experienced these problems and dangers firsthand. But almost all founders reported that interacting with transgender people and allies made them *more* aware of these problems and convinced them that something needed to be done. Comments in this vein emphasized that interactions led to a great deal of learning, which in turn led to a deeper understanding of just how much collective action was needed.

Julie Walsh, for example, told me that interacting with transgender people in various forums led her to "become aware" of the serious problems transgender people faced. After becoming aware of these problems, Julie met her spouse, a transgender man, and became yet more aware of these problems. She learned, for example, that her husband "needed a support group, [and] needed a physician." She subsequently reached out to more transgender people, and learned that her husband was not alone in his struggles. "They [the other transgender people I encountered] concurred," she told me. "They agreed that there was one physician in town, one mental health provider, and one support group, [and that this was not enough]." Her "scan" of the environment, Julie told me, convinced her that more needed to be done. Briefly, Julie learned a lot about what transgender people needed and what resources were available to them, and what she learned eventually convinced her to start her own group.

Joelle Ryan told me that interactions over the Internet educated her more on the issues facing transgender people and spurred her to consider starting a group: "[I], like many people just read [on the Internet] about the injustice." Learning more, she told me, convinced her that things were "unfair and [needed] to change" and led her on a search "to find conduits to channel [this] desire to create change." And Anonymous Respondent No. 2, who is now trying to get her currently Internet-only group off the ground, told me that when she decided to return to sports as an adult—a passion in her youth—she learned firsthand how hard it is for a gender-variant person to find an accepting adult sports league. She subsequently sought out other transgender athletes and learned from them that they faced similar challenges. "Sports are crucial to so many people," she told me, and she learned that like her, other "trans athletes are going through so much." "That's where the group came from," she told me. Transgender athletes, she told me, "need a group just to be able to have access [to opportunities in sports]."

Tony Barreto-Neto said something similar about how he came to found TOPS, his group focusing on transgender people in law enforcement. For years, he told me, he interacted with other transgender people in various forums. He learned that there was no extant group that focused on the needs of transgender people in law enforcement. One of the reasons Tony started TOPS, he told me, was "because I was in law enforcement and there were no support groups or any groups, really, that were looking out for the rights of transgender cops and firefighters." Dallas Denny and Riki Wilchins said words to this effect also, noting that when they began their activism and attended conferences, there were not a lot of other transgender groups around. Essentially, each said to herself: Something needs to be done, and I guess I am the one who needs to do it.

Conferences and the Internet were unquestionably important in fostering interaction between founders and other people. But no forums for interaction were more important than other organizations. As I note above, by "other organizations," I mean primarily LGB groups, LGBT groups, extant transgender advocacy groups, women's/feminist groups, and transgender support groups. Twenty-five of my respondents told me that interactions raised their awareness of the problems and threats facing transgender people and pushed them toward group founding. And all of these respondents told me also interactions with transgender people and allies *in other organizations* convinced them not only that action was needed, but also that extant organizations were not up to the task for various reasons. In other words, *working with and/or for other organizations convinced founders that there was an urgent need for new groups.* This refrain was especially strong among respondents who had extensive experience in LGB and/or LGBT advocacy groups before founding their own groups. The data are very clear: Experience within extant LGB and/or LGBT groups convinced founders that such groups were not sufficient to address the political and social needs of transgender people, and thus new groups were needed.

Interactions within Existing LGB and LGBT Groups

To get at the question of why the respondents who worked extensively within extant LGB, LGBT, and/or transgender rights groups chose to start their own groups rather than work within the existing groups they worked with, I asked my respondents the following question: "Did you ever consider working within an already existing LGB or LGBT or transgender rights group rather than starting your own group?" To put it mildly, all twenty-five founders who answered this question were emphatic that working within extant LGB, LGBT, or transgender rights groups was simply not an option for them. Turning first to founders who worked extensively within LGB or LGBT groups before group founding, twenty of the respondents told me that working in and with LGB groups and the larger LGB movement convinced them that the idea of working within an extant LGB or LGBT group to further transgender rights was a nonstarter. Joelle Ryan put it this way:

> [When I came out], there was ongoing, and this is really important to me personally, transphobia in the gay and lesbian and feminist communities. That was something that I really saw when I first came out, both as a women's studies student and as somebody in the queer community. [Of course], you would think that both of those places would be natural allies to trans people, [that] they'd be totally on board and say, "Let's all join together to go and fight the patriarchy." That wasn't necessarily the case. That frustration, I know for me and others, helped to push [me toward starting a group].

Several respondents cited "transphobia" in describing their decisions to start standalone transgender groups rather than work within LGB or LGBT groups. Thomi Clinton, for example, told me: "Anyone who thinks that the gay community doesn't have transphobia lives underneath a rock." Thomi said she felt compelled to start her own standalone transgender rights group because she simply could not forgive the bad behavior of the well-resourced LGB and LGBT groups that allegedly were on her side. "A lot of those organizations," she told me "tokenize trans people." She said:

> [These big LGB groups], they say, "Oh look here, [we're working hard for you!]" And I'm like, "What about three years ago when you threw us under the bus by refusing to include us in in some sort of [nondiscrimination] law? Now you're all cool with us because of Laverne Cox." It's still fresh, and even though you forgive, you don't forget.

Blake Alford was similarly unimpressed with LGB groups' commitment to transgender rights. "The LGB groups," he told me, "they still do not recognize the 'T' to this day, even when they say they do. Officially, they add the 'T' to their mission statements. But they don't represent transgender people." He continued:

> I was at this awards dinner the other night for LGB people in Atlanta. And there were no "T" awards given at all, not one! I talked to someone after the dinner, one of the big leaders of

> one of the largest LGB organizations there is, and I got blown off. They don't want to do anything. We are an embarrassment to them. Even though they are so gay and so proud of it, they don't want people to know who they are and what they are. So they don't want to walk down the street with [transgender people] who will make them look like they really are.

Brooke Cerda Guzman told me a similar story. Her experiences with other groups, she told me, convinced her that she needed to do something on her own. A local big city LGBT center she explored, she told me, provided "no jobs for black women," and the "Spanish-speaking neighborhood groups" in Jackson Heights were "disappointing." "I was very disappointed in these groups," she told me. She continued:

> I feel like they are very detrimental to our community because they gave a sense that something is being done for trans people [when it's not]. Everybody I talk to, they believe that we have arrived. They say, "Oh, transgender people, everything is done! You have marriage equality. It's all done!"

Tony Barreto-Neto, an early founder and activist, told me that he was involved in LGB groups for years but became convinced after a while that standalone transgender rights groups were absolutely necessary. What happened? He told me:

> Well, these [groups and the larger movement], they were not inclusive. They did not address the issues I thought were important. And I didn't see that working with any of these groups would change anything. We need our community, to be known as a community, ourselves. As for HRC, I have a real problem with them, especially when they "diss" transgender people. I think to myself, "Wait a minute, while you guys were in your closets, in your cushy jobs, we transgender people were going to jail and getting our tails beat."

I heard a version of this story from founders active in LGB and LGBT groups many times. To paraphrase Anonymous Respondent No. 3, the story goes like this: "I wanted to do something, so I became active and involved in LGB or LGBT groups. But then I learned that these groups were not doing enough on behalf of transgender people, so I decided to start a group myself." Stories like this were often accompanied by scornful commentaries on the (current and former) state of LGB and LGBT advocacy on transgender rights. No LGB or LGBT group attracted more scorn from my respondents than Human Rights Campaign (HRC) did. As I pointed out in chapter 2, HRC is viewed by many transgender people to this day as a "sell-out" for cutting transgender people out of its lobbying efforts for federal employment nondiscrimination legislation throughout the 1990s and early 2000s. Many transgender rights activists refuse either to forgive or forget HRC. Many of my founders noted that the behavior of HRC and other LGB groups pushed them toward founding standalone transgender rights groups. Dallas Denny, for example, told me:

> In the 1990s, things were getting a little more organized, and the trans community had lobby days in Washington. At one of the lobby days, there were all these activists from all over the country. But we found out that HRC had gone behind our backs and convinced the legislators and their aides to remove transinclusive language from the employment nondiscrimination bill. Everyone was in an uproar, and this put shame on HRC. HRC, they were really bad actors for many years.

It was not just HRC, however. Dallas, who had been active in transgender rights groups for many years even before the 1990s, told me that she had a similar experience with the national LGB organization PFLAG. She told me:

> So I went up to PFLAG one year. And this was before the HRC thing, probably around 1991 or 1992. I went up to the PFLAG people at Pride [a conference] in Atlanta, and I asked, "So what is your position on transgender people?" These people . . . they just went running around like chickens with their heads cut off. Finally, after a while one of them told me: "Well, if you are lesbian or gay I suppose it's all right." This wasn't a good enough answer for me.

No respondent was as contemptuous in her assessment of HRC and other LGB groups as Brooke Cerda Guzman was. She told me:

> [Sure], I give [these national groups] kudos for their creativity. I don't know how they do it, but they do everything to avoid

> the problems that affect black and brown trans women. They don't want to touch them with a ten-foot pole. They keep saying, "We're hiring trans women." But nothing. These groups, they don't care about us. . . . They live in gold and luxury and have millions of dollars. The HRC has millions of dollars. But they're never going to do anything for us.

But again, Brooke was not alone. The HRC clearly has done a lot since the 1990s to repair its relationship with transgender rights groups and transgender people, and several of my respondents told me that many national, well-resourced LGBT groups today are very good on transgender rights. But clearly this was not always the case. The shunning of transgender people by LGB groups and people from the 1950s to the 1990s clearly affected many of my sample founders directly and substantially and helped push many to start their own groups. But despite progress, the history of LGB and LGBT groups still pushes many people to work outside extant LGB and LGBT groups. For example, Eli Erlick, whose group is only a few years old, clearly had the option of working within an extant LGBT group when she first became politically active. In the end, she chose not to do so. And one of the reasons she chose not to do so was her disgust with the HRC and other LGB groups. She told me that after starting her group, she worked extensively with some LGBT groups including GLAAD and the It Gets Better project. Eli cautiously pointed out:

> We do work with them [now]. But I have always refused to work with HRC because of their incredibly violent history toward transgender people. It's not that these other organizations don't also have a history of ignoring us, but HRC stands out in the community as the most exclusive and most violent.

Pauline Park also found fault with the HRC, decrying its "assimilationist discourse."

It is certainly worth noting that not all respondents had bad things to say about HRC and other LGBT groups. Andrea Zekis, for example, told me that while "HRC has a terrible track record with the trans community," over the past few years she has aligned herself with the group and that the group has helped pay for some of her transgender rights work in Arkansas. HRC, she told me, has changed its ways. And Mara Keisling said that she does not have particularly hard feelings about the past behavior of some LGB groups. She told me:

> It doesn't really matter what we think [about the past]. [Today], we work very closely with a lot of LGBT groups. Some of the best work on trans issues has been done by these groups. We worked so hard to get them to represent us responsibly and to really rearrange their thinking. And I think everybody's stronger if everybody's stronger. [And people need to] understand that most of our wins in the first ten years were because of these LGBT groups.

Thus, it is not the case that my respondents universally dislike LGBT groups and what they do. But it is the case that for many of my founders, interactions with LGB groups that were not particularly friendly toward transgender people or transgender groups, in addition to learning about the history of such groups, led to the realization that working within extant LGBT groups was not an option.

Interactions in Other Transgender Groups

Some founders were active in extant, standalone transgender rights groups before starting their own organizations, and many of these founders found these groups lacking for some reason. Joelle Ryan, for example, told me that after she learned a great deal about the needs of transgender people, she became involved with several transgender-focused organizations. She learned, she said, that "there were local things going on piecemeal here and there," but nothing like "a statewide transgender presence." Local groups were great, she continued, but a statewide group was also necessary. This theme emerged from the accounts of other founders of state and local groups, including Rachel Crandall, Adrien Lawyer, Jacqueline Patterson, Marisa Richmond, Joelle Ryan, De Sube, Josephine Tittsworth, and Andrea Zekis. These founders essentially said that they had no choice but to start a group if they wanted substantial organizational involvement either where they lived (rather than, for example, in Washington DC) or in groups that focused on a certain level of government. The accounts of these founders indicate that many of them looked around and found organizations that worked for transgender rights but did not find an appropriate group that did what they wanted it to do. There were not, for example, state-level transgender rights groups in Indiana, Texas, Arkansas, or Tennessee at the time my founders started their own state-level groups in these places. If someone was highly motivated to become active in a transgender group in one of these places, he/she had to do it him/herself or not do it at all.

Several founders hit a similar but different note about their experiences with extant transgender rights groups, telling me that they started their own groups because of the focus of the extant transgender groups. Bamby Salcedo, for example, told me that during years of involvement in many groups, she learned that groups such as the "National Center for Transgender Equality, [and] the Transgender Law Center were trans-specific" but did not focus on the issues or people she was most interested in. She said that "a lot of their advocacy efforts and a lot of the things they were doing weren't really reflecting the needs and issues of trans-Latina immigrants specifically." In other words, extant groups were not addressing the issues of primary interest to her and others like her.

Masen Davis told me something similar about his (and others') decisions to start the FTM Alliance of Los Angeles. "[First of all], in the 1990s," he told me, "there were not that many trans groups to begin with." The local groups he did find, Masen told me, tended to focus on the needs of transgender women. "There was just a high level of invisibility of trans men at the time," he told me. "[Many] programs were designed for trans women, and rightfully so. [So much of the work being done] was focused on trans women, and so much was service focused." As a transgender man, Masen saw a need for an FTM group. "With trans guys," he told me, "if you didn't [at the time] say [what you were doing] was specifically for trans guys, they would just sit out. They'd say, 'this is going to be for trans women, I'm not going to find anything here for me.'" He decided, he told me, that what was needed was "something that was specific, to give [trans men] some space to talk about things that are unique to [our] experience." A handful of other founders, including Loree Cook Daniels, whose group focuses on the needs of aging transgender people; and Bamby Salcedo, whose group represents transgender Latinas, told me similar stories. The basic story goes like this: "Yes, there are transgender groups out there, but they are not focusing on the issues or constituencies that I am most interested in. So I must start my own group."

Interactions in Women's Rights and Feminist Groups

Six respondents told me that their experiences within women's rights/feminist groups pushed them toward group founding. The early organizer Nancy

Nangeroni was one of these founders. Nancy told me that she became active in women's rights groups before becoming active on the issue of transgender rights. She told me that she "always respected women's groups" and "always ceded women's places to women born women." But she also said that some of the women's groups she encountered, especially early on in her advocacy career, "were not particularly trans friendly." Nancy had nothing bad to say about women's groups, telling me that "women are embattled and long suffering," and that she felt "no need to crash someone else's party." But "it's terrible," she told me, for some of the people in these women's groups "to call trans women men." Nancy told me that today, "many women's groups are very accepting" and that good things almost always happen "when they are approached with respect." But this was not always the case.

De Sube told me a similar story. De told me, for example, about "the completely negative view toward transgender people" that "comes from the second wave of feminism." De was clear that she has wonderful relationships with many women's groups today, but that this was not always the case, and that some feminists and feminist organizations still exclude transgender people. Mara Keisling told me that her group had many wonderful supporters among women's groups, including the National Women's Law Center. But "trans-exclusive radical feminists" (TERFs), she told me, get a lot of press and make some transgender women feel unwelcome in feminist circles to this day. Few people know this more than Joelle Ryan, who has been attacked on-line repeatedly by TERFs, some of whom call her a man, and one of whom dedicated an entire odious website to attacking her called "privilegedenyingtranny." While it is true that many women's groups do great work on behalf of transgender people, the few feminists and women's groups in the past that were not trans friendly pushed some founders toward starting their own groups.

Anonymous Respondent No. 1 started his group solely in response to TERFs, whom he and a well-known transgender athlete felt were doing harm to the transgender community. This transgender athlete, he told me

> called me one day and told me that these trans-exclusive radical feminists were doing huge, huge damage to the trans community. They really want the gay, lesbian, and bi communities to be totally isolated from the trans community. And so [in conjunction with this person], I decided that we need our own inclusive movement, a diametrically opposed movement.

Interactions in Transgender Support Groups

Finally, it is worth noting that several respondents mentioned transgender support groups as important sources of interaction that spurred the founding decision. Many respondents told me that in support groups they learned that support was not all that they wanted or needed; they also wanted and needed political and societal change, and that for this, new groups were needed. Loree Cook Daniels, for example, told me that she has often thought of the role of support groups in the transgender movement. She laughed when I probed after she mentioned the importance of support groups:

> I am laughing because [in all the support groups we were a part of] both my partners and I were out to change the world. We still are. We want a world where people can be who they are, be supported for who they are, be able to blossom, and not be held back by trauma and oppression. To me support is helping people survive in a world that is not what we want it to be. So yes, [support groups and our current group] are about advocacy.

Loree told me that support groups are almost by definition political, whether people want them to be or not, or realize it or not. Anonymous Respondent No. 2 concurred, telling me:

> On the relationship between support groups and living as a trans person and policy, unfortunately, policy always comes up. [It comes up] in everything. So policy always comes up in support groups and everywhere else trans people go because of the way trans bodies are interacted with. Policy stuff comes up all the time. It always comes up. Basically, trans people have to be political to get access to the things they want and the things they need. There are policy barriers to access to everything, and you have to be political to get access.

And Mara Keisling told me:

> [Support groups] have been significantly important. I like to think of the trans movement as having three basic roles. One is policy change, two is public education, and three is providing

> support for existing and emerging transgender people. By the latter, I mean all sorts of kind of direct services, not just support groups. [But support groups are how] this first came together. [Recently], someone was telling me about a support group in the 1950s where they would get together at 8 p.m. on a Saturday, and everybody would come into the room, sit around in a circle, and they'd have a brown paper bag with them. They would take their high heels out of the brown paper bag and put them on. They would sit there and talk about it . . . talk about [being trans]. Back in those days, you could definitely die, you could definitely lose your job for being trans. You could be arrested. In fact, early trans activist Virginia Prince actually was arrested and convicted of pornography [for disseminating the magazine *Transvestia*]. Support groups were in fact political, whether they liked it or not. A lot of them worked really hard to not be. But around the time I got involved, around the turn of the century, the support groups were generally very much engaged, whether it was providing safety for people to come out or emerge and allow them to become activists, or just being a straight up activist group when you need something.

Riki Wilchins sounded a similar note, telling me that virtually any transgender support group inexorably either morphed into a political group or spawned a political group. She said that in the early days of trans organizing, "you had this gradual backbone of what were almost entirely social gatherings. But when you get a lot of oppressed and despised people together in a group, it is by definition political."

Marisa Richmond also told me that her involvement in support groups led her to become politically active and eventually nudged her toward starting her own group. She told me that she was involved in a group that "was not really a political group." Then she became involved in a support group called the Tennessee Vals, which she told me was primarily there "for people coming out of the closet." Involvement in these groups, Marisa told me, helped her immensely. But after a while, especially with the support group Tennessee Vals, Marisa said, "I felt we needed to go in an organizationally different direction to get more involved in politics and standing up for our rights."

Finally, Andrea Zekis provided a detailed account of how her involvement in a support group moved her toward political action and founding her own group. The story is a long one, but it nicely illustrates how involvement in nonpolitical groups can lead to political action and the founding decision. Andrea told me that for many years she was running a transgender support group for the Center for Artistic Revolution (CAR), a broad LGBT group in Little Rock. When she took over the group (at CAR's request), CAR worked mostly on LGB issues. She said that working with the support group was unsatisfying:

> It was a peer-led support group. And I was noticing over time that people were coming into the support group and then they would leave. And they would go back to, you know, a life of hiding! So I sort of got to the point where I realized that this just continues the cycle of people coming into a support group and then leaving, and they were not free to live their lives freely and openly and to be themselves.

Andrea then said that she herself came out as transgender. She continued to work with CAR but became increasingly dissatisfied. The group, she told me was

> not going to be anything beyond a support group. People [in the group] were divided on whether we should be political or not, and it was difficult. And in the meantime, I was making connections with other people who were doing really cool stuff. So I even applied for my own grants, and I was able to get a grant from the Trans Justice Funding Project. [But] I was not able to use that money for what I wanted!

Eventually, Andrea split with CAR to start her own group. She could not avoid, she told me, "getting political."

Interactions Provide Emotional Benefits

Fifteen founders told me that interactions provided them with intangible, emotional benefits that pushed them toward group founding. By emotional benefits, I mean feelings of confidence, efficacy, empowerment, enthusiasm, and inspiration, as well as fellowship and feelings of acceptance. Theorists of political participation have long argued that political efficacy spurs political activity (see, for example, Condon and Holleque 2013; Finkel 1985), and there is now a substantial body of literature on how emotions drive political participation (Brader 2006; Marcus, Neuman, and MacKuen 2000; Valentino et al. 2011; Valentino, Gregorowicz, and Groenendyk 2009). In addition, the expansive literature on social capital shows that connections between people and the "norms of reciprocity and trustworthiness that arise from them" lead to more participation (Putnam 2001, 19). Moreover, research suggests that interaction may create "strong ties" (Ganz 2000; Lichbach 1998) and "weak ties" (Diani and McAdam 2003) that also spur political activity.

Riki Wilchins was one of the founders who told me that interactions led to emotional benefits that spurred her founding decision. She told me that conferences in particular increased feelings of belonging among people who were used to being pariahs:

> Getting three hundred people from a despised identity together is by itself a political act. You may feel that you're a weirdo, a sex pervert. But when you see three hundred other people, many of whom are quite respectable, wonderful people, it's kind of hard to maintain that fiction.

Riki went on to tell me that interactions with other transgender people that gave rise to feelings of belonging and community were crucial in her own decision to start a group:

> The pivot for me [was when I went from] thinking, "There is something bad about me," to realizing, "Oh they hate all of us, it's not personal." When you suddenly realize that this is not about you, that this is not a personal issue, then you start to realize that it's about power, about politics, and about who holds power and how it is exercised and which people are accepted.

Andrea Zekis hit a similar note, telling me that what she called "trans spaces" such as conferences and Internet forums were crucial in her decision to start a group. Such spaces, she told me, tell transgender people "they have a place where they belong." And Mara Keisling told me that forming and maintaining a group is easier when interactions foster a sense of community among potential and actual supporters.

Once again, as important as conferences and the Internet were for interactions that provided emotional benefits, extant organizations were even more important. Nancy Nangeroni told me that the earliest days of organizing

Transexual Menace were important in her decision to remain active in the movement and later found Gender Education and Media, because interacting with other transgender people was empowering. I asked her about her earliest actions with Transexual Menace, and as I noted above, she told me "it was more the empowerment, the feeling that we were doing something." She also noted that support groups were crucial to the organizers of transgender rights groups in the early 1990s, not just because they empowered people, but also because they provided another invaluable benefit: They were *fun*. She told me: "There were a lot of local support groups, probably several hundred at that time nationwide. [And] we did enjoy it, we did have fun."

Marisa Richmond told me that though she had always been very political, support groups gave her the confidence "to be out." Founders in this vein tended to be active in non-transgender-focused groups such as civil rights groups, LGB groups, or women's groups. Melissa Alexander, for example, told me:

> I was very much a feminist as a teenager. I was an ERA supporter and a strong advocate for women's rights. And throughout my whole life I have drawn support from the civil rights movement. I drew inspiration from the women's movement and the civil rights movement. I became passionate.

Anonymous Respondent No. 1 told me that his prior work with a large LGB organization provided him "with the inspiration" to start his own group. Justus Eisfeld also used the word "inspiration" when speaking of his involvement in LGB groups. "I'd done some other organizing before [starting my own group]" he told me, and the connections he made allowed people to "share their experiences" with him. He told me he "learned from other activists" and "got a great deal of inspiration" from them.

Eli Erlick also mentioned inspiration. She told me that before she started her group, she "was a board member of a queer and trans youth conference in the local community." The experience, she told me, inspired her to get more involved. Early transgender activist Nancy Nangeroni also spoke of her experience in the LGB movement, saying that she joined the Lavender Alliance in Cambridge. Going to "gay spaces" and working with LGB groups provided Nancy with invaluable emotional benefits that gave her strength and resilience to continue her activism. To paraphrase, Nancy told me that before she became a transgender activist, she "loved" gay bars and also became active in LGB groups, partially because she felt accepted, safe, and empowered in "gay spaces." These feelings helped push her toward the founding decision.

Interactions Provide Founders with Knowledge of the "Nuts and Bolts" of Group Formation

Twelve founders told me that interactions at conferences, via the Internet, and in other organizations spurred the founding decision by providing practical knowledge about how to go about starting and running a group. Josephine Tittsworth was one of these founders; she told me that she came to activism after learning "how it was done." It all started, she told me, when she was an undergraduate in a social work program. The dean of students at the time asked her to work on "trying to get transgender inclusion" worked into some policies at her university. She agreed to do it despite her lack of activist experience, and she "created a small strategy group made up of faculty and staff" and a student representative, herself. This led her to "learn about the shared governance process" at the university and how "to get policies changed." Years later, she won her first battle, getting transgender people included in university discrimination policy. From there, Josephine attended graduate school, where she served as a senator in student government. There, she says she met and started working with "systemwide administrators." "Anyway," she told me, "I spent [some of my] time working on getting policies changed." Word started spreading at her university and others that she was good at this sort of thing, and in 2009, "people were asking an attorney friend of mine how to change policies on their campus, and she would always tell them to talk to me because I had learned a lot." In 2009, after these requests, Josephine decided to "start an organization."

Riki Wilchins also gained valuable knowledge about "how it was done" from her interactions with others at conferences and other venues. She told me that when she helped to form and design the direct-action group Transexual Menace, she patterned the group "directly off of the Lavender Menace," an early, informal 1970s lesbian rights group best known for its public demonstration at the Second Congress to Unite Women protesting the exclusion of lesbians by many prominent feminist organizations. Here, we see a direct demonstration effect.

Again, conferences and the Internet were undoubtedly important forums in which founders interacted with transgender people and allies. But once again, other organizations were particularly important for learning how things are done. Masen Davis, for example, told me that his interactions with other transgender people and allies in other organizations gave him invaluable information about "how it was done" and helped spur his founding decision. He and many of his cohorts, he told me, were active in other organizations before he founded FTM Alliance of Los Angeles. He and his friends, he said, "were politicized by, and learned from [the LGB movement] and groups like ACT UP." Masen also told me that his work with United Way helped him learn how to run an organization. He said:

> My background is in social work, and after my social work degree I went to United Way in part to get a bigger picture view of what was going on in the nonprofit sector and to learn and practice some fundraising skills. I worked at United Way when I was doing FTM Alliance, which was never a job for me [but] was just compassion. I would work at United Way in fundraising and grant making, and I did that for six years. Every night and weekend it would be all FTM Alliance. I learned so many things, from learning how to make a website, to figuring out our programs with our team.

Joelle Ryan told a similar story when I asked her about her founding. "I became a women's studies major as an undergrad," she told me, "and as you know I am now a women's studies professor." She continued: "[I learned] activism when I became an undergrad and started joining campus queer organizations and talking about feminism and social justice in my classes." "Learning activism," Joelle told me, meant quite literally learning how activist groups work. Adrien Lawyer also referred to learning about the logistics of group formation, telling me that he and his co-founder "learned from other civil rights movements [and organizations]." "I was in it," he told me. "I got to watch a lot of second-wave feminist stuff unfurl."

The early transgender activist Dallas Denny also gained valuable skills and experience by working with other groups, particularly LGB, before founding her own transgender group. As I note above, Dallas worked with an organization called the Montgomery Institute before starting her own groups. Shortly after going to work at the Institute, Dallas began a relationship with the LGB community. The Institute, she told me, "had been doing outreach to the gay community for years in Atlanta." Essentially, the Montgomery Institute reached out to the LGB community hoping to gain an ally. Dallas told me that as part of her outreach, she "started publishing articles in the gay press to educate gay people about transgender people." In other words, Dallas began doing the things for the Montgomery Institute that later became hallmarks of her transgender advocacy.

Another early transgender activist, Anthony Barreto-Neto, told me that he worked in the LGB movement for decades before getting involved in the transgender movement and founding his group. This provided him with invaluable insight about how groups form and survive. He told me:

> Well, I've [been] involved in this since the late 1960s and early 1970s. I was in New Orleans. "Transgender" did not exist then. I was working with gay and lesbian rights groups. Everybody [at that time] was gay. Nobody was a lesbian. Nobody was a homosexual, everybody was gay. That's how it started in New Orleans.

Anthony went on to tell me that he was "a gay rights activist, and a civil rights activist" as well. "But I started with lesbian rights in New Orleans, which was the best place to be [at the time]."

Julie Walsh was straightforward in her assessment of how working with LGB groups helped her when she decided to start her own group. "Work in the LGB [community]," she told me, "informed me in organizational development." She also told me that her work "in an AIDS service organization that had gender diverse clients" taught her a great deal about how to deal with transgender people. All of these experiences, she told me, contributed to her desire to start her own group and her ability to get it up and running.

And Anonymous Respondent No. 1 told me that he came to transgender activism partially from being active in the atheist community. "I stump on their behalf too," he told me. Some of the skills he uses in his atheist work come in handy in his work on behalf of transgender people.

Finally, Jacqueline Patterson told me about how her experience with an LGB group taught her a great deal about group development and helped to spur her on to found her own group:

> Through my employment, I became affiliated with [an LGB group] that worked on workplace equality. There, I was able to get a broader understanding of [the issues facing transgender people]. I got a lot of things shared with me that [were] coming out of different [places, including] academia, showing that the LGBT and transgender population had many needs. I thought, "Wow, this is the bigger picture, and this is what's happening

> and working in other parts of the country. We need to expand that here." [Working with this group] gave me a larger vision, and I realized that success for the transgender community most often comes from association with the larger LGB community as a whole. Where the LGB community has been active and entrenched or has gotten certain visibility and acceptance, we were able to be a part of that.

It is worth noting that one respondent, Julie Walsh, told me that she took quite a direct path to learning about organizational development. Specifically, she earned an MSW with a focus on leadership. She took courses on "non-profit management." She told me: "One course, Designing Transformational Programs, was [particularly helpful]. It was by far the best course I ever had during my graduate education. [The course helped me do] programming and helped me in founding. [It was] amazing."

Interactions Provide Encouragement

Finally, twelve founders said that their interactions with transgender people and allies actually led to, for lack of a better phrase, direct encouragement to start a group. Respondents in this vein alluded to a process by which a person or small group of people directly encouraged or emboldened them to start a group. Pauline Park, for example, shared with me that her group came about in the late 1990s when she "began circulating in the [transgender] community" and then met at a conference "a political scientist, who is actually now a tenured professor of political science, who suggested that we co-found an organization together." This direct encouragement was not the only factor in Pauline's decision to start a group, but it was an important one.

Early activist Riki Wilchins told me that she too was directly encouraged to start a group. She had been attending conferences and events for years before she started Transexual Menace, and people would approach her and say, "You have to get involved," and "You really need to come and do [something]." Later, she did. And Jacqueline Patterson, whose group focuses on health care issues in the transgender community, told me that her decision to start a group was influenced by people encouraging her to do so. She said:

> [During] my transition, I met quite a few people that had non-profit organizations of their own. I became concerned about the

> high incidence of HIV and addiction and incarceration [among] the transgender population. [I learned that there were] some health organizations out there, yes, but people in these organizations encouraged me to develop a singular, standalone organization that just represented the transgender community by itself.

Mara Kiesling did not say that someone asked her or encouraged her to start a group per se, but she did say that direct encouragement played a role in spurring her activism. Mara told me that she was active in a local support group and that at one meeting,

> a trans man said [to her], "I'm going up to State College this weekend to do a job fair career day for LGBT students." They were looking for trans Penn State grads to come up, but they couldn't find one. So they asked me, and I said, "Okay, I'm a trans Penn State grad." They said, "Oh, you should come with us." So I did.

From here, some of the people she met that day encouraged her to engage in more activism. She heeded the call.

One respondent who spoke to me about this without attribution, told me that she was involved in a number of support groups before deciding to start her own group and that several people in these groups essentially told her: "Please do something else, because we don't want to." She said that in these support groups, person after person told her that more political action was needed and that she, not them, needed to do it.

Conclusion: Interactions, Learning, and Social Connections

As chapter 3 shows, the data reveal that threats, grievances, and disturbances pushed my sample founders toward the founding decision. They did so indirectly, however, by pushing founders toward extensive interaction with transgender people and allies. Indeed, the data reveal that the development of connections between my founders and transgender people and allies partially spurred the group-founding decision *in all cases*. This finding supports a growing body of literature that tabs social networks, cross-movement effects, and spillover effects as crucial in the group-formation process. But what is it about interactions that spurred the founding decision by my founders?

The data reveal that interactions affected the founding decision among sample founders in four distinct ways. First, in almost all cases, just as sociologist Debra Minkoff and others would predict, interactions *raised founders' awareness* of the problems and threats facing transgender people in the United States. In sum, almost all of my founders reported having proverbial consciousness raising experiences as a result of their interactions with others at conferences, via the Internet, and in other organizations. Some founders said they learned how bad it really was out there for transgender people and this compelled them to act. Others, especially those with extensive experience in other organizations, told me that they learned that extant organizations simply were not sufficient to address the issues facing transgender people. Founders in this vein said they were pushed toward founding after becoming more aware of the threats facing transgender people, becoming involved in other organizations, and ultimately concluding for one reason or another that the groups in which they were involved were simply not "getting the job done."

Second, in many cases, interactions provided a spur to group formation by *providing founders with emotional benefits*. Founders who told me about the emotional benefits of interactions used words such as "inspiration," "empowerment," "fellowship," "belonging," and "confidence." The data reveal that feeling powerful, feeling safe, feeling accepted, and being inspired pushed many respondents toward group founding. This finding supports a growing body of literature showing that emotions can directly affect political behavior.

Third, some founders told me that interactions helped propel them toward group founding by *teaching them practical lessons about organizing*. In essence, some founders *learned how* to found groups via their involvement in other groups and their connections with other people. Several founders told me that interacting with others, especially in other organizations, provided them with valuable skills and experiences that came in handy during the group-formation process. The data show that just as studies of cross-movement and spillover effects predict, many founders were pushed toward the founding decision after learning skills in fundraising, organizational management, and even lobbying. Briefly, the data show that *learning how* was vital to the founding decision of many founders.

Finally, in some cases, interactions led to more or less direct encouragement to start a transgender rights advocacy group. In these cases, founders learned about the threats facing transgender people, started interacting with other activists and transgender people as a result ("circulating in the community," as Pauline Park put it), and were then encouraged by others they met to consider founding a group. In sum, in a handful of cases, *being asked* to start a group led directly to the decision to start a group.

Pluralists long ago averred that interactions are crucial for group formation, and a number of recent scholars of social connections, spillover effects, and cross-movement effects have affirmed this notion. My data, in turn, affirm the conclusions of these scholars. But while my data speak directly to the usefulness of pluralist theories of group formation, many extant studies take a decidedly dimmer view of such theories. Most prominent among such studies are those in the rational choice tradition. Rational choice-based studies look well beyond threats, grievances, and disturbances and the interactions they produce to explain group formation. It is to these studies and the degree to which the data support them that I turn next.

5

Overcoming the Collective-Action Problem

Chapters 3 and 4 present data revealing that just as pluralist thinkers of the midtwentieth century argued, threats, grievances, and disturbances contributed mightily to the process by which transgender-rights interest groups formed. They did so by pushing founders to seek out and interact with other people at conferences, via the Internet, and in other organizations. These interactions, for reasons I adumbrate in chapter 4, were proximate spurs to the founding decision. Yet while pluralist theories of group formation dominated political science in the 1950s and early 1960s and have experienced a bit of a resurgence recently (I will have more to say about this in subsequent chapters), pluralists came under withering attack in the 1960s, 1970s, and 1980s. The attacks came most prominently from scholars working in the rational-choice tradition.

In this chapter, I will put rational-choice theories of group formation to the test against my data. I will begin by outlining the basic rational-choice (or "incentive-theory") approach to explaining interest-group formation. Rational-choice theorists downplay the role of threats and grievances in group formation, emphasizing instead the process by which group leaders offer benefits to members and patrons in exchange for support. From here, I analyze the qualitative data in an effort to test notions drawn from rational-choice theories of group formation. In the end, the data indicate that rational-choice theories of group formation do indeed have a great deal to teach us about the process by which transgender rights groups mobilize, but they are far from sufficient to explain this process.

Mancur Olson, Rational Choice, and Incentive Theory

While it is fair to say that the pluralist view of interest-group formation was widely accepted by political scientists in the 1950s and 1960s, it attracted criticism from the very beginning. In 1964, for example, political scientist Murray Edelman argued that people do not remain politically activated for very long when their interests are threatened, as they are open to manipulation by skilled propagandists who can dissipate their commitment to a cause by deploying symbols. And in 1960, in a famous critique of pluralism's essential underpinnings, E. E. Schattschneider noted that many people—especially people for whom organizing arguably is most necessary, including the poor and the oppressed—do not organize politically when their interests are threatened. Numerous subsequent studies of political participation provided empirical support for this observation (see, for example, Rosenstone and Hansen 1993; Schlozman, Verba, and Brady 2012; Verba, Schlozman, and Brady 1995). Interestingly, pluralists themselves seemed to understand that in some cases individuals who share common interests may not form groups when these interests are threatened. In some cases, pluralists acknowledged, people lack the resources to join collective fights. In others, they do not interact much with other people who share their interests, and thus their actions remain individual rather than collective. But, in the end, pluralists were optimistic about the prospects of aggrieved and threatened individuals joining together in political organizations (Dahl 1956, 145; 1961, 228).

"Optimistic" is not a word that anyone would associate with Mancur Olson's critique of pluralism. In his *Logic of Collective Action* (1965) Olson attacked the notion that threats, grievances, and disturbances spark collective action and group formation. He did this by arguing that rational individuals are decidedly *not* inclined to act collectively either when their interests are threatened or when they are faced with disturbances. In fact, Olson argued, exactly the opposite is true; most people are *dis*inclined to act collectively when their interests are threatened or when they are "disturbed." Rational, self-interested individuals, Olson argued, realize that the costs they incur by acting collectively are likely to outweigh the personal benefits they derive from doing this. Ultimately, Olson averred, interest-group formation is unlikely as long as the collective benefits of joining a group are available to individual "free-riders." Olson did not argue that collective action is impossible. Instead, he argued that it relied upon the ability of an established group either to induce individuals to contribute and participate by offering them selective material and social benefits, or to coerce people to join.

Olson's basic argument, despite criticism that it underestimated the willingness of people to join political groups for reasons beyond narrow self-interest (see, for example, Cigler and Hansen 1983; Frohlich and Oppenheimer 1978; Godwin and Mitchell 1982; Hansen 1985; Hardin 1982; Marsh 1976; McFarland 1976; 1984; Moe 1980; Rothenberg 1988), was widely accepted almost immediately by political scientists, and it reframed how political scientists tended to study interest-group formation and survival. Specifically, subsequent to Olson, most scholars of interest-group formation took a decidedly supply-side approach, focusing on how groups could attract supporters who were disinclined to act collectively even in the face of disturbances and threats to their well-being. By the 1970s, Olsonian, supply-side, "incentive theory" replaced demand-side pluralist disturbance theory as the dominant paradigm for explaining group formation and survival. At the core of incentive theory is the straightforward notion that "the development of a political group involves a 'mutually satisfactory exchange,' with both leaders and followers experiencing a net gain from organizational involvement, as leaders offer incentives to members in exchange for support" (Cigler 1991, 110).

In the incentive-theory literature, contextual variables are downplayed as determinants of group formation, while the internal mechanics of groups and "the decision-making processes of individuals" are emphasized (Hojnacki et al. 2012, 383). Some research in this vein examines how nonmaterial social and expressive benefits can motivate people to act collectively (Clark and Wilson 1961; King and Walker 1992; Moe 1980; Salisbury 1969; Wilson 1974). Other studies focus on where interest groups might get resources (from, for example, patrons of political action) if they have trouble attracting members (Walker 1983; 1991).

One supply-side, internal group factor that looms large in the incentive-theory paradigm but has not received much research attention until recently is *leadership*. A core actor in the incentive-theory framework is the group leader—or group entrepreneur in Robert Salisbury's parlance (Salisbury 1969). Entrepreneurs, Salisbury wrote, are the interest-group leaders "who invest capital in a set of benefits, which they offer to prospective members at a price—membership" (1969, 2). It is entrepreneurs who start groups, find resources, and design incentive structures to attract support. And though treatments of interest groups published in the 1970s, 1980s and early 1990s dropped the names of exemplars such as Ralph Nader (various), Candy Lightner (Mothers Against Drunk Driving), César Chávez (United Farm Workers), and James Brady (Handgun Control, Inc.), leadership has received surprisingly little research attention from political scientists. I will have more to say about this later.

Resource Mobilization Theory in Sociology

In the 1970s, many sociologists—especially those in the "resource-mobilization" school—also adopted the basic incentive-theory framework to explain interest-group formation. For example, upon observing the surfeit of new, mostly left-leaning political organizations formed in the 1960s and early 1970s, sociologists McCarthy and Zald tabbed skilled and resourceful "movement entrepreneurs" who offered something to members in return for their support as the driving forces behind interest-group formation (McCarthy and Zald 1973). Like incentive theorists in political science, McCarthy and Zald argued that grievances alone are not enough to foster collective action. They and other resource mobilization theorists concluded that grievances had to be matched with resources if collective action is to occur and new interest groups are to form. And like incentive theorists, resource mobilization scholars argued that individual entrepreneurs are the promoters of this matching. Movement entrepreneurs are so important, in fact, that they can manipulate and even manufacture grievances to suit their organizational needs. "The definition of grievances," McCarthy and Zald wrote, "will expand to meet the funds and support personnel available" (1973, 13; see also Berry 1977; Jackson and Johnson 1974; Jenkins 1983; Jenkins and Perrow 1977; Schoenfeld, Meier, and Griffin 1979; Simcock 1979).

The Decline (or Acceptance?) of Incentive Theory

The number of political science studies of group development that focus on the internal workings of interest groups conducted in the last fifteen to twenty years is relatively small. In their discussions of group formation and maintenance, textbooks and general treatments continue to cite Mancur Olson and incentive theorists, including Salisbury (1969) and Walker (1983; 1991), but research using the incentive-theory paradigm has been limited. A number of empirical studies confirm the importance of patron subsidization for group formation (Lowry 1999; Nownes and Neeley 1996; Salamon 1995; Reckhow 2013; Vogel 1989), and others continue to examine how groups get individuals either to join or to remain as members (Djupe and Gilbert 2008; Djupe and Lewis 2015; Halpin 2010; Halpin and Daugbjerg 2015; Halpin and Jordan 2009; Halpin and Thomas 2012; Holyoke 2013; Jordan and Halpin 2004; Jordan and Maloney 1998a; 1998b; 2006). More than anything else, these studies show that supply-side considerations—especially leader decisions about what sorts of incentives and opportunities for participation to offer—are crucial in determining what interest groups actually look like. Incentive theory also appears in many case studies of both individual groups and interest-group populations, "sectors," or "guilds" (Bosso 2005; Flavin and Hartney 2015; Martin 2013; Williamson, Skocpol, and Coggin 2011; Skocpol and Williamson 2013; Wilcox 2009; Witko 2009; 2015).

One variable that is crucial in the incentive-theory paradigm that has attracted little attention overall but is beginning to receive more is *leadership*. One of the few political scientists to take interest-group leadership seriously is McGee Young, who has conducted several fine-grained studies of organizational development. In a series of studies, Young traces the development of four interest groups in the United States—the National Small Business Association (NSBA), the National Federation of Independent Business (NFIB), the Sierra Club, and the Natural Resources Defense Council (NRDC)—focusing on internal group decision making (Young 2008a; 2008b; 2010). In all four cases, Young shows that entrepreneurs were the driving forces behind group formation, thusly supporting his general declaration that "the organization of interest groups is, at root, entrepreneurial, motivated by the potential for benefits greater than that which could be achieved through individual effort alone" (Young 2008a, 187). Young also affirms the basic incentive-theory notion that successful group formation is all about entrepreneurs procuring capital and attracting supporters. The bulk of Young's work, however, is more about how the choices a group leader makes during organizational birth and development profoundly affect the group's subsequent trajectory and its ability to affect public policy than it is about group formation.

Political scientist Grant Jordan also takes leadership seriously. His recent empirical studies show that whether or not a group forms or survives in the long run is not simply a function of whether or not there is demand for the group, but rather is profoundly affected by what he calls "group manipulation" (Jordan and Maloney 1998b, 408). Interest-group leaders, Jordan and his collaborators have shown, actively work to manipulate people into joining their groups by trying to generate concern among the public for certain problems and by tinkering with incentive packages and recruitment strategies. Jordan's work is especially useful for showing that in the real world groups have leaders who engage in a number of important activities, one of which is trying to convince people to join or stay (Jordan and Maloney 1998a).

In sum, incentive theory is not dead, and recent studies of the importance of leadership comprise a positive development. What is not a positive development, however, is the overwhelming recent scholarly focus on interest-group *maintenance and development* rather than interest-group *formation*. In all, the studies I mention in this section have much more to say about group maintenance and survival than they do about initial group formation. In fact, none of the studies I mention in this section (Young is the clear exception) says much at all about how groups actually get up and running; not even the progenitor Olson says much about this. The question of how groups get up and running in the first place has been relegated to secondary or tertiary status while empiricists working in the incentive-theory tradition study how groups find ways to survive.

Money and Where It Comes From

Briefly, as interest-group scholar Allan Cigler has noted, the basic rational-choice, incentive-theory approach to group formation—the approach that dominated political science research on group formation for three decades after the publication of Mancur Olson's *Logic of Collective Action*—holds that "the development of a political group involves a 'mutually satisfactory exchange' " between a group entrepreneur and group members, as the former offers incentives and benefits to members "in exchange for support" (Cigler 1991, 110). The bare-bones incentive-theory framework, which posits the existence of a group entrepreneur and potential and actual group members, has been modified to account for the fact that many groups get support from patrons of political action in lieu of or in addition to support from members.

How well does incentive theory explain transgender rights interest-group formation? I now turn to this question.

Are Members and Other Supporters Necessary for Group Formation?

At the center of incentive theory is the notion that group formation occurs when an entrepreneur obtains capital from supporters. The entrepreneur obtains capital, either from members or patrons, by offering these supporters something they value. It is this notion I test first. To test this notion, I began by examining responses to this basic question: "Please tell me about the founding of [your group]? Can you briefly describe the origins of this organization? In other words, how did your group come about? Can you tell me what motivated you to start the group?" I also examined responses to the following set of follow-up questions:

> Now I would like to explore the "nuts and bolts" of group organizing with you. Thinking back on your experience founding [your group], can you tell me where you got the money to start this group? And precisely how did you go about securing these funds? I would also like to learn about the human resources you utilized to get this group off the ground. Did you have help founding your group? From whom? What did they do? How did you find these people?

Depending on what each respondent told me in response to these questions, I probed further, trying to learn as much as I could about the resources founders located and utilized to start their groups.

The data yielded four general findings. First, a majority of my respondents got their groups up and running using exclusively or almost exclusively their own money. Second, for a limited number of founders, patrons were important as initial funding sources. Third, in no cases were members important sources of start-up capital. Finally, the typical founder did not spend a great deal of money starting a group. In all, these findings do not provide much support for incentive theory.

Founders Themselves

Twenty-one founders told me they relied exclusively or almost exclusively on themselves for start-up capital, and twenty-four told me they provided at least *some* of their start-up money. In short, *founders relied heavily upon their own resources to get started.* Josephine Tittsworth, for example, whose group originated at a conference she organized, told me: "That first summit that we put together . . . that first summit, the money came out of my pocket!" Blake Alford of Transgender Health and Education Alliance similarly told me: "The shoestring [budget on which we started] came from everything I had in a savings account." Tony Barreto-Neto told me about TOPS, his law enforcement group: "We started with pretty much our own money. And even after we became more of a national movement, it was still our own money." And Rachel Crandall told me: "We have always had very little money. From the start, [the money has come from] me and my partner. We have had to rely on our own resources."

Of course, many of my respondents started groups that began and remain quite small, and this may partially explain why founders provided so much of the money themselves. But even Mara Keisling, who helped found and now leads one of the largest transgender rights groups in the country (and in the history of the United States), relied upon her own funds to get started. "We [the NCTE] were formed, initially," she told me, "by me and my savings and retirement." "It was all me," she told me, "for the first two or three years." Adrien Lawyer, the founder of another relatively large group, told me a similar story about the earliest days of his group, the Transgender Resource Center for New Mexico. He told me: "In the trans world, we're kind of big financially, you know?" At the beginning, however, according to Adrien, he and his partner had to "piece it together." Adrien told me he did not have a full-time job when he started his group, but his co-director and founder did. "For years and years," Adrien said, it was just the two of them. "He had to work his whole forty-hours-plus work week and do what he could for us. I had to work way more than that for no pay at all [to get the group up and running]." Adrien did go on to note that after a while his group got some grants (I will return to this later). It is important to note that even founders who did get some outside money used their own money to help found their groups.

Patrons

While founders almost invariably funded—either partially or fully—their own endeavors using their own resources, patrons were also important sources of funding for a handful of founders. Based on respondents' answers and some archival and news sources, I estimate that six of twenty-seven respondents received some start-up money from patrons. Pauline Park, for example, told me that in addition to using some of her own resources, she succeeded in getting some foundation support. She told me: "I have not totaled it all, but in the first few years I was able to get us $170,000 in funding." She continued:

> It came from several different foundations. Empire State Pride Agenda [a New York LGB group] gave us $3,000 for the work on legislation, but most of the money came from foundations. It came from the Open Society Institute, the Stonewall Community Foundation, and the Paul Rapaport Foundation. [The latter] is now defunct, but at the time it and the Stonewall Community Foundation were the only LGBT specific foundations in the city.

Pauline told me that she invested a lot of time and money in garnering these grants and that her group "got several decent-sized grants." "I wrote the grant proposals for all of them," she said, "so capacity building was also a big part of the work I was doing at the time." Melissa Alexander told me that she succeeded in getting grants to launch her group: "I have a legal background, and I got involved in this kind of stuff years ago." She continued:

> In fact, when I first started this, I urged the group to get 501 (c)(3) status. This way the group could make contributions tax deductible and could get contributions from foundations and companies and large contributors. It worked. I worked on it. I made it happen because of my legal background. My plan worked! On this basis, we were able to get, and continue to get, money from LGBT organizations outside of this state and inside. And we have received a lot of corporate support. We do a big symposium every year, and corporations help us pay for that. Basically, we look around and find companies that have helped T and LGBT groups before and ask them. And they help. They sponsor our symposium. We also get some help from national trans and national LGBT groups. That helps a lot.

I was quite conservative in my estimate that six founders relied upon patrons for start-up capital. If we assume that group formation is a process that lasts years, patrons loom larger. Eli Erlick, for example, started her group with her own money and that of her co-founder, but three years after getting the group up and running, she attracted outside support. She told me:

> In 2014, I was contacted by the organization Peace First, which is a youth-focused fellowship and grant organization. They gave us our first $25,000 grant to expand all of our work, which was really wonderful and very appreciated. Since then, we've been accepting donations and we became a 501(c)(3).

Jacqueline Patterson also reported that not too long after she started Indiana Transgender Wellness Alliance, she received outside funding. "The Department of Justice," she told me, "has a community resource program," which has provided her group some money. She said: "I go around Indiana, and I do training to law enforcement, which is a huge undertaking for transgender populations." Adrien Lawyer, who began with his and his partner's own money, told me, "Once we started to get a little traction, we were so lucky to get good support" from outside funders. "The Santa Fe Community Foundation," he told me, "was one that helped to open our first doors. They were just amazing and took such a big chance on us." He continued:

> The New Mexico Community AIDS Partnership was also one that gave us a small initial grant that helped us get started. [We have also gotten some funding from] certain divisions in the state Department of Health. We have been very fortunate to get some funding for HIV prevention programs.

When does group "formation" end and "maintenance" begin? This remains an open question, and one I will return to later. But for now, it will suffice to say that virtually all founders rely somewhat upon their own resources at the very beginning but that a few also attract outside support at the very beginning, and that a few more attract outside support later.

Members

Finally, I turn to members as sources of start-up capital. In sum, the data indicate that members were nonfactors in the founding of every group started by my sample founders. In fact, *not a single founder cited members as sources of start-up capital.* Moreover, only a few founders mentioned members *ever* being a substantial source of support, even years after formation. Founder after founder either failed to mention members at all when I asked them about start-up money or told me that they were not a source of support when they got their groups up and running. Mara Keisling summed it up well: "[Now] we get a bunch of people who give us thirty-five dollars or fifty dollars. But our movement is primarily not funded by transgender people. There has not been a culture of support for trans groups." Tony Barreto-Neto concurred: "With TOPS," he told me, "there was a membership fee after a while. It wasn't a large membership fee. And no, it did not sustain the organization." Julie Walsh told me that her group does not have and never has had "a membership model." The bulk of her group's money, she told me, comes from large individual contributors and private foundations.

When I asked follow-up questions about why founders did not get money from members, by far the most common answer (from seventeen founders) was that they did not really even try. Many simply left it at that, but a few gave me more information on why members were nonfactors in group formation. Three themes arose in these responses. First, some founders told me that they did not and could not rely on members because the transgender community is resource-poor. Second, several founders told me they eschewed seeking members early on because recruiting members is very difficult. Third, a number of founders told me that they did not seek the support of members early on because they simply did not want to.

Four founders cited (in one way or another) the *lack of resources among transgender people* as an explanation for why they did not seek members. Melissa Alexander, for example, told me:

> As for members, yes, we get some money from members [now]. But not a lot, to tell you the truth. From the start, we realized that keeping afloat was simply not possible by just relying on members. We have had to look elsewhere to stay alive. Individuals from time to time provide us with resources. We understand, and I understand, that this community—the trans community—is not the most prosperous community. A lot of people in the community face discrimination and, as a result, do not have work or good work. So many of our members and people who support us in the trans community are not in the position to give us money. We understand that.

Marisa Richmond told me:

> We've always struggled for money, and we continue to talk about this. Trans groups tend to be very poorly funded. We have great difficulty not only getting money from within our community, because so many people are underemployed and they're paying for medical care. The money has always been a problem.

And Joelle Ryan told me:

> As you know, the trans community is by and large an economically impoverished community. There's exceptions, but overall there's tremendous poverty. So the natural place [for] fundraising—the trans community itself—isn't a good bet in all of this, because when you're struggling to survive, right?

The second theme that arose about membership was that *recruiting members is difficult.* Eli Erlick, whose group focuses on students, put it succinctly when she told me: "It can be very hard to get young people engaged." Pauline Park agreed:

> [We have] tried to have regular membership meetings. It's so hard, it really is, to sell memberships. Well-established organizations can offer you all sorts of trinkets for membership. But if you're just a little startup, there isn't much you can do other than tell people they're helping to create a voice for the transgender community.

And Adrien Lawyer told me that he did not even consider recruiting members at the very beginning of his group, and that even now:

> That's been a hard thing for me, [and it is related to] my own fears about money. I've had to really look at a "poverty mentality" and some of my own really misguided ideas about the purity of struggling without having enough money, like that there's something holy about that when there just really isn't.

Finally, four founders gave me some variation of this answer to the question of why they did not seek members: "I didn't want to." Anonymous Respondent No. 1, for example, told me:

> I [never wanted to be a] traditional membership group, no. I don't want anybody to pay to be a member or pay a subscription to read what I have to write. If it came down to academic grants, sure. I would be open to that. If I'm able to teach people, and if some institute said, "Yes, this is relevant enough that we want you to continue your work, and we want you to grow your group, here, here's some money."

I should note that, at present, Anonymous Respondent No. 1's group remains a small, Internet-only group. Anonymous Respondent No. 3 told me: "I really did not want members because I wanted to do my own thing. It's easier that way. Members want things," meaning that members make demands upon leaders, and he was not prepared to deal with demands early on.

In short, my respondents did not, as many incentive-theory studies might predict, start their groups with the help of members. Not a single founder told me that he/she recruited members early on in an effort to raise capital for group formation. This is not to say, however, that founders ignored transgender people during the earliest stages of group formation. The precise opposite is true, actually, as founders told me that their primary activity during the earliest stages of group formation was *helping* transgender people. But *helping* is not *mobilizing*. And again, not a single founder reported receiving substantial support—financial or otherwise—from large numbers of transgender people in the earliest days of group formation. Thus, the data show that at the earliest stages of group organization, sample founders eschewed serious efforts to mobilize large numbers of others and/or collect money from others, especially transgender people. I do not have good data on this (primarily because I kept my questions almost solely to group formation and not group survival or development over time), but my sense is that in many cases this dynamic changed over time. Specifically, my data suggest that in many cases, once a founder made his/her initial efforts to get a group up and running, he/she subsequently worked to attract transgender people as members and/or supporters.

Many founders were quick to point out, however, that even after their groups were up and running, they did not necessarily need the direct support (financial or otherwise) of transgender people or to have transgender people as individual group members for their groups to remain going concerns. One respondent who told me that he/she did not want to be quoted as saying this told me: "We simply cannot rely on trans people to support this group." Many founders told me about some of the places they look for the resources they need to keep going. Adrien Lawyer, for example, who told me his group was not moving toward a membership model, told me that since his group has been up and running, he has considered a number of ways to attract money, including running a thrift shop, or opening "a queer coffee shop" or laundromat. Julie Walsh told me that at first she spent a lot of her own money, and did so partially because she did not "do much" to woo individual donors. After she began her group, however, she told me she received "some small grants from the Trans Justice Funding Project and the Tides Foundation." She also noted that her group received some financial remuneration from a local hospital at which the group helped run an adolescent gender clinic.

Around twenty respondents *did* manage to mobilize at least a few transgender people for political action and/or monetary support fairly early on, even if they eschewed completely seeking formal members. Among these founders, a theme emerged: *founders who managed to mobilize transgender people did not engage in recruitment per se.* Sample founders who managed to mobilize some transgender people for financial or other forms of support (and in no case was it a lot) told me that to the extent that they were able to get others on board, they did it by providing *opportunities* for transgender people and waiting for support to follow rather than by recruiting per se. No one described heavy-handed, aggressive, or even substantial recruiting efforts. In fact, no one described much recruitment activity at all, either early on or later. Respondents' words were very much along the lines of the old cliché: You can lead a horse to water, but you cannot make her/him drink.

When I queried Nancy Nangeroni about her efforts to recruit and mobilize supporters (financial or otherwise) either early on or after her group got off the ground, she told me:

> I am not an expert at motivating people. I was never brilliant at that. I did build things over time. But I don't know that I was really so much a motivator. I just don't know. I think where there is an injustice, people decide on their own that they want to do something about it. When you present an opportunity to do something about it, people respond. Maybe this is what it is: you present an opportunity to be heard, you outline the injustice, and things happen. And that is what I did. To the extent that I turned people out, that was how I did it.

Nancy was not the only person who told me something like this. Joelle Ryan told me that she focused her earliest efforts on "getting the word out" on transgender issues, not on getting others on board. Only later, she told me, did she consider any serious mobilization. She said:

> [Early on] I was so focused on wanting people to understand and have more knowledge on transgender issues that there wasn't as much effort on recruitment or fundraising, for instance. The goal was really to change the culture of New Hampshire by putting these issues on the map so that people would no longer be able to say, "I don't know any transgender people. There aren't transgender people in the state of New Hampshire. That's

> a phenomenon in New York or San Francisco." [I wanted] to make it local, and to get them to see that trans people are their neighbors, their coworkers, the people they go to church with, etc.

Jacqueline Patterson told me that the support she has received has come from "visibility." She told me that the work her group did was what convinced people to support her, not anything specifically she did to drum up support.

Masen Davis told me a story that was quite similar to those I heard from other founders. His group began, he told me, with a founding board. The board put together a request for support from a foundation in Los Angeles, and then set out to decide what to do next. "We did a survey in LA pretty early on," he told me. He continued:

> We did a survey on the health needs of trans guys to see what our priorities should be. And we had a lot of conversations with people. I've got the original report [on needs] somewhere around here. Our plan was to bring people in. To get them involved in the organization, to get them working on a campaign. And we tried to get them involved in some of our social events, and to get them engaging more, getting people to know each other. And we learned [early on] that more than anything else, people wanted support, and wanted engagement. It wasn't like we said, "You come support this thing and now we're going to turn you into a political person." It was much more subtle than that. If someone came to one of our "guys chats" on a weekend, we would make an announcement about [politics]. We didn't recruit. We didn't expect political action. We presented people with an opportunity. That's what we did, give people the opportunity.

Costs

In the end, the most important finding here is that by far, the dominant source of start-up funds for the founders in my study was founders themselves. After founders themselves, there were patrons. In addition to asking my respondents about where they got their money—a question that bears directly on incentive theory—I asked respondents for a broad estimate of how much money they spent getting their groups off the ground. My respondents followed my lead and seldom offered precise dollar amounts, but their responses, which I supplemented with material from on-line research, clearly support the following conclusion: *the vast majority (I estimate nineteen of twenty-four who provided information on costs) invested less than $1,000) to start their groups.* I should caution here that many respondents' answers to my budget questions confirmed (again) that there is no clear line between group formation and group maintenance in the minds of many respondents. Thus, my analysis of founding costs must be viewed as somewhat tentative, as founders repeatedly told me in one way or another that group founding is more of a lengthy process than a discrete event.

The data suggest that only four respondents out of twenty-four who gave me codeable responses about their initial investments initially raised or invested more than approximately $1,000. Thus, for most founders, the initial financial investment was very, very small. How small? Many respondents told me that their initial investment was a few hundred dollars or less. Anonymous Respondent No. 1, for example, told me: "Capital resources? [Well], I'm into it for about $100 a year! That's the way it has always been. My group is very low budget." He admitted that his group is still in its incipient stages and at this point was more or less an Internet-only operation. But he also noted that many people have read his work and responded well to it. Blake Alford of THEA+ told me that he started his group "on a shoestring." Joelle Ryan and Nancy Nangeroni said they started their groups with virtually no money. Nangeroni said she and other activists invested in flying all over the country to the locations of murders but did not spend tens of thousands of dollars doing it. Rachel Crandall told me that she started with very little money, and still has very little money, Marisa Richmond told me that her group has never taken in more than $2,000 in a year.

It is probably less than coincidental that the four respondents who reported investing relatively large sums of money initially presided over groups that had more financial success in the years that followed formation. Masen Davis, for example, who helped found the FTM Alliance of LA, told me that things with the group got off the ground with $15,000 that was left over from a conference in 1999. He told me:

> We worked together for about a year and a half to put together this conference; that was in 1999. We ended up having [some] resources left over at the end of that conference, which was very successful. We had a lot of people from around the country and

> world there. And I think we had about $15,000 left over, and the steering committee, the organizers of the conference, agreed that the members could put together proposals on how to use that resource. And one of the other transgender committee members, Daniel Gould and I, wrote a proposal to invest that to start creating an organization.

Riki Wilchins and her crew also started with a less modest sum of money than others in this sample—a few thousand dollars (which she and others collected in small amounts at a conference)—and GenderPAC became a much bigger organization in subsequent years and arguably the most successful national transgender rights interest group before NCTE. And Justus Eisfeld, who got some money from patrons, started with more than a few thousand dollars. It is also worth noting that archival materials suggest that two additional relatively large groups—the Sylvia Rivera Law Project and the Transgender Law Center—were also started with more than the "almost nothing" that many of my founders report spending.

All of this said, two of the largest groups in the sample (and two of the largest in the country) got started with very small sums of money. Adrien Lawyer of the Transgender Resource Center of New Mexico told me that it was all him and his partner at the beginning, and Mara Keisling of NCTE similarly reported that she did not start her group with much money (and again, it was mostly her money).

Leadership and Experience

Another key notion in incentive theory is that leadership is crucial to the formation and survival of interest groups. Incentive-theory studies do not go into great detail about what sorts of skills are necessary to form a group, but they do assign a lot of importance to the group entrepreneur who is the driving force behind group development. So to further explore the accuracy of incentive theory, I explored the issue of leadership with my respondents.

What sorts of leadership skills do the founders in this study possess? I cannot say for certain, but the interviews in combination with publically available information hint at an answer: *most founders are highly educated, highly skilled professionals.* The founders in my sample obtained skills in two primary ways: education and experience.

Education

I was able to acquire educational data on twenty-five founders. These data show that all of them graduated from high school, twenty-two of them graduated from college, and sixteen have graduate degrees (including two JDs and four PhDs). Of course, this in and of itself does not mean that founders have great organizational skills. Neither does it mean that education imparted organizational skills per se. But considering that today only around 30 percent of Americans have college undergraduate degrees, 9 percent have MA degrees, and about 1.5 percent have a PhD, these figures are telling.

I did not probe respondents deeply about how their education affected their ability to organize. But several respondents volunteered that their education helped them develop skills that then helped them in their group-founding endeavors. Melissa Alexander, for example, who has a law degree, told me that she thought that 501(c)(3) status (which makes fund-raising easier) would be good for her organization from the very start and that her legal background helped her make it happen. Nancy Nangeroni told me that the "technological skills" she obtained (partially) through her education as an engineer helped her "take advantage of these emerging tools [the Internet and email]" in the mid and late 1990s. "Between my personal financial security and my technological skills," she told me, "I was able to see how I could use these tools to reach out to a bunch of people for free or for cheap. And that was all a part of it." Dallas Denny, who has a BA in sociology and another in psychology, as well as an MA in applied behavioral analysis and behavioral biology, told me that the writing and editing skills (among others) she obtained as a student helped her in her group endeavors. And Eli Erlick told me that she learned computer programming at a very young age, which helped her get her group off the ground. "Like a lot of other trans women," she told me, "I've been programming since I was eight years old. I used that ability to work online." She continued: "I used that to work with others to put together [my] website and these resources. I mean, these skills have been very invaluable to TSER's creation."

Finally, Josephine Tittsworth told me about her time as an undergraduate at the University of Houston, Clear Lake:

> In my early years as an undergraduate student in the social work program, the Dean of Students asked me to work on trying to get transgender inclusion [to be a part of university policy]. I

> had never done something like that, so it was all brand-new stuff to me.

She went on to explain that she worked at this for years and learned a great deal, especially about "shared governance" at institutions of higher learning.

Experience

The data also reveal that many founders developed skills working with and for other organizations. All of my respondents reported *some* experience in other organizations before founding their own, and the data show that in virtually all cases this experience helped them in their founding endeavors. Jacqueline Patterson, for example, told me that after she came out, she became involved "with an organization [that worked on] workplace equality for LGBT people." She became a member of the "transgender advisory council" for the group, and using the resources of the group, she told me, she learned a great deal about "the needs of the LGBT population as well as the transgender population." She continued: "I thought, 'Wow, this is the bigger picture, and this is what's happening and working in other parts of the country. We need to expand that here.' " Rachel Crandall told me that before starting her group and before she transitioned, she "ran Alzheimer's groups and had lots of experience with other groups." This experience, she told me, "helped a lot, of course," when she founded her transgender group. Even Eli Erlick, who started her group as a teenager, had previous organizational experience.

Some founders even had previous experience founding groups. Dallas Denny, for example, is a serial organization starter, helping to found several groups. Pauline Park helped create Gay Asian and Pacific Islanders of Chicago before starting her group, and Nancy Nangeroni helped found the Boston chapter of Transexual Menace before she helped start Gender Education and Media. Joelle Ryan founded a group called the Transgender Liberation Coalition in the mid-1990s and then started a group called New Hampshire Transgender Resources for Education and Empowerment in 2000. She then took a break and started Transgender New Hampshire in "2008 or 2009." And, finally, De Sube told me that she started her own business before she founded her group, which gave her skills that came in very handy. In short, no founder reported that founding a group was his/her first foray into organizational work, and several told me they had started previous groups.

Privilege and Resources

Before leaving the topic of skills, I would like to note one other theme that emerged from the data: *affluence and privilege help*. It was impossible for me to discern precisely how wealthy my respondents were, and to be honest, I did not want to ask. Moreover, I did not ask respondents whether or not they considered themselves "elite" or "privileged." But, tellingly, thirteen of my twenty-seven respondents *extemporaneously* told me (that is, without being prompted by me) that they thought that their positions of relative privilege in society were important in their ability to get their groups off the ground. Nancy Nangeroni, for example, told me:

> I am a child of some privilege. [When I was doing things with Transexual Menace], I didn't have nearly as much to risk and didn't risk as much as so many other people did—people who risked their lives and their personal security in ways that I did not. So I am definitely not up there with the Sylvia Riveras [in the history of trans organizing]. I recognized early on that I was in a position to help. There were not a lot of other people in that position to help, people who were secure as I was. [I was a] relatively elite engineer. My continued employment was pretty well assured as well, as I didn't do anything terrible to my employers. In addition, I was able to take it down to working part-time but still keep a job. And this made me available to do this work. Finally, I had resources in terms of personal security and sufficient money to travel for the trans work.

Riki Wilchins told me a similar story. Starting a group, Riki told me, "was very expensive." But, as I mention above, she told me: "I was lucky in that I had a job that paid enough that I could afford to become an activist and found a group. Who gets empowered to engage in activism? People who have both sufficient economic means and sufficient viability socially to launch movements." And Adrien Lawyer said:

> I'm really privileged, and I'm white, and I have a college degree, and went to prep school. Of course, I have [had] my own challenges, and have been all around different socioeconomic groups at different times in my life. But mainly I carry a lot

> of white privilege and educational privilege and stuff like that around with me.

Adrien noted that this privilege did not mean that he had an easy go of things as a transgender person or as a group founder but that privilege helped. In sum, according to these respondents, privilege helped them in their founding endeavors.

Conclusion: Incentive Theory and Transgender Interest-Group Formation

In all, the data provide mixed support for the basic incentive-theory approach to explaining transgender interest-group formation. First, the data fail to support the notion drawn from incentive theory that transgender rights interest-group formation is a function of an entrepreneur (group leader) who offers benefits or incentives to members in exchange for their support. I have argued elsewhere that members are not important sources of start-up funds for citizen groups (Nownes and Neeley 1996), and the data here support this conclusion. Without exception, sample founders relied upon themselves, their friends and family, and to a much lesser extent patrons rather than members for start-up capital. *Not a single founder told me that he/she sought members or member support at group inception.* This casts doubt upon the entire incentive-theory approach to the understanding of group formation. To sum up, Mancur Olson's basic framework does not do a good job of explaining the formation of transgender rights groups. For the groups in my sample, there were no members, there was no exchange of benefits, and there were no "free riders" at group inception. None of this is to say that the Olsonian framework is useless for explaining group maintenance and development over time. But members were (and in many cases remain) nonentities in the groups founded by my respondents.

Second, the data provide mixed support for the notion drawn from incentive theory that transgender rights interest-group formation is a function of an entrepreneur (group leader) who obtains start-up capital from patrons. Incentive theory, as I note earlier in this chapter, was broadened by Jack Walker and others who argued that *patrons* rather than *members* are important sources of start-up funds for interest groups. Patrons were indeed important for some founders. Specifically, six of my founders reported getting some of their start-up money from patrons. Thus, my data show that the argument that patrons are important sources of seed money for interest groups is not altogether mistaken. But any theory or approach to group formation that identifies patrons as the primary drivers of group formation does not receive support here. Again and again, founders identified themselves, not outside patrons, as the sources of their start-up money. Of course, the obvious rejoinder to the claim that patrons are often not particularly important for group formation is that patrons may become more important later in a group's existence. And, in fact, my interviews provide some evidence for this claim. I did not ask my respondents about group-maintenance activities, so I cannot speak a great deal to this topic. But several respondents told me that after they got their groups off the ground, they were able to attract some patron support. Perhaps tellingly, this was especially true of the larger groups in the sample, including FORGE, the NCTE, and the Transgender Resource Center of New Mexico, all of which have received patron support in recent years. This is certainly an issue that deserves further attention.

Finally, my data support incentive theory's emphasis on leadership as an important determinant of group formation. Though the incentive-theory literature posits that group entrepreneurs are at the very center of the group formation process, few incentive-theory studies tell us much about exactly who these people are and what skills they must have to get groups up and running. Nonetheless, the implication is clear: a group entrepreneur must be a skilled leader with exceptional organizational abilities to get a group off the ground. The data provide support for this implication. I acknowledge that I do not have any direct measures of respondents' leadership abilities or organizational abilities. But the indirect evidence I present here is thoroughly suggestive: almost all of my sample founders are well-educated, many are *extremely* well-educated, virtually all have organizational experience, and many had prior founding experience. All told, the people who found transgender rights interest groups are overwhelmingly well-educated, highly skilled people.

Yet while my data may appear to support the basic incentive-theory notion that leaders are crucial to group formation, the whole picture is more complicated. I say this because incentive theory assumes that group entrepreneurs form groups at least partially for personal material gain. The classic expression of this assumption is found in Robert Salisbury's foundational 1969 study of interest-group formation, in which he states that in most cases, the group entrepreneur (founder or leader) "profits" from group formation. Specifically, Salisbury argues that the group entrepreneur gains something of tangible economic value from founding a group—he/she becomes a "salaried executive," or an "executive secretary or its equivalent," complete with monetary rewards and job security (Salisbury 1969, 26). My data suggest that any strict version of the role of the entrepreneur must be dismissed. For the most part, sample founders did not start their groups to realize personal gains. Many founders lost it all or lost most of what they had when they founded their groups. And almost all the founders in my sample have skills and credentials that make them eminently employable. All of this supports the conclusion that for virtually all sample founders, founding a group did not bring substantial economic benefits.

In all, the data I present here do not come close to fully confirming the basic incentive-theory approach to studying group formation. Of course, I am not the first person to cast doubt upon some of the notions at the center of incentive theory. Indeed, starting in the mid-1990s, a number of organizational scholars started to question the incentive-theory approach, raising particular concerns about its virtual disregard for demand-side and contextual variables that affect group formation. In the next chapter, I will summarize studies in this vein and examine how well they explain transgender rights interest-group formation.

6

A Return to Context

Population Ecology and Political Opportunity Structure

The data I present in chapter 5 cast doubt upon the basic incentive-theory framework that has dominated political-science treatments of group formation since the mid-1960s. This is not surprising, as a number of previous studies have cast doubt upon the framework as well. Perhaps most prominent among such studies are those that critique incentive theory's virtual disregard for demand-side and contextual variables that affect group formation. In this chapter, I begin by summarizing studies in this vein. As a whole, these studies, like earlier pluralist studies, put the external context in which groups form and develop at the center of the analysis of group formation, at the same time eschewing supply-side variables such as entrepreneurial activity and benefit packages. These newer demand-side studies of group formation fit into two broad categories: (1) population-ecology (PE) studies; and (2) political-opportunity-structure (POS) studies. After a brief precis on each of these approaches to the study of group formation, I examine the data in an effort to see if either approach helps us explain the process by which transgender rights interest groups have formed.

PE and POS Theory

"Despite important differences between organisms and organizations," political scientists David Lowery and Virginia Gray write, "both respond to environmental constraints" (1995, 5). In a series of studies in the 1990s, starting on a strong foundation built from earlier PE studies in sociology, Gray and Lowery began the process of "bringing the outside back in" to political-science treatments of interest-group formation. Like studies in the incentive-theory tradition, Gray and Lowery's PE work examines the group-level vital event of formation (birth) (Gray and Lowery 1996b; 2001; Lowery and Gray 1995). Unlike studies in the incentive-theory tradition, however, Gray and Lowery ignore the exchange of benefits between group entrepreneurs and group supporters, and instead focus on the larger environment in which groups within a population form, exist, and compete for resources.

ESA Theory

Gray and Lowery are perhaps best known for their energy-stability-area (ESA) model of group formation, which seeks to explain differences in group numbers across American states (Gray and Lowery 1996a; 1996b; 1997; Lowery and Gray 1995). The theory posits that the number of groups in a state is a function of the *energy* the state government provides to latent and extant groups (via policy attention mostly) and the *area* of the state (i.e., how big it is, how many "interests" it is home to, and how diverse and differentiated it and its economy are). Stability is not particularly important in the model, as Gray and Lowery argue that state boundaries have been stable for the past 150 years. The theory posits that increases in energy and area increase group numbers only up to a point, because at some point a state becomes saturated with interest groups, and competition between like groups for resources leaves little room for new organizations to form. In short, each state has an organizational "carrying capacity."

Density-Dependence Theory

For current purposes, the most important aspect of the PE research project is that, like earlier pluralist studies, it puts the external context in which groups operate at the center of the analysis of group formation and survival (Gray and Lowery 1996a; 1997; Lowery and Gray 1995). One particularly useful theory fragment that has come to us from PE is density-dependence theory, which speaks directly to the circumstances under which we should expect new groups to form. The theory begins with the premise that density—the number of organizations within a specific organizational population—affects both group formation (births) and group dissolution (deaths). Our focus here is on group formation. Density affects the foundings of new groups through the dueling sociological processes of competition and legitimation. The first of these processes, competition, is the extent to which groups in the same population (e.g., the population of nationally focused transgender rights interest groups in the United States) vie for the resources necessary to form and survive. Density-dependence theory posits a negative relationship between competition and the founding rate, as more groups mean more competition for resources, which means fewer resources available for new groups, which leads to fewer foundings (Hannan and Carroll 1995). The second of these processes, legitimation, is opaquer. Generally, PE scholars consider an organizational form "legitimate" when it is viewed by society at large as a widely accepted and appropriate way for political actors (be they individuals or groups of individuals) to work together to achieve collective ends. Density-dependence theory holds that there is a positive relationship between the level of legitimation and the organizational founding rate within a population (Hannan and Carroll 1995). More groups mean more legitimacy for the organizational form, and more legitimacy means that group entrepreneurs and leaders can spend more resources on organizing and mobilizing yet more resources, and fewer resources on justifying and explaining to a skeptical public what they are up to, which leads to an enhanced founding rate.

After establishing that competition and legitimation affect founding rates (legitimation positively, and competition negatively), the theory posits that density profoundly affects both processes. About competition, the theory holds that relatively high levels of density lead to more competition (in other words, more like-groups means more competition) but that the relationship between density and competition, while positive, is not linear. The theory holds that growing density intensifies competition at an increasing rate (Hannan and Carroll 1995, 117). So, for example, when density is two or three (that is, there are only two or three groups in a group population), the level of competition between the groups is vanishingly low, even when new groups enter the population. At some point, however, when the population grows larger (say, for example, it comprises a dozen or so groups), competitive pressures run high, and the founding of new groups is more difficult and puts considerable pressure on extant groups. This relationship between competition and density leads to the general proposition that in an organizational population, competition processes always exist but dominate population dynamics at high density.

As for legitimation, the theory holds that when group numbers are low (i.e., at low density), legitimation is problematic. This is simply another way of saying that the first entrants into an organizational population face a difficult road, as group entrepreneurs selling a "new product" to a skeptical world expend substantial resources on justification and explanation. At some point, however, when a population reaches considerable size, legitimation pressures abate, and group leaders and entrepreneurs are no longer forced to expend resources on justification and explanation. At this point, legitimation no longer affects the founding rate to any serious degree. This relationship between legitimation and density leads to the proposition that in an organizational population, legitimation processes dominate at low density.

Taken together, the postulates about the effects of legitimation and competition on foundings and the effects of density on legitimation and competition yield the following general prediction, which is at the core of density-dependence theory: within an organizational population, there is density dependence in the founding rate, which is "nonmonotonic in the general shape of an inverted U" (Hannan and Carroll 1995, 118).Thus, at the incipient stages of a group population's existence—that is, at a density near zero—increased density increases legitimation but has little effect on competition, and as such, the founding rate increases. Later in the population's history, increased density increases competition but has little impact on legitimation, which depresses the founding rate.

The Role of Political Opportunity

The theory of density dependence has received empirical support in sociology (Hannan and Freeman 1987; 1988; Minkoff 1995; 1997; Stretesky et al. 2011), political science (Gray and Lowery 2001; Nownes 2004), and several other fields (especially business studies). One of the most important things about density-dependence theory in particular and PE theories in general is that they force us to abjure a sole focus on the internal workings of groups to explain interest-group formation. PE studies irrefutably show that contextual variables affect group formation and development, just as pluralists said they do. Density-dependence theory emphasizes one of these contextual variables—density. But there are unquestionably others. In fact, following McCarthy and Zald and other resource-mobilization studies, a number of sociologists and a few political scientists noted the obvious flaws in the supply-side, incentive-theory approaches to the study of group formation and survival (McCarthy and Zald 1977). Particularly important here are studies of "political opportunity structure" (POS).

So-called political opportunity theorists, like PE theorists, argue for the return of context—which incentive theorists ignore—to the analysis of interest-group formation. There are different strands of political opportunity theory, but all emphasize the concept of the "political opportunity structure" (POS), which is broadly defined as "the institutional features or informal political alignments of a given political system" (McAdam 1995, 224). At the heart of POS theories of group formation and survival is the notion that "interest-group formation and survival reflects the external political environment," and when political opportunities expand, POS theorists argue, "new groups form and existing groups flourish" (Meyer and Imig 1993, 262). Conversely, when opportunities wane, fewer groups form and extant groups languish. It is important to note that POS theorists did not completely reject the "rational economic individual" who was at the center of incentive and resource-mobilization theories of group formation and maintenance. Rather, they noted that in the real world, organizational actors—entrepreneurs and real and potential supporters alike—respond to external incentives to mobilize and perceived opportunities for influence in addition to group-provided selective incentives. In other words, they simply noted that some of the costs and benefits of group participation (and collective action in general) were external to the group.

So what exactly constitutes the POS that interest groups face? Unfortunately, there is no good answer to this question. As sociologist Sidney Tarrow has noted, POS "may be discerned along so many directions and in so many ways that it is less a variable than a cluster of variables—some more readily observable than others" (1988, 430). Gamson and Meyer concur, noting that because POS is so difficult to define, it "threatens to become an all-encompassing fudge factor for all the conditions and circumstances that form the context of collective action" (1996, 275). Adding to the difficulty here is the fact that many political scientists who study interest-group formation tend to ignore the concept of political opportunity virtually altogether. And compounding this problem for us is the fact that most sociologists who study political opportunity empirically examine social movements rather than the interest groups that are parts of them. Still, there is undoubtedly something to the notion that the array of institutional factors facing potential leaders and supporters profoundly affects group formation.

So what can POS theories teach us about group formation other than that context matters, which we already know? To address this question, I will briefly consider a few studies that focus specifically on group formation and development. One of the best-known POS studies of interest-group formation comes from David Meyer and Douglas Imig (Meyer and Imig 1993). At a time when most scholars of interest-group formation and survival worked within the incentive-theory framework, Meyer and Imig focused on political context. They adopted the "interest-group sector" as their unit of analysis, which they defined as a "set of organized groups that share broadly similar policy concerns" (258). This concept of an "interest-group sector" is similar to that of the "interest-group population" in PE. To explore the effects of contextual variables, Meyer and Imig examined five interest-group sectors: "anti-poverty, civil rights, animal rights, child welfare, and consumer protection" (262). While each sector was unique, Meyer and Imig concluded that interest-group formation in all five sectors was affected by "national attention, government policy, and political economy." These variables were left largely undefined, but Meyer and Imig concluded that most new "social justice" groups formed in the wake of the "settlement house movement, the New Deal, and the Great Society Programs." Similarly, group formation in all five of the sectors coincided "with expansions of federal initiatives." "Expanded federal and private support," they also noted, also spawned new groups (264). Things get a little confusing when it comes to government policy, as Meyer and Imig show that President Reagan's efforts to "defund the left" succeeded in dampening group founding rates in the antipoverty, child welfare, and civil rights sectors, while cuts to domestic spending had the opposite effect.

David Meyer and Debra Minkoff also focus on the effects of political opportunities on group formation (they examine other aspects of social-movement development and activity as well). Specifically, they examine the formation of civil rights groups in the United States from 1955 through 1985. They conclude that civil rights–group "entrepreneurs are more likely to establish new organizations" when African American electoral strength (as measured by the number of registered African American voters) is high, during national election years, when the president is a Democrat, and when the media are paying attention to civil rights issues. Conversely, they conclude that group formation is less likely when "prior movement gains" (as measured by federal funding for civil rights) are high, when protest levels are low, and when electoral instability (as measured by the number of closely contested congressional elections) is high. In all, they conclude that group entrepreneurs are "more responsive to general factors in the political environment than to issue-specific conditions." They go on to say, "Both the presence of potential allies in power and the opportunities presented by routine shifts in the balance of power," promote the founding of new civil rights groups (2004, 1478). In the end, they conclude that group formation is closely linked to a "signaling process" in which entrepreneurs look for changes in the political environment that they see as signals to mobilize. In a number of other POS-focused studies, Debra Minkoff similarly finds that strong political allies (especially in government), electoral instability, and other supportive movements create opportunities for group formation (1995; 1997; 2002).

Two other studies of note come to conflicting conclusions about the merits of a POS approach to explaining interest-group formation. On the one hand, in a 2011 study of environmental group formation, Johnson and Frickel find, just as a pluralist might predict, that new environmental citizen groups form in the wake of objective environmental threats such as increases in air pollution and greenhouse gases and declines in animal populations. On the other hand, Carmichael, Jenkins, and Brulle find minimal support for POS effects on environmental interest-group formation, instead tabbing density effects and the effects of "discourse-creative activities of critical communities" as determinative (2012, 422).

Data Analysis: ESA, Density Dependence, and POS

So how well do PE and POS theories explain transgender rights interest-group formation? In the remainder of this chapter, I will address this question using both quantitative and qualitative data.

Area and Energy

I will begin with ESA theory, which as I note above, is a general theory predicting that the number of interest groups in a population is a function partially of energy and area. The energy term in the ESA model "refers to the policy issues of concern to interest organizations and the level of uncertainty about their solution" (Gray et al. 2015, 177). ESA studies generally operationalize energy with variables that measure the size of the governmental agenda concerning a particular issue and/or the level of party competition. As for area, it is generally conceptualized using a variable that measures the "potential number of constituents" or patron supporters for a specific organization or cause (Gray et al. 2015, 177).

Area

To discern the impact of area, I examined respondents' answers to my questions about why and how they started their groups, looking for answers suggesting that they considered size of potential group membership, and/or amount of patron or member support when they started their groups. In all, the data are broadly supportive of the notion that area affects group formation. I say this because as I show in previous chapters, every founder in my sample cited widespread *need* for representation as a partial spur to his/her decision to start a group. In other words, all my founders told me in one way or another that the decision to start a group was based partially on the realization that a group was needed to address the obstacles and threats that transgender Americans face in their lives. While the specific words that founders used varied, each founder gave me some variation of this generic statement: "I found out that there were lots of transgender people out there suffering, and I started my group to do something about it." Quotes to this effect are sprinkled throughout chapter 3.

Does this mean that my founders felt that there was *demand* for their groups and that this is what spurred them? Not exactly. Again, my founders consistently told me that what spurred their founding decisions was *need*, not *demand*. Thus, we must reject any strong version of the ESA-derived argument that it is manifest demand that spurs interest-group formation. Indeed, not a single founder told me that he/she started his/her group because he/she became convinced that there was now (whenever "now" was) a huge opportunity to capitalize on potential member or patron support. In other words, no founder said that he or she decided to start a group because lots of people were willing to support a transgender rights interest group at that time. Any strong version of ESA theory which purports that group entrepreneurs look for objective signs that the time is right for group formation because there are resources available to sustain a group must be rejected. Here, my data support a more relaxed version of the area hypothesis, one that holds that groups are more likely to form when founders learn that there are people out there like them who need representation.

Energy

To determine if energy was related to the decisions of my sample founders to start their groups, again I examined respondents' answers to my general, open-ended questions about group formation. Specifically, I scoured respondents' answers to my questions about why and how they started their groups, looking for answers suggesting that governmental attention to the issue of transgender rights, political uncertainty, and/or closely related variables such as salience and party competition played a role in their founding decisions. This, I believe, allows the qualitative data to speak directly to the role of energy in transgender rights interest-group formation. The generic energy hypothesis holds that groups are more likely to form when energy levels are high—when group founders are more likely to be able to "persuade potential members or sponsors that they have a stake in public policy meriting an expenditure of time, effort, and financial contributions" (Lowery and Brasher, 2004, 84).

So is there a relationship between the level of energy vis à vis transgender rights and the decision to start a transgender rights interest group? The results are mixed. On the one hand, eighteen of twenty-seven founders provided accounts of the founding decision that ignored energy-related factors completely. Again, in perusing respondents' accounts of their founding decisions, I was looking for information on anything related to government attention, political uncertainty, the likelihood of policy change on transgender rights, salience, and party competition. The majority of founders provided accounts that did not mention any of these things. On the other hand, nine respondents *did* cite (an) energy-related factor(s) as important in the founding decision. This is not a huge proportion of respondents, but it does indicate that energy helped spur group formation for a portion of sample founders.

Of the nine founders who cited energy as an influence on the founding decision, seven cited government activity, and three cited issue salience (one respondent cited both). Marisa Richmond falls into the first category of founders. As I explained in the last chapter, Marisa told me that she was spurred to start her group when the Nashville city/county government considered a nondiscrimination ordinance in 2003. Joelle Ryan told a similar story. She told me that her group, Transgender New Hampshire, formed in 2009 after the New Hampshire state legislature considered a bill that would add "gender identity" to its law banning discrimination in accommodations, housing, and employment based on sexual orientation. The bill, Joelle told me, "went down to defeat, because a simple non-discrimination bill got transformed into a 'bathroom bill'" by its opponents in state government. Transgender New Hampshire, she told me, came into existence partially as a result of the defeat.

In cases like these, a founder was spurred into action partially by government attention to the issue of transgender rights. In three other instances, founders explicitly cited the increased salience of transgender rights issues as a motivating factor in the founding decision. Anthony Barreto-Neto, for example, told me that his decision to start his law enforcement group TOPS (as well as his decision to help with the founding of Transexual Menace) was affected by the heightened salience of transgender rights in the wake of the heinous murder of Brandon Teena in 1993. What happened to Brandon, Anthony told me, brought "national attention" to the plight of transgender people throughout the country. Anthony had been involved in LGB rights and civil rights for decades, he told me, but Brandon's murder and the ensuing media attention helped convince him that something more needed to be done on transgender rights. He said that he and others wanted to make sure that Brandon Teena did not die in vain, and thus used the senseless murder as a rallying cry to form new organizations in the wake of unprecedented media attention and public interest in transgender rights.

Mara Keisling told me that one of the things that pushed her over the proverbial edge and caused her to help found NCTE was the fact that in 2001 and 2002, Congress once again considered a nondiscrimination bill that included sexual orientation (it had debated such bills since 1993, she told me). This time, she told me, the bill was "making progress," and the bill's supporters did not want to slow it down by including gender identity. She was incensed, of course, and went to Washington DC to try to do something about the bill's lack of protections for transgender people. Shortly after she visited with some lawmakers, she told me, she learned that "two young transgender people had been murdered in DC." "It was August 12, 2002," she told me, and the founding of the NCTE took place shortly thereafter.

Density Dependence in the Population of Transgender Rights Interest Groups

Table 2.1 lists the groups that comprise the population of nationally active transgender rights interest groups in the United States. Figure 6.1 below is a graph of the data in table 2.1. It plots the number of groups over time (density), as well as the number of foundings over time.

To recap, the population began with the formation of the EEF in 1964. The National Transsexual Counseling United (NTCU) was formed in 1968, and an additional pioneering group—the Transsexual Action Organization—was formed in 1970. Two other groups were founded later in the 1970s. From 1964 through 1980, the population began to vanish, and by 1980 there were only two groups left. There was an uptick in births in the late 1980s, and during the 1990s, the population doubled in size from five groups (at the beginning of 1990) to eleven (at the end of 1999). Figure 6.1 shows that from 2000 through 2010 was the "golden age" of transgender organizing. Not only did the population almost double in size from eleven groups in 2000 to twenty-two in 2010, but it was during this period that many of the most powerful and effective groups were formed, including the Sylvia Rivera Law Project (2002), the Transgender Law Center (2002), the National Center for Transgender Equality (2003), and FORGE (2009). Since 2009, a number of new groups have formed, but the population has remained quite stable in size, as some groups have vanished.

The density series in figure 6.1 displays the familiar S so common in graphs of organizational populations, which suggests that the population of nationally active transgender rights interest groups in the United States evolved in a fairly predictable way. The foundings series is not nearly as well behaved as the density series is. It remains quite flat from 1964 through

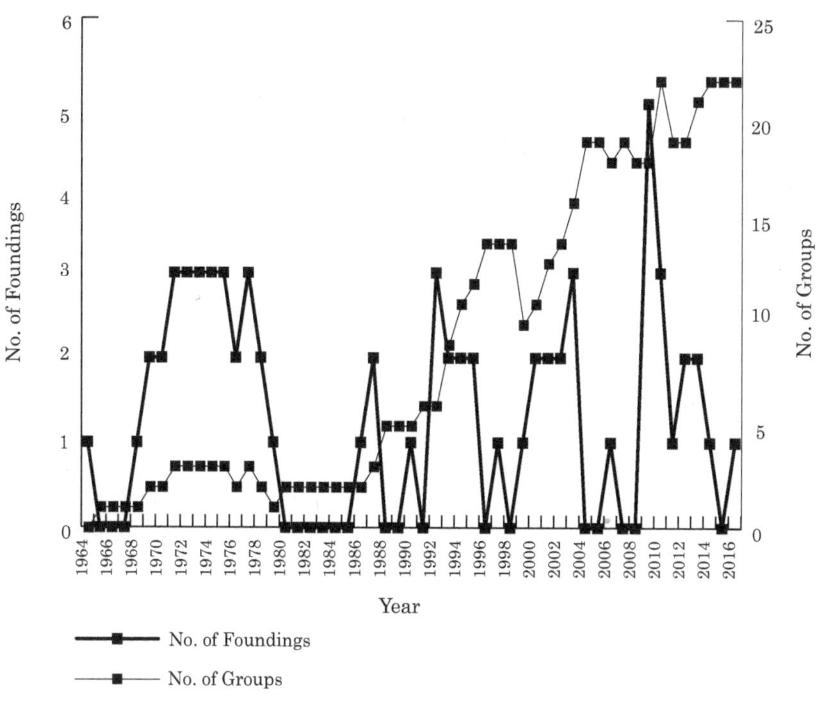

Figure 6.1. The number and foundings of nationally active transgender rights interest groups in the United States, 1964–2016. *Source:* Author's data.

1985, then jumps up and down from 1986 through 2003. The period from 2000 through 2010 was quite good for group formation, though proliferation occurred most during the early and late portions. From 2004 to 2008, only one new group was formed. But there was a spate of foundings in 2010, and several after 2010.

The quantitative data used to create figure 6.1 are ideal for testing density-dependence theory. Applying density-dependence theory to the population under study here yields the following straightforward hypothesis: the relationship between the number of nationally active transgender rights interest groups in the United States and the founding rate of these groups is nonmonotonic in the shape of an inverted U. To test this hypothesis here, I model organizational foundings using Poisson regression, which assumes that the founding of each new group is the realization of an arrival process.[1] This method is appropriate here, as my data are classic event-count data, and the founding rate does not evince overdispersion.[2]

I began by creating a dependent variable, *Foundings* (range = 0–5, mean = .846, s.d. = 1.11), which is defined as the number of transgender rights interest groups entering the population during a given year. Next, I created two independent variables: (1) *Density* (range = 1–22, mean = 9.06, s.d. = 7.57), which is a yearly count of the total number of transgender rights interest groups in the population at the beginning of a year; and (2) *DensitySq* (range = 1–484, mean = 138.25, s.d. = 167.08), which is the second-order density term. Both of these variables are calculated using the groups listed in table 2.1. I used these independent variables to model the density-dependent effects of legitimation and competition on the foundings of new nationally focused transgender rights interest groups, as measured by *Foundings*.

Table 6.1 presents the results of my statistical tests. Specifically, model 1 represents *Foundings* using the two density measures. The results—the positive and statistically significant coefficient on the density term, and the negative and statistically significant coefficient on the squared density term—support the density-dependence hypothesis. In short, the model reveals that density affected the founding rate of transgender rights interest groups during the period under study exactly as the theory of density dependence predicts. The first-order effect of density is positive, and the second-order effect is negative, which indicates that density dependence displays the nonmonotonic pattern that the theory predicts.

These results strongly support density-dependence theory. Thus, we can safely conclude that one contextual variable that has affected transgender

Table 6.1. Poisson regression results: foundings of nationally active transgender rights interest groups in the United States, 1964–2016.

Independent Variable	Dependent Variable: *Foundings*
Constant	–1.66 (.473)***
Density	.328 (.097)***
DensitySq	–.012 (.004)***
N	51
Log-likelihood	–58.430
Pseudo R^2	.127
Prob>chi^2	.0002

Notes: (1) Independent variables are lagged one year. (2) Cells represent the unstandardized coefficients of a Poisson regression model. Standard errors are in parentheses. (3) ***p<.01 (two-tailed test).

Source: Author's data.

rights interest-group formation over the years is density—the number of transgender rights interest groups in the population. In other words, the size of the population that potential groups will enter clearly affects patterns of transgender rights interest-group formation.

The Role of Political Opportunity

Finally, I turn to the role of POS in the formation of transgender rights interest groups. As I note above, POS theorists posit that interest-group formation is partially a function of the external political and institutional environment. When political opportunities expand, the theory goes, new groups form. When political opportunities contract, new groups do not form, and existing groups are endangered. To determine the impact of the POS on sample founders' group-founding decisions, I examined the qualitative data for indications that political considerations factored into these decisions. I coded respondents' answers quite liberally, essentially considering *any* statement citing the larger governmental or political world as an impetus for group formation as a statement supportive of POS theory.

The data here are decidedly mixed. In all, nine of twenty-seven founders explicitly cited POS factors as important in spurring the founding decision. These are the same nine founders I cite above as providing answers supportive of the energy-related prediction of ESA theory. As I mention above, seven founders cited government activity as a spur to group formation, and three others cited increased issue salience. I conceptualize POS very broadly here and thus consider these nine founders' words at least somewhat supportive of POS theory.

If we conceptualize POS more narrowly to encompass *only* perceived government openness to the claims of transgender rights supporters and groups, the data are not strongly supportive of POS theory. Only four respondents alluded to changes in perceived government openness to transgender rights claims as at all important in their founding decisions. Joelle Ryan is one of these founders. She told me that when New Hampshire's state legislature considered but ultimately rejected a bill banning discrimination against transgender people in 2009, she saw this as evidence that the state government might ultimately be open to supporting "transfriendly" legislation. Three other respondents—all of whom started their groups after 2008—cited the election of Barack Obama as president as a spur to group formation. To paraphrase one of these sample founders who wished to remain anonymous: "I knew Barack Obama was supportive of trans rights, even before he publically admitted it. And his election was part of the reason I started this group."

In sum, the vast majority of respondents did not mention the perceived openness of the government to transgender rights claims, the existence of allies in government, the existence of a "window of opportunity" to win on transgender rights, the passage of new policies supportive of transgender rights, the consideration of new policy proposals supportive of transgender rights, the provision of more government funds for transgender rights initiatives (or people), or anything remotely similar to any of these things as factors in their founding decisions. Thus, if we conceptualize POS as a perceived or actual openness of government to transgender rights claims, the qualitative data provide very modest support for POS theories of interest-group formation.

The quantitative data present us with an additional opportunity to put POS theory to the test. Specifically, we can expand the basic density-dependence model to include a few variables that measure the relative openness of the POS facing transgender rights groups during the period under study. Unfortunately, finding variables that correspond to the national POS facing transgender rights interest groups is not easy. I say this because some obvious measures are simply not available to us. For example, a yearly variable such as *Number of transgender rights bills before Congress* would be ideal for measuring the willingness of Congress to consider the demands of transgender groups. But this measure would have a value of 0 for every year in the dataset but one or two (the most recent one or two), and thus is not suitable. Another candidate for use here would be something like *Democratic president*, which would be a dummy variable for years in which a Democrat was president. This would reflect the fact that Democrats are friendlier to transgender rights than are Republicans. But this variable too is inappropriate, as presidents of both parties have been, for most of our history, decidedly opposed to transgender rights.

In the end, while recognizing that testing POS theories here would not be easy, I proceeded nonetheless. I must caution, however, that the results of this test must be considered tentative rather than in any way conclusive. I settled on three independent variables that I believe in some way reflect the POS facing transgender rights interest groups. First, to measure the general openness of the population to the demands of transgender rights interest groups, I used James Stimson's widely utilized policy mood measure.[3] This measure is a summative, yearly measure of policy liberalism among the public. This measure can also be viewed as a basic indicator of the *area* available to transgender rights interest groups, because it provides some idea of the number of American citizens likely to be supportive of transgender rights at any given time. The specific variable I use here is *Policy mood* (range = 51.96–66.73, mean = 60.53, s.d. = 3.94). Higher values indicate a more liberal electorate, and lower values indicate a more conservative electorate.

Second, to measure the openness of the federal government (which can also be viewed as a measure of *energy*) to transgender rights claims, I created a yearly dummy variable called *Obama* (range = 0–1, mean = .154, s.d. = .364), which takes a value of 1 for every year Barack Obama was president and a value of 0 for every other year. President Obama is the only president in American history to mention transgender Americans in a public speech, and unlike virtually every other president in American history, he pushed a number of policies favorable to transgender Americans during his presidency. *Obama* is a far-from-perfect measure of either the openness of the POS to transgender rights claims or energy. But clearly there was more federal government attention to transgender rights during the Obama years than there was during any other era in US history.

Third, similar to Dusso (2010), I created the variable *Issue salience*, which is a yearly measure of the amount of attention transgender rights issues receive in the media. I assume that media in the United States play an important agenda-setting role and thus that more media attention means a more open POS (and more energy) for interest-group formation. To create *Issue salience*, first, for each year under study, I counted the total number of articles in the *New York Times* (using the *New York Times Index*) containing any of the following words: "transsexual," "transsexual," "transgender." From here, I took each year's article count and divided it by the total number of pages in the *New York Times Index* for that year. The result was *Issue salience*, which has a range of 0-.137, a mean of .029, and a standard deviation of .029.

Table 6.2 contains the results of two Poisson regression models designed to measure the effects of the POS facing transgender rights interest groups (as well as the effects of energy and area) on group formation. Model 1 contains the two density measures, as well as the three POS variables. Once again, the coefficients on the two density terms are in the expected direction and are statistically significant, which again supports the predictions of density-dependence theory. Model 1 also provides some support for the predictions of POS theory, as the coefficient on *Policy mood* is in the

Table 6.2. Poisson regression results: foundings of nationally active transgender rights interest groups in the United States, 1965–2016.

Independent Variable	Dependent Variable: *Foundings*	
	(Model 1)	(Model 2)
Constant	–6.94 (3.00)**	–7.26 (2.94)**
Density	.377 (.124)***	.420 (.119)***
DensitySq	–.018 (.006)***	–.019 (.006)***
Policy mood	.084 (.048)*	.089 (.047)*
Obama	.788 (.742)	1.18 (.560)**
Issue salience	8.92 (11.07)	——
N	49	50
Log–likelihood	–53.097	–53.95
Pseudo R^2	.183	.181
Prob>chi^2	.000	.000

Notes: (1) Independent variables are lagged one year. (2) Cells represent the unstandardized coefficients of a Poisson regression model. Standard errors are in parentheses. (3) ***p<.01 (two–tailed test); **p<.05 (two–tailed test). (4) Model 1 excludes the last three years of the data series due to missing data. Model 2 excludes last two years from the data series due to missing data.

Source: Author's data.

expected direction and is statistically significant at the .10 level (two-tailed test). However, the remaining results cast doubt upon POS theory, as the coefficients on *Obama* and *Issue salience* are not statistically significant.

Model 2 is identical to model 1 except that it excludes the salience variable. I excluded the salience variable because in no specification of the model (alternative specifications are not shown here) was the coefficient on *Issue salience* statistically significant. When *Issue salience* is removed from the model, the coefficient on *Policy mood* is still significant ($p<.10$, two-tailed test), which provides further support for POS theory, and *Obama* becomes statistically significant as well ($p<.05$, two-tailed test).

In all, the data provide mixed support for POS theories of group formation. On the one hand, only a few respondents cited the POS facing transgender rights activists as an important factor in the founding decision. On the other hand, the quantitative data give at least a modicum of support to the idea that the formation of new transgender rights interest groups was positively related to a more liberal public and the presidency of Barack Obama.

Conclusion: PE, ESA, and POS

While rational-choice approaches to explaining group formation dominated the pages of political science journals from 1965 through 2000, a number of scholars pushed back against the notion that supply-side, internal group variables were the only types of variables that mattered for interest-group formation. Foremost among these studies were those citing area, energy, density, and POS factors as affecting group formation. In this chapter, using both quantitative and qualitative data, I have attempted to put notions drawn from these approaches to the test against data on the founding of transgender rights interest groups. What do the results reveal?

First and most generally, the data clearly show that external conditions exerted a strong impact on transgender rights interest-group formation. Theories of interest-group formation (and maintenance) must take the context in which groups form and survive into account. As for which specific approach garners support here, the most obvious answer is density-dependence theory. The quantitative data show that the trajectory of the transgender rights interest-group population, which is affected partially by the formation of new groups (but also by group deaths), has been profoundly affected by the dueling density-dependent processes of legitimation and competition.

In summary, in the population under study, as density rose from low to high, the founding rate rose at first but eventually decreased. This finding supports the general argument that legitimation, which dominates at low densities, works to encourage and increase interest-group formation, while competition, which dominates at higher densities, constrains the number of new groups formed.

But density is not the only external factor that affects group formation. Both the quantitative and qualitative data provide some, albeit limited and tentative, support for the view that transgender rights interest-group formation was pushed along somewhat by a growing policy liberalism among Americans during the period under study, as well as by the presidency of Barack Obama. It is important to note here that two of the variables I used to test POS theory—*Policy mood* and *Obama*—are also reasonable candidates for testing ESA theory. Specifically, *Policy mood* can be seen as a reasonable indicator of area, while *Obama* is an indicator of energy. Thus, the quantitative data analyses can also be viewed as broadly supportive of ESA theory.

In toto, the data I examine in this chapter show that like pluralist theories of group formation, PE and POS theories are helpful in explaining the formation of transgender rights interest groups. However, scholars in the new social movement tradition say that these approaches, like incentive theory, miss a great deal of the action in group formation. Specifically, NSM scholars argue that macrolevel POS and PE theories leave the policy demands and attitudes and behavior of actual people—the people that groups purport to represent—out of the picture almost completely. In the next chapter, I explore the effects of one variable that NSM scholars have identified as particularly important in group formation—collective identity.

7

The Role of Collective Identity

Rational-choice studies of interest-group formation do not say a great deal about the role of *interests* in this process. Similarly, many PE and POS studies of group formation do not say much about the actual *interests* of the people whom interest groups purport to represent. It was partially because so many approaches to interest-group formation did not say a great deal about how the interests that help give rise to interest groups form, that a number of sociologists turned their attention to questions of *identity* in the mid-1990s. In this chapter, I consider the effects of collective identity on transgender rights interest-group formation. I begin with a brief overview of theoretical work that posits a role for collective identity in the rise of new interests and subsequently new interest groups. From here, I examine the qualitative data to address this question: What is the role of collective identity in the formation of transgender rights interest groups?

Collective Identity and New Social Movements

While political science treatments of group formation have virtually ignored the concept of collective identity, sociologists have long posited its importance for collective action. The idea that collective identity is important in collective action comes from what is often called the "new social movement" (NSM) perspective. The NSM perspective arose (mostly in Europe) from the inability of Marxist, rational choice, and other (including PE and POS) perspectives to adequately account for collective action that was not related to economic issues (Buechler 1995). In an early formulation, Melucci noted that traditional theories of social movements—especially those that tabbed class consciousness or economic variables (which pluralist theories often tabbed) as key determinants of individual decisions to engage in collective action—were ill-equipped to deal with "new social movements" that arose not around economic issues, but around other issues such as civil rights, the environment, peace, and women's rights (Melucci, 1980; 1988; 1995; 1996).

Collective Identity in NSM Research

The NSM literature is expansive, and I am concerned here only with its emphasis on collective identity. Collective identity is defined in different ways by different scholars. One definition explains collective identity as an individual-level variable—as "an individual's cognitive, moral, and emotional connection with a broader community, category, practice, or institution" (Polletta and Jasper 2001, 285). Another defines collective identity as something that is located *between* individuals, as "a shared sense of 'one-ness' or 'we-ness' anchored in real or imagined shared attributes and experiences among those who comprise the collectivity and in relation or contrast to one or more actual or imagined sets of 'others' " (Snow 2001). A similar definition comes from Taylor and Whittier, who define collective identity as "the shared definition of a group that derives from members' common interests, experiences, and solidarity" (1992, 105).

No matter the definition, scholars concur that collective identity arises from emotions and affective ties between individuals. Several empirical studies show that emotional ties between activists are crucial to the formation of a collective identity within a movement (Adams 2003; Hetherington 1998; Yang 2000). Also crucial to the formation of collective identity is what some sociologists call "boundary work," which essentially is the process of determining who is "us" and who is "them" (Gamson 1995; Hunt and Benford 2004; Taylor and Whittier 1992). Finally, many scholars who work within the NSM paradigm argue that collective identity formation within a new social movement is by definition "*oppositional to dominant cultural practices.*" This aspect of collective identity is crucial to movements that seek to "resist or restructure existing systems of domination" facing long-oppressed groups (Fominaya 2010, 396; italics in original).

There is much more to the collective-identity concept and scholarship than this, but for now this will have to suffice. The reason I am interested in collective identity is that many studies suggest that collective action (such as group formation) is more likely to take place (or to continue) among people who have a strong sense of collective identity. Another way to put this is that "collective action is unlikely to happen without a collective identity" (Jian and King-Chi Chan 2016, 108). Or as Fominaya states: "Collective identity is generally thought of as necessary to strengthen and sustain movements" (2010, 398). While scholars of collective identity agree that it is important for collective action, they do not agree on whether it necessarily precedes it or flows from it. Numerous studies show that collective identity is formed or strengthened by collective efforts (Barr and Drury 2009; Gamson 1991; Gamson, Fireman, and Rytina 1982; Seel and Plows 2000; Tarrow 1989; Taylor and Whittier 1992; Whittier 1995) as interactions between movement participants foster and reinforce solidarity and commitment to the cause. However, other studies show that collective identities can be created or at least molded by movement activists (Della Porta and Diani 2016; Kelly and Breinlinger 1995; Polletta and Jasper 2001). In some cases, people already share certain attributes or beliefs or feelings that are the raw materials for collective identity, while in other cases they do not. In either case, a collective identity among individuals arises through "an act of perception and construction as well as the discovery of preexisting bonds, interests, and boundaries" (Polletta and Jasper 2001, 298). Activists such as group entrepreneurs and leaders are parts of this construction process, and within movements they work hard to foster collective identity in an attempt to mobilize supporters and members.

Collective Identity and LGB and Transgender Rights

Collective identity is cited often by scholars of the gay rights movement, a movement that clearly has some parallels to the transgender rights movement. For example, in his germinal treatise of the gay rights movement, historian John D'Emilio traces the development of the movement in the United States to the World War II mobilization, the subsequent brutal crackdown on gay people during the McCarthy era, and the medical categorization of those with same sex desires as "deviants" (D'Emilio 1983). In the face of all this hardship and persecution, gay "deviants," he writes, developed a sense of community and subsequently formed groups in reaction to shared oppression based on sexual orientation. One of the studies I mention above—that by Schrock, Holden, and Reid—offers a somewhat similar (though partial) explanation for the participation of many people in transgender rights groups (Schrock, Holden, and Reid 2004). Specifically, the authors studied transgender support groups and found that participation in such groups fostered emotional states that pushed people toward activism by making them more receptive to appeals from what they called "social movement organizations" (a.k.a., interest groups). Participation in a transgender support group, Schrock and her colleagues found, fostered feelings of solidarity with other transgender people, as well as feelings of efficacy and authenticity, which led to the formation of a collective identity as "transgender."

The Role of Collective Identity in Transgender Rights Interest-Group Formation

I conclude my data analysis with an examination of how the rise of a transgender collective identity might have affected transgender rights interest-group formation. In what follows, I test the basic notion drawn from studies of collective identity that collective action such as group formation is more likely to take place (or continue) among people who have a strong sense of collective identity than it is otherwise.

Collective Identity in a Broad Sense Is Always Important

If we define collective identity very broadly as an individual-level sense that there are others out there like me who have had similar experiences and are suffering, then it is fair to say that all of my respondents believe that the existence of a transgender collective identity played some role in the founding decision. I say this because as I note in previous chapters, in their responses to my general questions about the origins of their groups, all of my respondents in one way or another told me that they started their groups partially because they came to the realization that there was a need for them and that this realization flowed from a sense that there were others out there like them. To summarize, in the broadest sense, all of the talk of a realization of need borne of interaction among sample founders supports the view that collective identity acts as a spur to group formation. The data show that to some degree, the basic, generic calculus of each and every group founder was something like this, as articulated by Anonymous Respondent No. 3:

> I knew who I was, and I knew it was difficult living in the world this way. I knew what my interests, experiences, and needs were. At some point, I found out that there were others who shared at least some of my interests and experiences and needs, and I learned that we as a group of transgender people had a lot in common. This learning experience, among other things, pushed me toward my decision to found a group. I started my group partially because I realized that there were other people like me in need.

A More Nuanced View of the Role of Collective Identity

If we define the term "collective identity" more narrowly as "an individual-level understanding that at a specific point in time there exists a population of people who share attributes and experiences and who are united in some way," then the data are less supportive of the view that collective identity acts as a spur to group formation. After each of my respondents told me that the realization of need borne of interaction partially spurred him/her toward group formation, I probed further with this questionnaire item:

> Some scholars argue that the rise of a collective identity is necessary for a group and/or social movement to get up and running. By collective identity I mean a shared recognition among a group of people—in this case transgender people—that they have certain orientations and experiences in common. Another way to put this is that people develop a sense of community. Other scholars do not assign much importance to collective identity in the rise of groups or social movements. Thinking back on your own experience in starting your group, do you believe that a collective identity among transgender people existed when you got started?

I did not originally intend to read this questionnaire item to all respondents, but rather I intended it as a "probe" that I would read to respondents who either implicitly or explicitly mentioned collective identity as a spur to the group-founding decision. But since every respondent in some way cited collective identity (though they might not have used this term) broadly defined, I ended up exploring this with all my respondents.

In coding responses to my queries about collective identity, a theme emerged from the data. Specifically, I found that *respondents were decidedly ambivalent about the role of collective identity in group formation and survival.* I say this because sixteen of twenty respondents who gave me codable answers to this query (seven respondents gave ambiguous answers) evinced decidedly mixed or outright negative feelings about its role in group formation and in the rise of the transgender movement in general. What do I mean by mixed or downright negative feelings? A few examples will illustrate.

I will start with Loree Cook Daniels, who told me that while "questions of identity are important to a lot of people," she was not sure the rise of a transgender collective identity was good for either her group or the larger movement. She told me:

> I laugh [when I think about collective identity]! I laugh because I have taken a lot of crap around this one. At this point in my life, I am in transition. I am moving into becoming a human. I am changing my language, and I am no longer participating in the gender binary. The divisions we are putting ourselves into . . . I have come to [the] conclusion that they are inherently destructive, inherently dangerous.

Loree went on to explain that part of her ambivalence (if not hostility) toward the notion of a transgender collective identity came from her personal experiences at transgender group meetings and conferences. She explained that earlier in her life, she ended up with a transgender man as a partner, and that after discussing things with him, she decided she "wanted to go [with him] to some FTM conferences." However, she said,

> People [at these gatherings] were not ready for me. I had complained loudly about how the partners of transgender people were treated [at these gatherings and conferences], and people came back at me and said things like, "You and your partner might have been equal back when you were lesbians, but now he's a man and you're a woman, and you have different interests." I am in middle of what I call the SOFFA [significant others, friends, family, and allies] wars, in which people fight over what to do with partners like me.

Loree told me that currently there are many people within the larger transgender movement who "will allow [her] under the trans umbrella as some sort of genderqueer." But others, she noted, are not so accepting and, essentially, tell her that she is not part of their movement. She concluded: "At this point, I no longer give a shit."

Mara Keisling, who had earlier told me that a transgender collective identity existed, to some extent, when she founded her group, told me that questions of collective identity nonetheless often divide people. She spoke to me at length about the idea:

> Trying to convince people of the collective identity is what the first eight years of NCTE were all about! But it was trying to convince *gay* people of [our] collective identity; to convince [them] that gay and transgender people shared a history, shared safe space, shared friends and enemies, and shared 98 percent of our collective agenda. We [in the transgender movement] thought we understood that transgender people were an identity. But this has shifted so dramatically and so many times in the last fifteen years. Let me give you an example. Recently, a friend of mine . . . I'm fifty-six, [and my friend is my age . . . we] were co-doing a workshop with a young person [who identified] as genderqueer. My friend introduced herself, [and this young person said to the group,] "Mostly what you all need to know is her, right there, she's an old-style transgender person. That's not where it is right now. *Real* transgender people now are gender fluid, they're not just transsexual." She just went on in a totally asshole-ish manner.

In Mara's case then, not only did she have a different notion of collective identity than many people in the transgender movement do (who did not see transgender people and LGB people as sharing mostly the same interests), but she also thought that collective identity was sometimes destructive to the larger cause and the rise of new groups rather than constructive.

This theme recurred. Riki Wilchins also displayed profound ambivalence about the role of collective identity in the movement in general and her group in particular. On the one hand, she said that being part of a larger community of people—"being with other people like you," as she put it—was "tremendously healing" and crucial to, and valuable in, her organizing and founding efforts. On the other hand, she told me that she believes that any time a group of people gloms onto a collective identity, the results can be ugly. She noted, for example, that though much of the earliest known transgender organizing was done by groups of cross-dressers, cross-dressers are now more or less absent from the contemporary transgender movement because the leaders and supporters of the movement and its organizations do not view them as actual transgender people. She was blunt: "There is not a transgender movement," she told me. She continued:

> There is a *transsexual* movement. The other half of the movement [at least as it originated], the lion's share of the movement, the people who actually started the conference culture that gave rise to the larger movement, are the cross-dressers. They remain in the closet. The transspecific groups do not talk at all about cross-dressers. None of the current groups have protested the lack of representation of cross-dressers. There may be a half a million transsexuals in this country. There are millions and millions of cross-dressing individuals. I just find this omission kind of stark. Every movement has its own hierarchies and stratifications, and very often you end up reproducing the hierarchies of power that are in the dominant culture.

Of course, Riki Wilchins is *sui generis* in the history of transgender organizing. By her own account, after years in more or less straightforwardly transgender-specific advocacy, she began (within her own group, GenderPAC, and without) "pushing for a non-identity-based approach that looked at the issue of oppression around the expression of gender." She continued at length:

> [When] I started out, I was specifically identity-based. [But then the more] I dug into it, I learned that lesbians were being harassed in the women's room. Drag queens were talking about being unwelcome. And then I realized that gender regimes are the bigger issue. Gender regimes . . . that is what I spend my day job doing now. Sure, you have groups like NCTE that are trans specific. I won't say that this was never my vision, but once you see that [gender regimes] affect other people beyond just trans people, it's very hard to turn your back on them.

Eventually, Riki Wilchins split from the transgender movement she helped jump start. Her group GenderPAC morphed into what is today TrueChild, a group that through training, briefings, white-paper reports, and other means works to help "funders, policy-makers and practitioners challenge rigid gender norms and inequities through intersectional approaches that reconnect race, class and gender" (TrueChild n.d.).

Jacqueline Patterson also evinced a strong ambivalence about transgender collective identity. On the one hand, she told me that she thought her own group and others like it arose when they did partially as a result of the rise of a transgender collective identity. "We [were] beginning to be recognized under a bigger umbrella," she said. On the other hand, she and other leaders saw and continue to "see the trans community as very fragmented." She explained:

> Some people say, "I am a trans man, so you could not possibly know what I need." [Others say], "I'm a trans woman, it's way harder to transition." [And then there are those who say], "I'm nonbinary, and we have a whole set of circumstances there." I was in the military, then in business. How does [an organization] really get to where it needs to be? Well, that's by bringing people *together* under one common theme of progress and change.

Adrien Lawyer also showed a great deal of ambivalence about the role of collective identity in the transgender movement. He told me that as early as age two, he knew he was male. It was the 1980s, however, so Adrien said he identified as a lesbian. Later, when he learned more, Adrien began to identify as transgender. But as a group leader and activist, Adrien says he sees a downside of collective identity:

> Increasingly, I feel that this sort of fixed identity type of politics is dangerous. It makes us really unwilling to see when we don't live up to that identity, and it makes us so quick to cut off members of our group if they don't meet it. I remember from my lesbian days that we would sometimes have a really good friend [a sister] who then would end up in [a] relationship with a man. And then everybody hated her! "But that's our sister, right? What are you talking about? We can't hate her now; she's our person." It's [the same way with] transgender people who detransition, right? What about these transgender people who regret transitioning and change their minds and medically go back or try to go back? What are we going to do [about them]? Are we going to be ashamed of them? Are we going to be embarrassed? Are we

> going to try to bury their narrative so that nobody knows that sometimes people change their minds? It gets scary when we get too attached to a collective identity, you know?

Brooke Cerda Guzman had some strong words about the way battles over collective identity weaken the overall transgender movement, create schisms, and lead to all sorts of trouble. She told me that people within the transgender movement and within some transgender groups spend time policing who belongs and who does not and attempt to draw sharp boundaries around the transgender community:

> Basically, the transgender community has declared war on binaries. I said it before, I am a woman, 100 percent woman. [But] I feel like a lot of time my own community is against us. They have declared war on binaries. We are constantly attacked and ridiculed. When we are disrespected as women, they just roll their eyes and say, "Oh, lighten up." I just want them to know what it is that I'm talking about from my own experience as a woman of trans experience. To understand the full trans experience, you have to talk to gender nonconforming, gender fluid, genderqueer, two spirit people; the list goes on and on. When I hear "transgender," I feel like I don't really know exactly what people are talking about.

The "boundary work" that some transgender people are doing, Brooke told me, incenses her.

Again, Adrien Lawyer was another respondent who has serious doubts about the role of collective identity in the transgender movement. He told me that collective identity did *not* play a role in his founding decision because there was (and is) no transgender collective identity:

> Of course, I've met a lot of guys who have stories [like mine]. I've met a lot of guys, where we all have these photos of ourselves at three years old with little dresses and Mary Janes and tear-streaked faces. And I also know other transgender men who were fine and very girly and fit in really well getting the love that they needed. We can't all be the same, what does that even mean? Where there is no group of people that doesn't contain transgender people, how could we possibly hold a collective identity?

And in his concluding statements about collective identity, Adrien was quite blunt: "We do not have a collective identity." Justus Eisfeld told me something similar. When he started his group, he told me, there was not a single collective identity, but rather "a large number of collective identities." He continued:

> There were transvestites, the transsexuals, there were the "Harry Benjamin Syndrome" sufferers, and there were the transgender people. And all of these identities were in flux. And then there were the genderqueer folks. All of these identities were also linked to age and socioeconomic status and educational background.

Later, he told me: "People were very invested in their specific identities." Josephine Tittsworth chafed at the very notion of a collective identity. She told me:

> Labels are not important for myself and people like myself. Labels are not important to us. The reason labels exist in relation to this community is so cisgender—the people outside the transgender community—can come to grips and start gaining some understanding. That's what labels are for.

All told, many respondents displayed a strong ambivalence toward the role of collective identity in group formation and development.

Collective Identity Is Tricky but Necessary

So what are we to make of all this? My analysis of the interview data leads me to conclude that the data provide a moderate degree of support for the conclusion that the rise of a transgender collective identity helped to spur group formation. Of course, each individual founder is unique. But my sense, after looking at all the founders' stories, is that collective identity worked something like this. For all twenty founders who gave me codable answers about collective identity, collective identity in the broadest sense—*the individually experienced sense that there are others out there at least somewhat like me*—played some role in spurring the group-founding decision. Time after time, founders told me that the decision to start a group followed the discovery, borne of interaction, that they had some shared interests with other people. But the data show clearly that it was not the case that my founders believed that there was a group of people out there called "transgender people" who were unified and who shared a large number of common interests and experiences. Instead, my founders' sense of collective identity was based on the belief that there was a group of people out there who were different in their approach to how they saw their gender. This group was anything but unified and did not manifest solidarity as we usually define it. In short, most of my founders, even those who said collective identity was an important spur to the group-founding decision, seemed to suggest that they defined themselves and their fellow activists and supporters as different from others more than as similar to one another.

As each founder learned that there were others out there like him/her in the sense that they were different from the majority of people and the way they viewed gender and gender norms, he/she drew a line around "us" and "them." The line, however, was not particularly well defined. Based on the accounts of my respondents, I would describe the situation as one in which sample founders could not necessarily define at the time of group founding who precisely "us" was, but they knew when they encountered a person whether or not that person was "one of us" or "one of them." This knowledge that there was an "us" and a "them" undoubtedly played a role in most of my founders' decisions to form a group. In this sense, collective identity in a broad sense helped to spur group formation.

But after group formation and some sustained involvement in transgender advocacy, navigating the proverbial waters of collective identity became more difficult for my founders. It appears that after first deciding that there was indeed an "us" and a "them," and then gathering people together under the banner of "us," founders had to do the more difficult and time-consuming work of determining exactly who was part of "us." Once the boundary work begun, things got difficult. Among my founders, for example, it led to the virtual disbandment of GenderPAC, one of the most influential and important early transgender rights interest groups. It also led, at least according to the founder of GenderPAC, to the virtual disappearance of cross-dressers from the transgender movement. More recently, the continued dialogue on collective identity has led to the formation of many "niche" groups, about which I will say more later in this chapter. All of this continued dialogue and in some cases conflict over precisely who the transgender movement and transgender interest groups represent explains the ambivalence and, in some cases, outright hostility toward the role of collective identity in transgender politics.

Of course, all of this begs the question: Is the rise of a collective identity *necessary* for group formation? My data suggest that the answer is "Yes." It is hard to imagine any of my founders deciding to found a group in the absence of ironclad evidence that there was an "us" out there and not just a "me." But as Blake Alford noted, "transgender people have been around since dirt." So why are transgender rights interest groups a relatively recent phenomenon? One partial answer, as I implied in Chapter 3, lies in the rise of technology, especially air travel and the Internet, which allowed transgender people to find other transgender people—which was crucial for the development of a transgender identity. By all accounts, there are relatively few Americans who identify as transgender. And clearly transgender people have been around forever. But in his/her daily life, for most of American history, a transgender person was quite unlikely to encounter another transgender person. Part of this is due to the fact that culturally, transgender people were not accepted. But part of the reason they were not accepted is because they were hidden. In addition, it is probably the case that for most of American history, transgender people were unaware that there were other transgender people out there. And even if they were aware that there were others out there, they certainly did not interact with them. Many of my sample founders—especially the older ones—described their repeated and sometimes herculean attempts to find and connect with other transgender people in the 1960s and 1970s. Joelle Ryan was one of these founders. She told me that like many transgender people, she had a difficult childhood. She said:

> I can remember being in high school and going to the school library and searching desperately for anything I could find about the issue of transgender. I could find maybe two or three books, and they were in the "sexual disorder" section, around books on things like pedophilia. Then when I did take the books off the shelf, I went to the school carrel and hid, essentially, and what I found was stuff that was very pathologizing about trans [people] and written by nontrans people who were sometimes not particularly enthusiastic about our group, if not downright hostile.

But Joelle continued her search, eventually learning, mostly via the Internet, that there were other people out there like her; that she was not alone.

Dallas Denny, an early transgender organizer, told me of the lengths she went to trying to find other transgender people:

> Essentially, before I started my group I'd been looking for resources my whole life and not finding them. In fact, I never met another transsexual person. I went to the gender program at Vanderbilt

> University in the 1970s, and they told me they would not help me transition and they would not put me in touch with any other transgender people. And when I went out, the clubs in Nashville would not let any person in who was cross-dressed. I didn't know any transgender people until I was forty! Then I found out there was an organization started by a transgender person called Virginia Prince, the founder of Tri-Ess, who was popularizing the notion, which was radical at the time, that it was possible to be heterosexual and be a cross-dresser. Unfortunately, she chose to implement a very restrictive policy in her group, Tri-Ess—no transsexuals and no gay people. I did not join the organization because of that policy, because I wanted to respect it. I actually wrote the organization and told them that I realized I didn't qualify for membership, but I was desperate for information. Could they please put me in touch with someone who knew about transsexualism? They gave my letter to Virginia Prince, who wrote a letter back, and that popped my bubble about my dreams. [Author's note: Elsewhere, Dallas Denny has written that Virginia Prince wrote her back and essentially told her that she was "crazy."] But I was still looking. In fact, I was on hormones shortly after that, and finally about ten years later I said, "I realize I still don't qualify for membership in Tri-Ess, but there have to be people like me out there, so maybe if I join I will, through this organization, find my people. And that's what happened. About four or five months later, someone showed me a magazine called *Tapestry*, which was later called *Transgender Tapestry*]. Inside there was a listing of organizations for all kinds of gender-variant people. I was living in the South, and about the only thing in the South at the time was an organization in Atlanta called the Montgomery Institute. I worked as a behavior specialist at the time, and I had no information at all except this organization in Atlanta which was called Montgomery Medical and Psychological Institute, which I found out was a support group run by a transsexual man and his wife who he had met when he had come into the gender clinic in Atlanta. I called the Montgomery Institute for a month, and finally someone answered the phone.

Dallas went on to say that she finally reached the Montgomery Institute, the leaders of which invited her to visit. She visited, and while she was there, the leaders offered her a job. "They were so impressed by my credentials," she told me, "that within a month or two they had convinced me to run the group." She eventually moved to Atlanta and took even more of a role in the group. She told me:

> I had no intentions when I moved to Atlanta of doing anything more than getting the support and information I needed to get through my transition. But after working at the Montgomery Institute for a while, I decided that there were so many people out there who were just desperately needing and seeking information, and I could not go into that goodnight with a good conscious. I had to help people. So I founded AEGIS, which became national in scope.

Dallas' search for others like her took years. And when she found them, her career as a leader and group founder began.

Josephine Tittsworth described a similar dynamic that took place in her life. "Thirty years ago," she told me, "we [transgender people] would go to the public library and go to the card index and slip a card into the card index under T, and that's how we got in touch with other people." Josephine eventually reached other transgender people by first writing to *Playboy* after it published an article about cross-dressers and getting the names of others like her, then meeting personally with other cross-dressers, then starting a chapter of Tri-Ess. But this was not easy, and it took time. She told me that after she received the name of the cross-dresser from Los Angeles, the cross-dresser sent her "a list of names and addresses of people in the Houston Area who were cross-dressers." "Then," she told me, "I wrote letters to every one of them and informed them that I reserved a suite at the La Quinta Inn in Houston, and I will be there on such and such a date and such and such a time, and [you're] welcome to join me." Again, Josephine searched to find people like her, and it took a very long time for her search to bear fruit.

Before the Internet, it was difficult for transgender people to find each other. To be sure, they were out there, but they were not easy to find. There were those who worked very hard to find other people like them, and they succeeded. Some of my sample founders are among these people, and when they found others like them, this helped spur the founding decision.

In the end, what I am arguing here is that the data suggest that collective identity played a role in the founding decisions of a large chunk of my sample founders, and this collective identity flowed directly from interactions among founders and others, which were made easier by technological advances, especially the Internet. Interestingly and not coincidentally, David Truman, a protopluralist, recognized the importance of technology in his classic *The Governmental Process*. "The mass newspaper, telephone, telegraph, radio, and motion pictures, not to mention the various drastic changes in the speed of transportation have facilitated the interactions of men [*sic*] and the development of groups only slightly dependent, if at all, upon face to face contact" (1951, 55). Truman did not talk about collective identity *per se*, but he recognized that for individuals to get a sense of connection to others, interaction, which was made easier by technology, was crucial.

Niche Considerations and Collective Identity

The conclusion that the rise of a transgender collective identity spurred group formation to some extent, but then led to difficult "boundary work" that caused tension and fissures among transgender rights groups and activists within the larger movement, is supported by evidence that on the whole, interest groups founded late in a population's history are much more likely to be "niche" groups than are groups founded earlier. Here, by "niche group," I mean a group that focuses not on the broad issues or interests of the transgender community as a whole, but rather on some narrower (often very narrow) set of issues or interests of some segment of the transgender community.

Table 7.1 contains a list of nationally active transgender rights groups founded since 2005, when the population hit its first peak. In all, seven of the sixteen groups listed in the table are clearly niche groups—Black Trans Advocacy, Trans People of Color Coalition, TransLatin@ Coalition, Brown Boi Project, Trans Student Educational Resources, Trans Athlete, and Trans Women of Color Collective. Three others arguably are niche groups—Trans Justice Funding Project, Gender Proud, and GATE. Each of these groups defines itself as an organization that aims to represent not the transgender community as a whole, but rather some specific portion of it. The agendas of these groups clearly are more limited than those of general groups such as the National Center for Transgender Equality, the National Transgender Advocacy Coalition, FORGE, and the Transgender Law Center. Also telling is the fact that while five of these seven groups are organized along ethnicity/racial lines, not a single transgender rights group founded before 2006

Table 7.1. Groups in the population of nationally active transgender rights interest groups founded after 2005.

Group	*Year Founded–Year Died*
TransYouth Family Allies	2006–2014
Black Trans Advocacy (Black Transmen and Black Transwomen are affiliates)	2009–
Trans People of Color Coalition	2009–
TransLatin@ Coalition	2009–
Global Action for Trans*Equality	2009–
FORGE	2009– (originally founded in 1994)
Brown Boi Project	2010–
National Coalition of Transgender Advocacy Groups	2010–2011
Trans Advocacy Network	2010–2015
Trans Student Educational Resources	2011–
Trans Justice Funding Project	2012–
United States Transgender Advocacy	2012–
Trans Athlete	2013–
Trans Women of Color Collective	2013–
Gender Proud	2014–
Trans United Fund	2016–

Source: Author's data.

was organized among such lines. Surely this is not a coincidence. Among the sixteen groups in table 7.1, there are three additional groups that can reasonably be categorized as specialists. First, there is the Trans Justice Funding Project, which does not have an issue niche (that is, it focuses on broad issues of interest to all transgender Americans) but does have what I will call an "operational" niche. The Trans Justice Funding Project is the only group in the population that works solely through grants to other organizations. Second, there is Gender Proud, which has sought an institutional niche; it focuses on media strategies. Third, GATE focuses on international as well as national issues, which is unique among groups in the population.

Using a very expansive definition of "niche group," I categorized only eight of thirty groups founded before 2007 as niche groups. All of this suggests that there is something to the notion that niche groups are more likely to form and survive late in a population's history than they are early in a population's history. One school of thought about niche-seeking behavior among interest groups holds that such behavior is purposeful, as group leaders seek specialized niches that eliminate competition with other like-groups (Bosso 2005; Browne 1988; 1990; Gray and Lowery 1998; Hansen 1991; Halpin and Jordan 2009; Heaney 2004; 2007). Studies in this vein often refer to "resource partitioning," which is the process by which groups in the same population divvy up resources by specializing in different things. Resource-partitioning studies are particularly noteworthy because just as the data here show, they hold that niche-seeking behavior among interest groups within the same population is much more common when density is high (that is, later in the population's history) than it is when density is low (Downey and Rohlinger 2008; Halpin and Thomas 2012; Lowery et al. 2012; Soule and King 2008). But I believe that something else explains the rise of niche groups in the population under study here since the mid-2000s. Specifically, I do not believe that the founders of these late-stage niche groups said to themselves, "I am going to found this group and focus narrowly because focusing broadly would lead to my group's failure." Instead, the qualitative data indicate that *founders' decisions to focus narrowly arose out of their attempts to navigate the choppy waters of collective identity.*

Serendipitously for an examination of niche considerations and transgender rights group foundings, I interviewed the founders of three niche groups—Trans Women of Color Collective (Brooke Cerda Guzman), TransLatin@ Coalition (Bamby Salcedo), and Trans Student Educational Resources (Eli Erlick). These founders' words reveal that they did not choose to focus narrowly on the needs of one segment of the transgender community because they thought that doing so would be good for their groups' fortunes. Instead, it was their experiences navigating the world of collective identity that led them to focus on the needs of a specific population. In other words, the data suggest that niche-seeking was a by-product of the movementwide work to define a transgender collective identity that ensued after the movement and attendant groups got up and running. After transgender rights groups were established, they, their supporters, and other transgender people started debating what it meant to be "transgender." This communitywide discussion and navigation led to the creation of boundaries that inevitably excluded certain people or groups of people from the proverbial club—or at least made some people feel more welcome than others—and led some founders to seek representation elsewhere, in their own groups.

Bamby Salcedo, founder of TransLatin@ Coalition, was straightforward about why she felt the need to start a group that focused on the needs of transgender Latinas. She said that in 2009, there was really no consideration of the issues facing trans-Latina immigrants. There was no representation by extant groups of the specific needs of this community. Bamby went on to say:

> At that time, we knew that there [were] organizations that were trans-specific, like the National Center for Transgender Equality and the Transgender Law Center. They were trans-specific, but a lot of their advocacy efforts and a lot of the things that they were doing weren't really reflecting the needs and issues of trans-Latino immigrants specifically.

Many general transgender groups, Brooke told me, "marginalized" people like her. This led her to start her own group.

Eli Erlick was succinct about why she founded a group focused on the needs of transgender students rather than all transgender people. Her group, she told me, "is heavily focused on being a youth-led organization focusing on young transgender people." Eli told me she looked around (at a young age, obviously) at the universe of groups before she founded her own group and found that "there [were] no other organizations out there focusing specifically on trans students at every level of education." "This was huge," she told me, in her decision to start her group. She went on to note, "Yes, there were smaller student groups out there," but they were "for the larger queer and trans student community, and that means mostly gay, rich, white, cisgender men." But no one, she told me, was doing what she wanted to do.

Finally, the words of Brooke Cerda Guzman are perhaps most illustrative of the point I am trying to make here. Brooke told me that when she first became active in transgender politics, many people in the transgender community began to dismiss her because she was "binary." This exclusion, she said, spurred her to create her own group, one that respected binary as well as nonbinary women. Ironically, however, Brooke did her own intragroup boundary work, focusing on the needs of "black and brown trans women," whom the "nonprofit industry, [including] all the community-based organizations and larger trans organizations," ignored and marginalized.

Overall, the quantitative data on group foundings, as well as the words of founders, provide some support for the notion that a population's late-comers are more likely to be specialized niche groups than are a population's earliest entrants. I do not believe that niche groups are formed by founders who first decide to found a group and then after surveying the organizational landscape make the conscious decision to focus narrowly to avoid competition with other groups. Rather, my qualitative data suggest that a narrow focus flows more or less naturally from population dynamics. After legitimation takes hold in a population, groups within the population and their supporters begin a communitywide discussion about collective identity. This discussion draws firmer and firmer lines around who is "in" and who is "out." This leads to the drawing of lines and the creation of categories both within and without of the community represented by extant groups. As these categories take shape, some people begin to identify more narrowly. And when they do, some begin to believe that they are not being served by extant groups and consider starting newer, narrower groups to serve their needs. In addition, after legitimation has taken hold, and the population begins to grow, extant groups *work*—they start to do things. And as interest-group scholar Dana Strolovitch (2007) reminds us, groups choose to work on some issues and not others. And when they make these choices, some groups of people—specifically, people who care about the issues that groups pay little or no attention to—start to believe that newer, narrower groups are necessary to pay attention to issues that the larger, older, more established groups ignore.

Conclusion: Collective Identity, Group Formation, and Niches

In this chapter, I have discussed the role of collective identity in transgender rights interest-group formation. On this, the data are somewhat vexing. On the one hand, the data suggest that in the very broadest sense, collective identity affected many founders' decisions to start groups. Once again, the data show that *need* was important to virtually all of my sample founders. On the other hand, there is little in the data suggesting that founders started their groups because they were convinced that there was a well-defined population of people who were unified and shared certain attributes and characteristics. In fact, a large number of founders were quite emphatic in stating that the rise of a transgender collective identity did *not* affect the founding decision. An even larger number were perceptibly ambivalent about the role of collective identity. Specifically, many founders noted that there really never has been, and there may still not be, a transgender collective identity. Instead, the whole notion of what it means to be transgender is hotly contested and has been for some time. In addition, many founders told me that the battle over a transgender collective identity was actually a deterrent to group formation and a detriment to the larger transgender movement. Some founders inferred that perhaps there would be more transgender interest groups if notions of identity were not so fraught.

In all, the data lead me to conclude that collective identity in the way of an individually experienced sense of emotional connection to others contributed to the decisions of many sample founders to start their groups. This emotional connection was based on the general notion that there were others out there who were, in the words of one of my respondents, "differently gendered." This connection led founders (and others) to draw a very loose boundary between themselves and others. But this boundary was indeed very far from firm. And once the boundary existed, it became contested; thus, among my founders, figuring out who "they" were was easier than figuring out who "we" were. Collective identity was important in the founding decisions of my sample founders. But navigating the choppy waters of collective identity has been difficult and has caused problems for individual groups and the movement.

This navigation has led recently to the formation of many "niche groups." I believe that the paucity of niche groups early in the population's history and the surfeit of such groups later are explained partially by founders' and activists' attempts to traverse the choppy waters of collective identity. Once the population was off the ground and the organizational form, "transgender rights interest group," obtained widespread legitimacy, founders, leaders, and activists started boundary work. This work led some people to feel like they were "in," and others to feel like they were "out." It also led extant groups to work on some issues and ignore others. And all of this almost inevitably led to the formation of specialist, niche organizations.

Before leaving the topic of collective identity, it is worth considering what queer theory might say about all this. I have eschewed queer theory completely in this book up until now, primarily because though it is making inroads in the discipline of political science, it speaks very little to the topic of interest-group development. Queer theory might, however, have something to say about the topic of this chapter—collective identity and its role in collective action. What might queer theory have to add here? First, there is an argument to be made that queer theory (or more accurately, queer theorists) actually helped *engender* the development of a transgender collective identity by shining a light on "the variety of possible 'sexualities'" that exist in the real world (Boyd 2005, 103). An argument along these lines would posit that queer theory, which "is not a singular or systematic conceptual or methodological framework, but a collection of intellectual engagements with the relations between sex, gender, and sexual desire" (Spargo 1999, 9), helped create and/or maintain space for the category of transgender to arise as an independent one quite separate from the categories of lesbian, gay, and bisexual (not to mention man and woman). Unfortunately, my data cannot and do not speak to this argument in any satisfactory way, but it is certainly an argument worth considering. Briefly, it may well be the case that queer theorists themselves played a role in the development of a transgender collective identity, broad and poorly-defined as some of my respondents suggest it was during the early days of transgender organizing (and perhaps remains to this day).

Second, many queer theorists argue (in contrast to essentialist views) that gender roles and gender identity are social and/or historical constructs. This is important here, because as Meyerowitz (2002) has brilliantly shown, the categories of transsexual and then transgender came into public parlance slowly over the course of the twentieth century (these are my words, not hers). If we take the idea that gender identity is socially and/or historically constructed, it is not a large leap to conclude that only with the rise of the socially and historically constructed transgender collective identity was the formation of transgender rights interest groups possible. In short, here, the argument is that the social and historical construction of a transgender identity separate from a lesbian or gay or bisexual identity created space, especially early on in the history of transgender rights organizing, for the formation of transgender rights interest groups. Again, unfortunately, my data cannot speak to this argument. But, certainly, a close reading of Meyerowitz's history is in order for anyone who wishes to understand transgender politics in its many forms.

Finally, it is worth considering that from a queer theoretical perspective, it is unquestionably the case that the activists, founders, and interest groups I discuss in this book are themselves part of the queer project, as they work to construct, deconstruct, and rearticulate the category of transgender.[1] Precisely what transgender means, who is and is not transgender, and what interests transgender rights groups represent and do not represent, is nowhere carved in stone. Transgender interest groups and activists are working on this project every day.

With this chapter, I conclude my analysis of the data. It is now time to step back and see what the data, taken as a whole, can teach us about how the transgender rights interest groups I study here managed to mobilize in the face of substantial barriers to formation and survival.

8

Conclusion

The Formation of Transgender Rights Interest Groups in the United States

I began this book by recounting the American Psychiatric Association's 2013 decision to update its *DSM-5* to replace the term "gender identity disorder" with "gender dysphoria." This was hardly the only victory for transgender Americans in the past five years. In May 2016, the Department of Justice directed all school districts in the United States to allow transgender students to use the bathroom consistent with their gender identity. In the same month and year, the Department of Health and Human Services adopted a rule stipulating that healthcare providers who receive federal money are barred from denying transition-related care to transgender people, including surgery and hormone treatments. This followed the Obama administration's 2014 declaration that Title IX protected transgender students, a 2014 executive order barring discrimination against transgender people by federal contractors, and the State Department's 2010 decision to allow people to change the gender markers on their passports with only a physician's note (rather than proof of reassignment surgery). And by 2016, twenty states and the District of Columbia, as well as hundreds of local jurisdictions, had laws on the books banning at least some forms of discrimination against transgender Americans.

Of course, all of the news is not good. The early days of the Trump presidency have not been good for transgender Americans. President Trump rescinded President Obama's protections for transgender students very early on, Trump's Justice Department has made it clear that pursuing cases of discrimination against transgender students is not a top priority, members of the Trump administration have publicly talked of rescinding President Obama's ban on transgender discrimination by federal contractors, and President Trump has appointed several people, including Attorney General Jeff Sessions, who are not, to say the least, particularly supportive of transgender rights. But none of this can overshadow the fact that many things, including public policies (at least in some places), have gotten better for transgender Americans in the United States in the last decade. Moreover, for the first time in American history, there is now an ongoing national discussion about transgender rights. It is the premise of this book that none of this would have been possible without the rise of transgender rights interest groups. In other words, the groups I list in tables 2.1 and 2.2 have been an integral part of the larger transgender rights movement that has changed the politics of transgender rights in this country.

The primary question I address in this book is: How did these groups manage to mobilize in the face of substantial barriers to group formation? It was my hope that by addressing this question, I could gather clues that might help us answer several others, including the following: How did transgender rights advocacy groups go from virtually nonexistent in the 1950s, 1960s, and 1970s, to more numerous in the 2000s and 2010s? Why does the universe of transgender rights interest groups in the United States today look the way it does? And what can the rise of transgender rights interest groups tell us about how oppressed and marginalized people can overcome the barriers to collective action and form viable organizations to represent their interests before government? In this concluding chapter, I will attempt to put all of my findings together to formulate reasonably comprehensive answers to these questions.

How Did Transgender Rights Interest Groups Manage to Mobilize in the Face of Substantial Barriers to Formation?

If there is one thing the political science literature on interest-group formation has taught us, it is that we cannot take interest-group formation for granted. There are barriers to the formation of organized interest groups, including the "free-rider" instinct among individuals, cost (group formation invariably costs money, as well as time and effort), and an often-unwelcoming political system. So how did the groups listed in tables 2.1 and 2.2 manage to overcome the seemingly substantial barriers to group formation? There is no one formula for successful group formation, and thus there is no single, all-inclusive answer to this question. The transgender rights interest groups I study in this book have their origins with the actual, identifiable human beings who started them, and I interviewed twenty-seven of these people in an attempt to answer this question. I also looked briefly at quantitative data on transgender rights group foundings over time looking for answers to this question. What do the data tell us?

It Does Not Take a Village

Without exception, my sample founders did a great deal of the work necessary for group formation themselves. Theoretical and empirical studies of group formation may endlessly debate where the money comes from, how group entrepreneurs manage to convince people to support their groups, what kinds of incentives and benefits do and do not work to attract members, what kinds of interest groups patrons such as foundations and large donors do and do not support, and what sorts of people do and do not join organizations that represent their interests. But my data show that in many cases, these concerns are largely irrelevant. For the most part, the transgender rights interest-group founders I study here started their groups either alone or with help from a few other people. None of my sample founders recruited members, designed incentive packages to attract supporters, or schemed to overcome the "free-rider" problem. Only a handful received patron support from the very beginning, and for these founders the patrons appeared to have come to them rather than the other way around. My sample founders relied primarily upon their own money, their own hard work, and their own efforts to get their groups up and running. A few had some help from patrons, and many had help from close friends and family. But the data are clear: for the most part, transgender rights interest groups in the United States originated with individual leaders who did a lot of the work themselves, eschewing any large-scale efforts to bring others on board.

The obvious retort to this is that groups that begin like this—that is, underresourced and very small—probably do/did not survive for long or become particularly powerful. I know of no extant scholarly study showing either that groups cannot survive in the long term unless they form with abundant resources or that only groups that form with abundant resources will become effective eventually. In fact, the data I analyze here and the history of transgender rights organizing suggest that groups that start small and not-very-powerful *can* become relatively large and influential after a time. I say this because the largest and most powerful transgender rights groups in American history—the National Center for Transgender Equality, the Transgender Law Center, the Transgender Resource Center of New Mexico, FORGE, and GenderPAC—originated with hard-charging founders who did a great deal of the early work of group formation themselves. Moreover, with the exception of the Transgender Law Center, these groups were started with relatively little money.

It Does Not Cost That Much Money to Start a Group, and Perhaps the Barriers to Group Formation Simply Are Not as Great as Many Theories Assume They Are

It is somewhat surprising that with all the attention paid to interest-group formation by political scientists and sociologists, very few scholars pay much attention to the quantity of resources—financial and human—it actually takes to start an interest group. My data show that starting a group takes time, money, and human resources. But my data also show that starting a group does *not* take *huge* amounts of money and/or human resources (time, yes). Most of the groups I study were founded on what respondents themselves called "a shoestring." As long as a person can start a group on a proverbial shoestring, individual founders willing to devote their own time and money and effort to group formation will be able to overcome the seemingly substantial barriers to group formation with relative ease. Survival over the long term, of course, is a different matter, and though my data are incomplete on this issue, many of the groups I study here—especially the largest ones—did indeed receive infusions of money from outside sources (e.g., large individual donors, foundations, and even members) after being in business for a while. But the data show that *any theory or approach that views large amounts of money, patronage, members, or human resources as essential for group formation is flawed.*

None of this is to say that founders can start groups with next to nothing, or that anyone can start a group. Almost without exception, the founders I interviewed for this book (as well as many I identified, contacted, and tried to interview) are well-educated, reasonably affluent, impressive people. The data suggest that starting an interest group takes money, skill, and hard work. And again, almost without exception, my founders were in possession of the first two and were in a position to do the third. Founders told me that they invested their own money during the earliest stages of group formation. So having *some* money seems like a prerequisite to forming a group. Many of my sample founders had enough in the bank to get their groups up and running and to pay travel expenses, website registration fees, and mailing and printing costs. Moreover, most of my respondents had the kinds of jobs that allowed them some flexibility and time to start interest groups. And not coincidentally, again almost without exception, my founders have substantial organizational skills. Among my founders are JDs, PhDs, MAs, and other thoroughly skilled and talented people who decided at some point in their lives to put their skills and talents to work trying to represent transgender Americans.

Some sociologists might classify my respondents as people with high levels of "cultural capital." While political scientists have been slow to embrace the concept of "cultural capital"—which broadly comprises social assets such as knowledge, intellect, skills, mores, manners, tastes and behaviors that a person acquires through membership in a certain social class—some sociologists deploy it to explain political, social, and economic outcomes, including social movement and/or group development. Starting with Pierre Bourdieu (1979), a number of sociologists have argued that people with high levels of cultural capital (that is, people with high levels of the social assets valued by and shared with members of the upper classes) have an easier time succeeding in stratified societies than do people with low levels of cultural capital. It is certainly not a large leap from this general notion to the conclusion that high levels of cultural capital render some people more able than others to start interest groups. Indeed, my data support such a conclusion. Thus, again, it is certainly not the case that my data support the idea that anyone can start a transgender rights interest group. Clearly, founding a group takes knowledge, skill, intelligence and education. What it does not take is a great deal of money.

In sum, the data support the conclusion that starting an interest group is the purview of the well-educated, the relatively well-off, and the resourceful. One of the more discouraging implications of this is that unorganized groups of people who do not have at least some affluent, well-educated, relatively "privileged" people in their midst probably are going to be woefully underrepresented by interest groups. Groups of "welfare" recipients, the unemployed, the homeless, children, and the desperately sick are among the groups of people I have in mind here.

While we are on the subject of cost, it is also worth noting that my data imply that the cost of starting an interest group is perhaps lower now than it ever has been. As many of my sample founders pointed out, the Internet now does for free what used to cost large sums of money—it reaches billions of people directly and instantly. Almost all of the founders who started groups after the advent of widespread Internet use reported using the Internet to promulgate their views, to get the word out that there was "a new group in town," to raise money or other resources, and to interact with other transgender people and supporters. Starting a group does not take a great deal of money.

Threats and Grievances Inspire Founders to Start Interest Groups, But Only after Interaction

If it is indeed the case that founders rely to a large extent on themselves and their friends and family for the resources and effort necessary to start a group, this begs the obvious question: *Why do they do it?* The data indicate perhaps first and foremost that founders do *not* do it—as the strictest versions of incentive theory or resource-mobilization theory might predict—for the money or the job security or the fame. My sample founders were and are unquestionably committed to transgender rights; they did not start their groups to "tap into a market." The life stories of virtually all of my founders—not just according to them, but also according to archival sources and news reports—show that starting a transgender rights group is not the road to fame, fortune, or job security. Moreover, for many founders, starting a transgender rights group brought with it serious and substantial risks. One underappreciated risk of starting an interest group is financial ruin. One anonymous founder told me that starting a group resulted in the founder's bankruptcy, and two others told me that they either "went broke" or "almost went broke" after quitting their jobs.

According to my data, the sorts of things that pluralist theories and grievance theories of interest-group formation and collective action tab as important *are* unquestionably important in motivating people to start groups. By this, I mean that threats, grievances, and disturbing events do indeed act as spurs to group formation. But as I have pointed out time and time again in these pages, *threats, grievances, and disturbing events alone are not enough to spur group formation and the founding decision.* Instead, the data show that *threats, grievances, and disturbances coupled with interaction spur group formation, as they push individuals toward the founding decision.* Without exception, sample founders told me that they were aware—due to personal experience and a variety of other means—of the fact that transgender people suffer in the United States and virtually always have. Indeed, founder after founder used words such as "discrimination," "violence," "isolation," "threats," and "danger" during my interviews, and some founders shared with me horrible stories about things that happened to them and/or transgender people they knew. And all of this clearly made a difference in the group-founding decision. For most founders, however, it was *not* knowledge or even direct experience of the threats and dangers facing them and transgender people in general that led to the ultimate decision to start a new group. Rather, this knowledge and/or direct experience led my sample founders to seek out interaction with transgender people (and allies), and once they found the interaction they wanted—that is, once they made contact with transgender people (and to a lesser extent, allies)—the idea to start a transgender rights group began to take shape.

My founders located other people by a variety of means. Founders whose work began in the 1960s or 1970s physically looked for other transgender people in places they heard were safe. Many sent letters and made telephone calls, joined LGB groups and women's and civil rights groups, and went to meetings of transgender support groups. Once conferences got up and running, they went to these too. Later on, younger founders relied less on these forums for interaction and turned to the Internet to make contact with other transgender people. This contact—which founders sought after becoming convinced that transgender people were threatened, and after deciding that they wanted to learn more about transgender issues to get the support they needed and wanted—is what spurred founders to start their interest groups.

It is impossible to understate the role of interactions and connections in my founders' decisions to start their groups. Interactions and connections inspired group founders, fueled their passion and excitement about transgender advocacy, raised their awareness of the multiple needs of transgender people, convinced them that extant LGB and in some cases other transgender rights groups were not enough, persuaded them of the need for effective group representation, and in some cases taught them skills that came in handy during the group founding process. All of this is another way of saying that at some point in their lives after (correctly, of course) coming to the conclusion that transgender people (including themselves in some but not all cases) are under threat from many quarters, my founders went searching for something. This "something" generally was information and support, but sometimes was friendship, communion, and understanding. What each of my founders learned during this search convinced them that starting a group was necessary, if not vital. In sum, the data show that for my founders, threats, grievances, and experiences led to searching, searching led to other people and organizations, interactions with these other people and organizations led to inspiration and learning and encouragement, and inspiration and learning and encouragement led to group formation.

It is impossible to say on the basis of my data that for an individual, the realization of threat coupled with interactions that lead to learning of various kinds *will inevitably* lead to the decision to start an interest group. At this point, all I am prepared to conclude is that for a person who experiences them, the conditions I identify here increase the probability that he/she will start a group. This, of course, begs yet another important question: *What is it that makes founders different?* In other words, why do some people start interest groups while almost every other person on the planet does not? Unfortunately, my data do not allow me to answer this question. I believe I can build a profile of the type of person most likely to start an interest group, but there are undoubtedly millions of Americans who fit this profile (i.e., well-educated, relatively "privileged," very skilled, hard-working, subject to discrimination and threats) yet who never start groups. Ultimately, this means that if social scientists are ever going to truly understand group formation, they are going to have to redouble their efforts to learn more about *leadership*. My sense after reading extensively on social movements and interest groups is that many social scientists are loathe to assign too much importance to leadership and individual leaders in the group formation process. The words of one of my respondents, who wished to remain anonymous, sum up this attitude. To paraphrase: "I don't subscribe to the 'great-man' theory of history. Anyone could do what I have done, and to assign too much importance to any one member of a group or movement is unwise." But this founder, like my other founders, is too humble. Moreover, she is probably incorrect when she says that anyone could have done what she did—that is, start a major transgender rights interest group virtually out of whole cloth. What is it about this woman that made her do what she did? What is it that causes some people to not just become predisposed to become leaders, but also to go on to start a new group and then lead it? What role do variables such as temperament and personality and upbringing play? After speaking with my founders, I became convinced that *there is something special about them*. They are different from most of us, and they are even different than the most politically active among us. I believe we have to learn much more about how leaders and founders are different from the rest of us if we are ever truly going to understand completely where interest groups come from.

How Did Transgender Rights Advocacy Groups Go from Virtually Nonexistent in the 1950s, 1960s, and 1970s, to More Numerous in the 2000s and 2010s?

The EEF was the first truly national transgender rights interest group in American history. Its activities are virtually legendary. From 1965 to 1986, only six new groups entered the population of nationally active groups. From 1987 to 1997 that number rose to thirteen. Then from 1998 to 2010, the number rose to nineteen. Since 2010, seven new groups have entered the population. In this section, I will briefly recount the history of the population of nationally active transgender rights groups in American history, attempting to account for the patterns we see in figure 6.1. Again, since I do not have good, over-time data on the numbers and foundings of subnational transgender rights interest groups over time, I speak primarily to the trajectory of the population of nationally active groups here. I will, however, occasionally reference the trajectory of the population of subnational groups as well.

The EEF and After: 1964–1986

I do not think we will ever truly know why Reed Erickson started the EEF or why he started the EEF when he did rather than earlier or later. But the data do give us a clue as to why very few new groups followed in the twenty years after the EEF formed. The quantitative data suggest that just as ESA theory and density-dependence theory predict, new groups were not forthcoming partially because the idea of a "transgender rights interest group" simply was not a widely accepted thing. To sum up, early in the population's history, legitimation pressures were manifest.

It is also safe to say, based on the interview data, that the lack of contact between transgender people, and the difficulty transgender people had connecting and interacting with each other, probably contributed to the low founding rate during this period as well. Clearly there were transgender people in this country during this period (as there always have been). And the qualitative data (as well as a wealth of data from other sources) show unequivocally that transgender people were in peril during this period (as they always had been). But if a transgender person sought out other transgender people during this period in American history, that person was not likely to have a great deal of success. After all, there were (and are) not many transgender people to begin with, and they were (and are) scattered throughout the United States. Where would a transgender person look for other transgender people in 1969? Where would he/she get information and support? In short, the lack of venues for interactions among transgender people—especially the lack of conferences, support groups, and the Internet—probably acted to dampen rates of group formation during this period. Finally, there was nothing in the larger political environment to spur group formation. The notion of a transgender collective identity did not exist, LGB groups had not made many waves or had much success, the public was quite conservative, and transgender rights issues received very little attention from either the public or governments.

But during this early period in the population's history, the seeds of future group formation were being sown, most obviously by LGB groups. During this period, some early founders *did* find people who were at least somewhat like them. That is, they found their fellow "outcasts," gay and lesbian Americans. This did not necessarily push people over the edge to start groups, but it gave early founders a start. In addition, the qualitative data suggest that slowly but surely during this period, support groups started popping up all over the country. In sum, while interactions between transgender people were not extensive during this period, they were increasing.

The Rumblings of Prolific Group Representation: 1987–1998

Several new groups formed from 1987 through 1998, and many of these groups, including Transexual Menace, It's Time America, and Survivor Project made quite a splash despite limited resources. What happened during this period to spur group formation?

First, as with the previous period, there was a need for new transgender rights groups, as transgender people faced widespread threats and discrimination. But again, threats to the well-being of transgender people were not sufficient to spur people to start new transgender rights groups. It was the second factor—increased interactions and connections among transgender people—that directly spurred group formation. During this period the "conference culture" took hold among transgender people and began to propel many founders toward group founding. Conferences were immensely important forums in which transgender people interacted with other transgender people, and conferences did not exist on a large scale before this period. It is not coincidental that of the seven sample founders who began their groups during this period, six told me that conferences where important settings in which they met and interacted with other transgender people before group founding. During this period, support groups were also important places where transgender people interacted with each other. Six of seven respondents who founded their groups during this period told me that support groups were important forums in which they interacted with other transgender people before they founded their groups. And toward the end of this period, the Internet became a feature of group formation as well. Of the seven sample founders who started their groups during this period, three reported using the Internet as a forum for interaction before founding their groups. Third, by 1987, six nationally active transgender rights groups had managed to get off the ground and become going concerns. Only two of them were left by the beginning of 1987, but these six provided some (albeit limited) evidence that the idea of starting a "transgender rights interest group" was not necessarily ridiculous or foolhardy. In other words, legitimation pressures had abated a bit by the beginning of this period.

Fourth, by the mid-1980s, there were large numbers of robust and active LGB and AIDS groups in the United States, which served as virtual training grounds for activists. Some of the people active in these groups before this period migrated toward transgender rights organizing. It is not coincidental that all seven of the sample founders I interviewed who founded their groups during this period reported having some experience working for and with LGB groups before founding their own groups. All told, the qualitative data show that during this period, the pool of potential founders became larger than it previously had been owing to the successful work of LGB groups (and to a lesser extent, women's groups).

Fifth, the notion of a transgender collective identity was beginning to take hold. The term "transgender" was on the way in, and the term "transsexual" was on the way out. There began to be a sense among transgender people that though they were not exactly sure in what ways they were different, they were indeed different. This sense probably contributed to group proliferation, as three of six sample founders who started their groups during this period told me that the rise of a transgender collective identity preceded their founding decisions. The qualitative data suggest that during this period, some founders of transgender groups began to believe that there really was an "us" out there. This feeling contributed to their group-founding decisions. The data do not show that founders believed that there was a unified group of people who were transgender, nor do the data show that the rise of a transgender collective identity convinced founders that there was an untapped market of transgender people out there ready to be mobilized. Rather, the qualitative data suggest that the notion that a transgender collective identity was forming worked to convince founders that the need for transgender rights interest groups was acute.

Sixth, and probably least important, there was at least one development in the political world that may have contributed to group formation in a few cases. Specifically, public opinion moved in a liberal direction for the first five years of this period.

The Rise of the Heavyweights: 1999–2008

Eleven new national groups were formed during this period, including the heavyweights NCTE, the Transgender Law Center, and the Sylvia Rivera Law Project. What happened to spur group proliferation during this period? First, as always, the need for groups was acute. But again, this need was not sufficient to lead to group formation; interaction and connections were crucial. Conferences and support groups continued and remained crucial settings in which transgender people became politically activated. Some of the activists decided to start new groups. Of the six sample founders who started their groups during this period, all six reported experience in support groups, and four cited experience at conferences. There is evidence that the Internet was starting to make a difference as well. Three sample founders cited the Internet as an important forum for interaction. Several founders told me that the interactions that led to their founding decisions—interactions that raised their awareness of need, provided inspiration, and allowed them to reach untold millions of people—were fostered by the Internet. Interestingly, though I have not said a great deal about this up until now, founders did not just use the Internet to reach people. For many founders of this era, the Internet substituted for the brick and mortar buildings that previously had indicated that a group was real. For the first time ever, a person with a little bit of money could start an interest group with nothing but a website. Thus, not only did the Internet help to spur the group founding decision; it drove down the cost of starting a new group. Given that most of the groups in the population were founded on small budgets, this is an important development.

The quantitative data suggest that legitimation pressures had more or less disappeared by the beginning of this period. The formation and success of transgender rights groups probably continued to signal to potential founders that a transgender rights interest group could indeed be a going concern. In addition, as in the previous period, this period was characterized by substantial LGB and AIDS group activity. Many founders came from LGB and AIDS groups, which numbered in the hundreds by the 1990s, and had been active for a decade or more before. Five founders reported LGB group experience. As for collective identity, the term "transgender" was gradually replacing the outdated term "transsexual," and a transgender collective identity was developing. Three of five sample founders who founded groups during this period reported that collective identity played a role in founding.

The political world probably did not contribute a great deal to group formation during this period. Public opinion began trending in a conservative direction in the mid-1990s, and the federal government continued to pay virtually no attention to transgender rights.

Two other points deserve mention. First, by 1998, the specter of competition had begun to rear its head. Specifically, the data indicate that one nationally active group died in 1997, and four died in 1998. This took away a substantial chunk of the population very quickly. Legitimation pressures had subsided, but there is some evidence that competition was beginning to be a factor in the size of the population. One group died in 2001, one died in 2005, and one died in 2007. This is not a high death rate, but coupled with the four deaths in 1998, this is seven dead groups in ten years. Second, for the first time, patrons became important for transgender rights interest-group formation. Of the six sample founders who received patronage, four of them started their groups during this period. The other two founded their groups in the next period.

Stability and Obama: 2009–Present

The period since 2009 has been a strong one for national transgender rights interest-group formation, as fifteen new groups were founded between 2009 and 2016. As always, need clearly was a factor. All of the sample founders who started their groups during this period, just like all of the sample founders who founded their groups during all the other periods, cited need as a factor in their decisions. In addition, interactions and connections were easier and more prevalent than ever, largely due to the explosion of the Internet. Eleven of fifteen sample founders reported substantial Internet contact with transgender people and/or allies before group founding. This, along with the continued vigor of the LGB and LGBT movements, led to a large pool of potential transgender rights group founders.

Three additional factors stand out as important during this period—the presidency of Barack Obama, the rise of experience in the transgender rights movement, and the rise of transgender rights interest-group patrons. Several respondents, as I note in chapter 6, cited the presidency of Barack Obama as important in their decisions to start groups. Obama's presidency pumped energy into the system, and it also signaled that for the first time, the federal government was somewhat open to the claims of transgender rights interest groups. President Obama is the first president in American history to pay any positive attention to transgender rights issues. Three sample founders who started their groups after 2008 reported that the presidency of Barack Obama contributed to their decisions. Second, for the first time, a group of founders reported gaining experience in the transgender movement itself before founding their groups. A large proportion of my founders, probably all of them, had some contact with at least one transgender organization of some kind before founding their groups. But based on interview data and archival sources, I concluded that six of my founders had very extensive experience in other transgender rights groups before founding their own. Of these six, four founded their groups after 2008. Thus, during this period, other transgender rights groups themselves became important settings in which new leaders were inspired and encouraged and trained to become group founders. Finally, patronage remained a factor in new group formation. Two of the six sample founders who received patronage started their groups during this period.

There is not much evidence in the data that competitive pressures depressed foundings after 2008. The fact that density has remained stable since 2008 in the population of national groups owes much more to an increased death rate than to a depressed founding rate. Since 2008, eleven of the groups listed in table 2.1 have died. This is almost half of all group deaths. To put this number in perspective, only three groups died in the previous period. While competitive pressures did not appear to depress the founding rate much during this period, there is some evidence that they might have led to resource partitioning, in which many new groups founded during this period tended to specialize rather than to focus broadly.

Why Does the Universe of Transgender Rights Interest Groups in the United States Today Look the Way It Does?

Before I address this question, I need to answer one more: Just how does the universe of transgender rights interest groups look today? This is a broad question, but several characteristics of the transgender rights interest-group population are apparent at this point.

First, the population is small. There are approximately twenty nationally active transgender rights interest groups, and there have been about this many for the last five to seven years. The population of state, local, and regional transgender interest groups probably stands at around a few hundred. These are not huge numbers. In contrast, it is safe to say that the universe of nationally active LGB groups is probably five times as big as that of nationally active transgender rights groups, and the universe of subnational LGB groups is probably several times larger as well. Other populations of groups, including the populations of civil rights groups, and environmental groups, are also larger.

Second, the population of nationally active transgender rights interest groups (and probably the population of subnational groups as well) does not hold a truly massive organizational player. The groups themselves that comprise the population, like the population, are quite small. There are some groups with six-digit budgets, such as the National Center for Transgender Equality and the Transgender Law Center, but the population does not hold a colossal organization such as the National Rifle Association or the National Wildlife Federation.

Third, the population of nationally active transgender rights interest groups does not appear to be growing at this point. The population has stayed about the same size for the last seven years. It is impossible, unfortunately, to say whether or not the population of subnational groups is growing.

Fourth, the population of nationally active transgender rights interest groups has, of late, gained several new "niche" entrants. As I note in chapter 7, several new and interesting group entrants into the transgender rights group population have been niche groups—groups that focus not on the needs of the transgender community as a whole, but rather on the needs of some subset of the larger transgender community. For example, the Trans Women of Color Collective (2013), Brown Boi Project (2010), Black Trans Advocacy (2009), and TransLatin@ Coalition (2009) focus on the needs of racial and ethnic minority transgender people. Trans Student Educational Resources (2011) focuses on the needs of transgender students, Trans Athlete (2013) focuses on the needs of transgender athletes, and the Trans Justice Founding Project (2012) exists to fund other transgender groups.

What explains the characteristics of the population of nationally active transgender rights interest groups today?

The Population Is Small Because Most Citizen-Group Populations Are Small

The data provide us with some straightforward and obvious answers to this question. First, as many of my founders pointed out, there simply are not that many transgender people in the United States. Estimates vary, but one respondent who is in a very good position to know but did not want to be quoted, cited a figure of around one million, which is well under 1 percent of the American population. Second, again as many founders pointed out, transgender people are not particularly affluent. It is tempting to conclude that these two facts explain why the population of transgender rights groups is so much smaller than, for example, the population of environmental groups or LGBT groups.

But this is not an adequate explanation. In fact, the only reasonable way to finish the sentence "The population is small because . . ." is "almost all populations of citizen groups are small." In other words, the population of transgender rights interest groups is small because populations of citizen groups are almost all invariably quite small. There are exceptions, of course. For instance, there are several hundred nationally active environmental groups in the United States, and (as I mention above), around one hundred nationally active LGB and LGBT groups. But it does not take much work to find that there are not large numbers of "gun-rights" groups (despite the presence of the NRA), "prochoice" or "prolife" groups (again, despite some pretty big groups such as National Right to Life and NARAL Pro-Choice America), consumer groups, civil-rights groups, taxpayer groups, retired-people groups (despite the presence of the massive AARP). Most citizen group populations are quite small, even if they have one or more "big players." The fact is that the population of transgender rights interest groups is not that much smaller than the populations of many other types of citizen groups.

The Population Does Not Have a Truly Massive Organizational Player Because Transgender People Are Not Numerous, and They Do Not Have a Lot of Money

In sum, the population of nationally active transgender rights interest groups is not particularly small compared to most other populations of citizen groups. There are lots of LGB and LGBT groups and environmental groups, but on a huge range of other issues including abortion, consumer protections, guns, immigration, taxes, and women's rights, there are not huge numbers of active groups. Thus, what appears to set the transgender rights interest-group population apart from other populations of citizen groups is not its small size, but rather it is its lack of a truly large organizational player such as AARP (over $2 billion in assets) or NRA (over $200 million in assets) or even National Right to Life (over $4 million in assets).

This is probably where the small number of transgender people and the relative lack of affluence among them come in. It may not take a lot of resources to start a transgender rights interest group, but by definition it takes a lot of resources to make a transgender rights interest group resource-rich. Again, as my respondents pointed out, there are not huge numbers of transgender people in the United States, and as a group, transgender people are not affluent.

The Population Is Not Growing Because the Population Has Reached Its Carrying Capacity

The population of nationally active transgender rights groups in the United States does not appear to be growing because it has reached its proverbial carrying capacity. The ESA model of interest-group population density and the general model of density dependence hold that populations of interest groups have limited carrying capacities. That is to say, interest-group populations are self-limiting. At some point, an interest-group population gets so large that competitive pressures dampen birth rates and increase death rates. It appears that the population of nationally active transgender rights groups (again it is hard to say with subnational groups) has reached this point. The statistical models I estimate in chapter 6 clearly show that density has reached a point at which new groups are being founded at a relatively low rate.

However, with this version of events seemingly flies in the face of my earlier findings about how little money it costs to start a new transgender rights interest group. After all, ESA theory and density-dependence theory hold that it is competition among groups for resources that depresses founding rates late in a population's history. So if it does not take very many resources to start a new transgender rights interest group, why would competitive pressures stop a budding founder from starting a new group? After all, if all he/she needs is her/his own resources to start a group, it does not matter that resources are being soaked up by extant groups. So do my findings about how few resources it takes to start a transgender rights interest group contradict the basic logic of ESA theory and density-dependence theory? Not necessarily. On the basis of my qualitative data, I have reached the following two conclusions about density-dependent population growth.

"Need" and New Groups

First, late in a population's history when the population has reached a certain size (that is, at or near its carrying capacity), it is not necessarily resource competition that dampens founding rates, but rather it is another form of competition that I will call representational competition. When the population of transgender rights groups was very small—say, in the mid-1980s—a person interested in founding a new group could look around and see that there were not very many other groups in the population. In doing this, her/his decision to start a group would be affirmed. His/her logic was: "I should follow through on my decision to start a group. There are no other groups out there doing what I want to do." In contrast, a person who wanted to start a new, generalist transgender rights interest group today might do some research and reach the opposite conclusion—that starting a new group might not be necessary, as there already are several, well-established, relatively well-resourced groups out there fighting the good fight. That is to say, an environmental scan might cause the budding founder to rethink his/her decision to start a group. The founder would not, however, rethink her/his decision because he/she felt that competition made failure more likely. His/her decision to rethink founding a new group would be based on the notion that a new group simply was not needed.

The theme of "need" recurred throughout my interviews. In sum, virtually every founder told me in one way or another that he/she started her/his group because there was a need for the group. The argument I am making here is that a founder is much less likely to look around and conclude that a new group is needed later in a population's history than he/she is to do so earlier in a population's history. In other words, the "need" for a new group is simply not as great in mature populations as it is newer populations.

Maintenance Concerns

Second, it may be the case that founders are dissuaded from starting new groups late in a population's history because they realize that once they get their groups off the ground, resources for maintenance and development may not be forthcoming. Unfortunately, I do not have data that speak directly to this issue. But I do have data showing that many (especially the most successful) sample founders managed to attract outside resources (that is, resources beyond their own) after they got their groups up and running. It might be the case that group founders in crowded interest-group populations look around and say to themselves, "I may well be able to get this group off the ground, but once I get it started, the resources I will need to grow the group are not available, as they are being soaked up by extant groups." I have no direct evidence that founders in mature interest-group populations think this way, but I think it is quite reasonable to believe that they do, as they are almost universally intelligent people.

We Really Don't Know Why Density Dependence Occurs

Before leaving this topic, I wish to make one more point. Empirically, we know that density-dependent growth occurs in populations of interest groups. The literature showing this to be the case is voluminous. But this literature stops short of explaining precisely *why* founding rates fall late in a population's history. Density-dependence theory predicts that founding rates are density dependent, and it bases this prediction on the *assumption* that competitive pressures kick in late in a population's history. But direct evidence that it is indeed competition that depresses founding rates at a certain point in a population's history is scant. It may well be the case that it is something other than resource competition that causes founding rates to fall at a certain point in a population's history. At this point, all the data tell us for certain is that populations, including the population I study here, tend to have carrying capacities and, as such, reach a point where the founding rate is relatively low. Precisely why this is the case remains an open question that deserves further scrutiny.

The Population Has Recently Gained Many "Niche" Entrants Because the Population Is Mature

As I point out in chapter 7, the recent entry of many "niche" groups into the population of transgender rights interest groups might be due to what scholars call "resource partitioning." In short, there is a great deal of evidence that when resources become somewhat scarce later in a population's history, new population entrants are more narrowly focused than are early entrants. Here, my data suggest that this specialization is not so much a function of individual founders' decisions to focus narrowly to avoid conflict with other older and larger groups, but rather is a function of founders' attempts to navigate the choppy waters of collective identity. For the first thirty-five to forty years of the population's history, transgender rights founders, activists, and groups attempted to draw blurry boundaries between "us" and "them." Their work was successful, my data suggest, in drawing this vague boundary. But the boundary did a much better job of defining who "they" were than it did defining who "we" were. After this boundary took hold (at least in the minds of founders and activists), the more difficult work of trying to figure out who precisely we were began. And this work led many new founders to decide that who wewere was a little narrower than who extant groups *said* we were.

Another dynamic was at work as well. As I point out in chapter 7, interest-group scholar Dana Strolovitch points out that interest groups cannot and do not work on every specific issue that has to do with their broader mission. Instead, they pick and choose which specific issues to focus upon. In the course of doing this, some issues are addressed and others are not. Once a population is firmly entrenched in the organizational landscape, people notice which issues are and are not being addressed. In our case, fifty years after the population of transgender rights groups was born, the organizational form "transgender rights interest group" had become established as legitimate, a number of prominent groups had demonstrated their staying power, and transgender rights issues were being addressed. But some issues were "left behind." In the minds of some of my sample founders—Eli Erlick, Brook Cerda Guzman, and Bamby Salcedo, for example—issues of primary interest to transgender students, and transgender women of color, respectively, were not being sufficiently addressed. As such, "niche" groups were formed.

There have always been "niche" groups in the population of transgender rights interest groups. Groups such as Tony Barreto-Neto's law-enforcement group TOPS (as well as its successor, TCOPS) and FTM International come to mind here. Thus, we cannot make too much of the fact that many latter-day population entrants are "niche" groups. But it is far from coincidental that so many of the most recent entrants to the population focus on the needs of a subset of transgender Americans.

What Can the Rise of Transgender Rights Interest Groups Tell Us about How Oppressed and Marginalized People Can Overcome the Barriers to Collective Action and Form Viable Organizations to Represent Their Interests before Government?

The data I present in this book show that oppressed and marginalized people can indeed overcome the barriers to group formation in particular and collective action generally to form viable organizations. The number of transgender people in the United States is not large. Transgender Americans as a group appear to be less affluent than average. Transgender Americans have been oppressed, persecuted, and subject to violence and discrimination throughout American history. It is not hard to guess what a scholar working in the basic incentive-theory framework might conclude about the probability of transgender Americans successfully overcoming the barriers to collective action and forming a set of interest groups capable of attracting resources and attention and some level of influence in the political system. And though I do not wish to overstate either the power of transgender rights groups or the size of the transgender rights interest-group population, the data show that transgender Americans now have a set of interest groups that represent their interests before government and in the public sphere.

Of course, I am hardly the first person to reach the conclusion that the allegedly substantial barriers to interest-group formation may not be as delimiting as Mancur Olson and subsequent rational-choice theorists might predict. But reiterating that marginalized people are capable of overcoming these barriers is important. More important, however, is understanding *how* marginalized people overcome these barriers. Perhaps the primary lesson of the qualitative data is that connections and interactions are crucial to the process by which people representing marginalized and oppressed people decide to form new interest groups. Oppressed and marginalized people always have an incentive to form interest groups to protect their interests. But the data show that need is not enough. The spark that led to the formation of all the groups whose founders I interviewed for this book was contact with transgender people (and in a few cases, allies). Interaction has manifold effects (which I discuss repeatedly in the chapters preceding this one) on people, and when it occurs, it increases the size of the pool of potential group founders. This is good news for oppressed and marginalized people in one sense, as it is clearly the case that it is easier today than perhaps ever before for groups of marginalized and oppressed people to reach other people like them, due to the Internet. It was not just face-to-face contact that pushed my founders toward group formation; it was *virtual* contact in many cases. Unfortunately, this has a downside—the Internet also makes it easier for the people who would continue to oppress groups of marginalized people to organize. Still, because interaction is so crucial to spurring group-founding decisions, the Internet has revolutionized the process by which new groups come into existence, and today it plays an important role in the process by which groups of oppressed and marginalized people organize for political action.

The data have a few lessons for us about how groups of marginalized people *do not* overcome the barriers to collective action. If my data are reflective of larger trends, founders of groups of marginalized and oppressed people do not necessarily need to mobilize large numbers of members to start new groups. Most of the groups I study here were started by someone (perhaps with the help of a few others) working tirelessly and investing time, effort, and money in group formation. Designing benefit packages and recruiting members is not necessary for group formation. It is certainly possible that mobilizing large numbers of people as members is a superior path to group formation than the path taken by most of the founders I describe here. But it is also possible that the only real alternative to the path described by most of my founders is *nothing*; that is, it may be the case that an alternative approach that relies on member recruitment and large-scale mobilization would not and could not work.

The data also show that patronage is not necessary for group formation. Most of my founders did not receive patronage early on. A few founders, however, did receive patron support at the very beginning, which suggests that the interests of America's patrons of political action do indeed manifest themselves in political organizations. Thus, to some probably small extent, the extent of organizational representation of oppressed and marginalized people is dependent upon the desires and activities of private foundations, the government, and large individual donors.

The data suggest that the larger political environment in which marginalized and oppressed people live is probably less important in group formation than many treatments of group formation posit. To be sure, there is some evidence here that political factors mattered in the formation of transgender rights interest groups. The quantitative data suggest that the presence of Barack Obama in the White House and a more liberal public contributed to transgender rights interest-group formation. And in the qualitative data, government attention to transgender issues was cited by a handful of founders as an important spur to group formation. But in the qualitative data, factors such as these loomed much smaller than other factors, especially need and increased interaction. Moreover, there is some evidence that group formation is far ahead of policy change. I say this because the data show that almost all nationally active transgender rights groups were founded decades before the federal government paid any attention to transgender rights issues.

The data also show that groups of oppressed and marginalized people can benefit from the mobilization of other groups of oppressed and marginalized people. The qualitative data support the conclusion that cross-movement effects are real and substantial. The large numbers of LGB groups that had previously managed to form and survive served as training grounds for transgender activists. Relatively stable and long-standing LGB groups had interests that aligned somewhat closely with those of transgender people, including my sample founders, and they became important training grounds for transgender people interested in political action. We cannot say for certain what might have become of my sample founders had they not had the opportunity to work within extant LGB groups, but the data suggest that these groups played a vital, indirect role in the formation of many transgender rights groups by providing forums for interaction, encouragement, inspiration, more awareness of the problems facing transgender people, and in a few cases even organizational skills.

Finally, my data indicate that the rise of a collective identity among a marginalized and oppressed group of people contributes to group formation. The qualitative data support the notion that the rise of a transgender collective identity led to more group formation. Unfortunately, because there is no quantitative measure of "transgender collective identity," I could not test the effect of the rise of a transgender collective identity on group formation using the quantitative data. But my interview data suggest that as transgender people began to interact with each other extensively starting in the mid-1980s, they began to get a sense that they were indeed a "we." This led several founders to more seriously contemplate founding an interest group. But the data also suggest that the rise of collective identity brings with it serious risks. After determining who they *are not*, groups of oppressed and marginalized people may have trouble determining exactly who they *are*. This may lead to splintering, infighting, and conflict. And it may also lead to the founding of niche groups.

Closing Thought

There was a time when people who studied interest-group formation more or less dismissed the possibility of truly oppressed and marginalized people mobilizing and forming interest groups to protect their interests before government. That time has passed. Today, in both political science and sociology, it is not a question of *if* people can act collectively, it is a question of *how* they find ways to overcome barriers to collective action and form interest groups. Here, I have drawn upon the experiences of the people who have founded transgender rights interest groups in America to illuminate the process by which these groups got off the ground. My respondents' accounts show that many theoretical approaches to explaining interest-group formation are useful, but that no single approach does a satisfactory job. Rather, explaining the creation of transgender rights interest groups requires us to look to various approaches for clues. Indeed, the data reveal that pluralist theories are correct that threats, grievances, and disturbances and the interactions they produce matter, while incentive-theory approaches are correct that entrepreneurship is crucial to new group formation. PE theories are correct that density, area, and energy affect group formation, and POS approaches are correct that the larger political environment matters to some extent. And NSM theories that identify collective identity as crucial to collective action also receive some support here.

My hope is that in these pages, by drawing upon a variety of approaches and testing a variety of predictions about interest-group formation, I have isolated the variables that are most important in explaining how transgender people have gained political representation in America and how other groups of oppressed and marginalized people might do so.

Appendix A

The Questionnaire Protocol

Introduction

Hello, thank you so much for agreeing to talk with me today. I will start by giving you a brief overview of what I am up to here. (Provide overview of project).

Before I begin, I want to make sure it is all right with you that I tape record our conversation. I assure you complete confidentiality and anonymity, unless you explicitly specify otherwise, in keeping with the code of conduct of the American Political Science Association. The results of this interview may be presented in professional papers and in scholarly publications such as books. But again, I will never use either your organization's name or your name unless you explicitly give me permission to do so.

General Questions

1. Please tell me about the founding of [your group]? Can you briefly describe the origins of this organization? In other words, how did your group come about? Can you tell me what motivated you to start the group? (Probes here).
2. Now I would like to explore the "nuts and bolts" of group organizing with you. Thinking back on your experience founding [your group], can you tell me approximately where you got the money to start this group?

a. And precisely how did you go about securing these funds?

b. I would also like to learn about the human resources you utilized to get this group off the ground. Did you have help founding your group? From whom? What did they do? How did you find these people? (Probes here).

c. Approximately how much money did you spend getting your group off the ground? I know you may not remember or may not know a precise amount. Thus, just a broad estimate would be great. (Probes here).

d. Can you tell me what your initial organizing activities actually looked like? What exactly were you doing? (Probes here).

3. Did you ever consider working within an already existing LGB or LGBT or transgender rights group rather than starting your own group? (Probes here).

4. Some scholars argue that the rise of a collective identity is necessary for a group and/or social movement to get up and running. By collective identity I mean a shared recognition among a group of people—in this case transgender people—that they have certain orientations and experiences in common. Another way to put this is that people develop a sense of community. Other scholars do not assign much importance to collective identity in the rise of groups or social movements. Thinking back on your own experience in starting your group, do you believe that a collective identity among transgender people existed when you got started? (Probes here).

5. Over the years, I have spoken with and interviewed many activists who have started groups, and many who have failed. Can you tell me what you think allowed your effort to succeed—that is, what accounts for your success at mobilizing while many others have failed? (Probes here).

6. I would like to learn as much as I can about you background and your experiences. Can you tell me about yourself? (Probes here).

Appendix B

Data and Methods

The Quantitative Data

To create table 2.1 and figures 2.1 and 6.1 and to conduct the quantitative data analyses found in chapter 6, I utilized my first dataset—an aggregation of the life histories of nationally active transgender rights interest groups in the United States founded between 1964 and 2016. I start with 1964 because it is the year that the first nationally active transgender rights interest group in American history—the Erickson Educational Foundation (EEF)—was founded. I stop in 2016 because that is when I began to write this book. As I state in chapter 1, I define the term *transgender rights interest group* as "an interest group whose primary political purpose is to advocate on behalf of transgender people." To be considered *nationally active*, a group must have (or have had) an overtly national orientation rather than a state, local, or regional orientation. This means that a group must engage or have engaged in at least some political activity and/or states/stated clearly in its material and/or public pronouncements that national policy is/was a concern. As I point out in chapter 1, my definition of *transgender rights interest group* excludes from the population under study LGBT groups, broad-based civil rights and/or liberties groups, and organizations that only periodically weigh in on transgender issues.

To build an initial master list of groups in the population, I began with the *Encyclopedia of Associations* (Gale Cengage Research, various years). For each volume of the *Encyclopedia*, I examined the index entries for "transgender" and "transsexual." After making an initial master population list,

I set out to locate groups the *Encyclopedia* might have missed. I embarked upon an extensive data collection odyssey that comprised the following:

1. scouring written histories of transgender politics (these histories were especially useful for identifying pioneers of transgender rights organizing; see, for example, Califia 2003; Feinberg 1996; Meyerowitz 2004; Stryker 2008);
2. scanning multiple websites of interest to transgender people (for example, ABGender.com, caitlynjenner.com, lgbtcenters.org, masstpc.org, and TSroadmap.com);
3. searching the guidestar.org database of nonprofit organizations in the United States;
4. reviewing thousands of scholarly and news articles on transgender issues, politics, and organizations via the expansive Factiva database;
5. locating and analyzing archival materials such as transcripts or oral histories, and ephemera issued by transgender groups, found in repositories and archives throughout the country;[1] and
6. speaking with transgender rights activists and asking them for the names of groups I might have missed.

In all, I went to great lengths to ensure the accuracy of my population list. Gathering population-level data is fraught with problems. But I believe that my list of nationally active US transgender rights interest groups is the most complete and accurate list there is.

Before moving on, I want to explain why my quantitative dataset includes only data on nationally active transgender rights interest groups rather than data on nationally active groups *and* subnationally active groups (that is, groups active at the state, local or regional level). When I began this project, I fully intended to create two master lists of organizations—one of nationally active groups, and another of state and local and regional groups. But it became clear very early on that obtaining an accurate, over-time population list of subnational groups was virtually impossible. The information on numbers of nationally active transgender rights interest groups is spotty but serviceable, and it enabled me to put together a solid population list of nationally active groups. But over-time records on state and local and regional transgender rights interest groups are more than spotty; for the most part they are nonexistent. I made serious efforts to make a comprehensive list of subnational transgender rights groups (table 2.2 reflects these efforts), but I was not successful. Thus, unfortunately, the primary quantitative dataset under study here does not contain data on subnational groups.

The Qualitative Data

For the bulk of my analyses, I relied upon my second data set—transcripts of interviews with twenty-seven founders of transgender rights interest groups in the United States.

I collected my qualitative data by *elite interviewing*, a "specialized case of interviewing that focuses on a particular type of interviewee" (Marshall and Rossman 2006, 105). Elites are defined as the "influential, prominent, and/or well-informed" people "in an organization or community" and are selected as research subjects "on the basis of their expertise in areas relevant to the research" (Marshall and Rossman 2006, 105). In this case, being an elite meant being a transgender rights interest-group founder—a person who was active in the formation of a transgender rights interest group.

Most practitioners of elite interviewing agree that the best way to ensure that a study's conclusions are accurate is to randomly select interviewees from the population under study. Unfortunately, true random sampling of transgender rights interest-group founders was not an option here, because there is no extant comprehensive list of transgender rights interest-group founders in the United States. As such, my first task was to try to build such a list. To do this, I followed essentially the same steps I followed to gather the names of transgender rights interest groups. Specifically, I searched archival sources, blogs, books, magazine and newspaper articles, organizational websites, and virtually anything else I could find to discover the names of people who started transgender rights interest groups anywhere in the United States. This yielded a list of 119 verifiable founders of transgender rights interest groups. From here, I attempted to locate contact information for each person on the list. I succeeded in finding contact information for 69 of 119 founders. For a variety of reasons, contact information on the other 50 was unavailable (some of these people were deceased, while others were impossible to locate). Next, I sent each of these 69 people an email explaining that I was conducting research on transgender rights activism, and that I was interested in scheduling an interview. If a respondent got back to me and expressed an interest in participating, I scheduled an interview with him or her. One or two days before the interview, I sent the respondent an informed consent form. On the day of the interview, I called the respondent at the designated time, asked if he or she had read the informed consent form and agreed to abide by its stipulations, and proceeded to conduct the interview. In the end, I interviewed twenty-seven founders, which means that 39 percent of the people I contacted agreed to be interviewed. Twenty-four respondents let me record their interviews for later transcription. For the other three, I took notes and transcribed the interview after the fact.

Only three respondents whom I interviewed for this book asked not to be identified by name. I call these respondents Anonymous Respondents Nos. 1, 2, and 3. Table 1.1 contains basic information about the founders I interviewed for this book: a name, the name of the founder's group(s), an indicator of the primary level of government at which the group focuses (or focused), and some other explanatory notes (if necessary).

Why Elite Interviewing?

There are two primary reasons I chose to study transgender rights interest-group formation primarily by using qualitative, interview data. First and most obvious, my interviews enabled me to gather an enormous amount of data about the formation of transgender rights interest groups. My interviews resulted in 417 single-spaced pages (more than 192,000 words) of interview data. These data, I believe, are invaluable for (1) discerning the motivations of the people who start transgender rights interest groups; (2) illuminating the actual processes by which groups are formed; (3) understanding how group founders find the financial and human capital necessary to make groups viable concerns; and (4) illuminating the relationships between founders and their supporters.

Overall, I believed that this approach would yield the most valuable information about transgender rights interest-group formation. One leading proponent of elite interviews notes that they can produce valuable and otherwise unattainable information about "an organization or its relationship to other organizations," and detailed data on things such an organization's "legal and financial structures" (Marshall and Rossman 2006, 105). As political scientist Glenn Beamer puts it, elites—in this case transgender interest-group founders—"may have special insight into the causal processes of politics," and elite interviews yield data that allow "for a richer description of political processes" and that are "reliable and valid data for inferential purposes" (2002, 87). In short, I rely here primarily upon interview data because this allowed me to complement my rough-hewn quantitative data with fine-grained qualitative data. Together, the two types of data can do much more to illuminate the process by which transgender rights interest groups form and survive than any single type of data can do alone.

Threats to Validity and Reliability

Elite interviewing is not without its drawbacks. Paramount here are validity and reliability problems. To try to minimize these problems, I took several concrete steps. First, before each interview, I engaged in advance preparation (Johnson and Reynolds 2005, ch. 10). In practice, this meant spending considerable time first learning about transgender politics, and then learning about each individual respondent and the group(s) he or she founded. My advance preparation work consisted mainly of consulting archival sources, newspaper and magazine articles, blog posts, books, and organization websites. Qualitative methodologists note that advance preparation allows an interviewer to impress respondents with his/her knowledge (thus establishing credibility), to put respondents' answers into context, and to check each respondent's version of events against other competing version (Johnson and Reynolds 2005, ch. 10).

Second, I relied heavily in my interviews on what veteran interest-group scholar and elite interviewer Jeffrey Berry calls "probing." I began all of my interviews with a questionnaire template (see appendix A) comprising a handful of broad, open-ended questions, and then formulated probing follow-up questions from there. In elite interviewing, probing is beneficial because it "allows the researcher to make decisions about what additional questions to ask" as the interview proceeds and allows respondents themselves to "tell the interviewer what's relevant and what's important rather than being restricted by the researchers' preconceived notions about what is important" (Berry 2002, 681). My interviews lasted an average of about sixty-five minutes, though several stretched to several hours.

Third, I protected each respondent's identity. Specifically, before each interview, I told each interviewee that neither his or her name nor the name of his or her organization would be revealed to anyone without permission. In addition, after the rough draft of this book was completed, I allowed each respondent to clarify his or her input. Moreover, during each interview I allowed each respondent to declare any statement "off the record" at any time. All of this was designed to encourage candor among respondents, which is essential to useful elite interviewing (Berry 2002; Goldstein 2002). As I mention above, all but three interviewees waived their right to anonymity. However, seventeen respondents told me at one point or another during my interview that something they were about to say was not for attribution.

Finally, I conducted all the interviews myself to make sure that each respondent was questioned in essentially the same way.

A Few Other Notes on the Interviews

As table 1.1 indicates, I conducted interviews with the founders of subnational groups as well as national groups. Thus, my data speak to the formation of national and subnational transgender rights interest groups. I mention this here because as I state above, my quantitative data come exclusively from national organizations. In chapters 3 through 7, I analyze qualitative data from elite interviews with national *and* subnational transgender rights interest-group founders to test a number of predictions and ideas (drawn from several approaches to the study of interest-group formation) about the motivations, activities, and opinions of the founders of transgender rights groups. None of the hypotheses I test or predictions I examine are jurisdiction specific; in other words, testing and exploring them does not require me to separate national group founders from subnational group founders. Thus, I do not believe that including subnational group founders in the population under study is problematic.

Second, only two of the sixty-nine people I contacted for inclusion in this study actively declined to take part. I did not receive a response from the others I did not interview. In some cases, this might have constituted a rejection, but in others it is possible that my email did not reach its intended recipient.

Is My Sample of Founders Representative?

I cannot say how representative my sample of transgender rights interest-group founders is. However, I interviewed a substantial proportion of all the people who have ever founded transgender rights interest groups in the United States. The number of transgender rights interest groups in the United States has never been large, which means that the population of founders of such groups is also not large. There are at most a few hundred individuals who have founded transgender rights interest groups in the history of the

United States. By interviewing twenty-seven of them, I interviewed a fairly large proportion of this population. I am fairly certain that this is the largest set of interest-group founders that has ever been extensively interviewed about their group-formation activities.

Nonetheless, I cannot pretend that my sample is truly representative. First of all, my sample probably underrepresents people who founded groups that failed early on or never truly got off the ground. This is a type of selection bias. This said, many of the founders listed in table 1.1 *did* found or try to found groups that did not actually take off, so this helps with the selection bias problem. I asked my respondents about the groups that made it, but in probing, I also asked them about efforts that failed. Second, my sample does not contain founders of groups founded before the 1980s, many of whom are either deceased, difficult to locate, or unable (due to health reasons) to talk about their experiences. Finally, there is no way to know if my sample accurately reflects the distribution of founders and groups across the three levels of government—national, state, and local. As I mentioned earlier, I made a conscious effort to talk with founders of groups that operate at all levels of government, but nowhere is there a comprehensive list of groups at all three levels, so it is impossible to say if my sample reflects the proportion of groups that have been founded at each level.

A Word about Data Reporting

In chapters 3 through 7, I occasionally describe and explain major themes that emerged from the interview data. In doing so, I periodically make quantitative assertions. By this, I mean I make statements akin to this hypothetical one: "Fifteen of twenty-seven sample respondents told me that they were ostracized by their families when they decided to start a transgender rights interest group." When I do this, I will not always identify precisely which (in this case) fifteen of the respondents gave me answers that I coded as "family ostracization." As I mention in chapter 1, all but three respondents chose to forgo anonymity and confidentiality. But many respondents, in the course of my interview, gave me statements that they told me they did not want attributed to them by name. Here is a hypothetical example of what I mean by this. Say one of my respondents told me: "After I started my group, my father and mother called and told me they never wanted to speak to me again." Shortly after making this statement, this respondent said: "Please don't quote me on that or share that with anyone." In this case, I would note on a spreadsheet that this respondent cited "family ostracization" in her description of her group formation activities, but I would *not* identify her by name anywhere as one of the fifteen respondents who cited "family ostracization." (Nor, of course, would I reproduce her quote). In other words, I would report these data in *group form* only, protecting the confidentiality and anonymity of respondents when necessary, and then use supportive statements that *were* made for attribution to illustrate the overall theme. I came to the conclusion at the outset of this project that this was the best way to get the most information across without ever coming close to betraying anyone's confidence.

Notes

Chapter 2

1. Determining which groups are truly national, visible, and politically active is very difficult. I say more about this in appendix B. Here, I consider TAO part of this population of groups, but not QLF or STAR.

2. I collected these data for another project. See Nownes (2004).

3. Some radical feminists do not like this term.

4. Activist Dallas Denny shares the view that by the late 1980s, these three groups were virtually the only transgender-rights groups with any national presence. See Denny (2010).

5. Phyllis Randolph Frye is now a municipal court judge in Houston, Texas.

6. All of the budget, income, and staff figures in the chapter come from documents found at guidestar.com.

Chapter 6

1. For more information on Poisson models, see Cameron and Trivedi (1986).

2. This section is essentially an extension of my previous analysis, which can be found in Nownes (2010).

3. I found the latest version of Dr. Stimson's mood dataset at http://kelizabethcoggins.com/mood-policy-agendas. Accessed February 14, 2017.

Chapter 7

1. I am indebted to an anonymous reviewer for pointing this out to me.

Appendix B

1. Among the archives I consulted are the following: the Transgender Archives at the University of Victoria (Canada) at http://www.uvic.ca/transgenderarchives/; the Digital Transgender Archive at https://archive.org/details/digitaltransgenderarchive; and the Transgender Foundation of America's archive of transgender history at http://tfahouston.com/.

References

Adams, Jacqueline. 2003. "The Bitter End: Emotions at a Movement's Conclusion." *Sociological Inquiry* 73 (1): 84–113.

Allen, Morgan. 2015. "The State of Transgender Rights in the United States." *The Hilltop Monitor*, May 8, 2015. https://hilltopmonitor.jewell.edu/the-state-of-transgender-rights-in-the-united-states/.

BambySalcedo.com. n.d. "Bamby Salcedo." Accessed July 21, 2016. http://bambysalcedo.com/#bio.

Barr, Dermot, and John Drury. 2009. "Activist Identity as a Motivational Resource: Dynamics of (Dis)empowerment at the G8 Direct Actions, Gleneagles, 2005." *Social Movement Studies* 8 (3): 243–60.

Batliwala, Srilatha. 2012. *Changing Their World: Concepts and Practices of Women's Movements*, 2nd edition. Toronto: The Association for Women's Rights in Development (AWID).

Beamer, Glenn. 2002. "Elite Interviews and State Politics Research." *State Politics and Policy Quarterly* 2 (1): 86–96.

Beemyn, Genny. 2014. "US History." In *Trans Bodies Trans Selves: A Resource for the Transgender Community*, edited by Laura Erickson-Schroth, 501–36. New York: Oxford University Press.

Bello, Ada. n.d. "Reed Erickson, Pioneering Transgender Activist and Philanthropist." *Outhistory*.org. http://outhistory.org/exhibits/show/erickson/essay.

Beredjick, Camille. 2012. "DSM-V To Rename Gender Identity Disorder 'Gender Dysphoria.'" *The Advocate*, July 23, 2012. http://www.advocate.com/politics/transgender/2012/07/23/dsm-replaces-gender-identity-disorder-gender-dysphoria.

Berry, Jeffrey M. 1977. *Lobbying for the People: The Political Behavior of Public Interest Groups*. Princeton, NJ: Princeton University Press.

———. 2002. "Validity and Reliability Issues in Elite Interviewing." *PS: Political Science and Politics* 35 (4): 679–82.

Bolich, G. G. 2007. *Today's Transgender Realities: Crossdressing in Context*, vol. 2. Raleigh, NC: Pscyhe's Press.

Bosso, Christopher J. 2005. *Environment, Inc.: From Grassroots to Beltway*. Lawrence: University Press of Kansas.

Bourdieu, Pierre. 1979. *La Distinction: Critique Sociale du Jugement*. Paris, France. Les Editions de Minuit.

Boyd, Nan Alamilla. 2005. "What Does Queer Studies Offer Women's Studies? The Problem and Promise of Instability." In *Women's Studies for the Future: Foundations, Interrogations, Politics*, edited by Elizabeth Lapovsky Kennedy and Agatha Beins, 97–108. New Brunswick, JN: Rutgers University Press.

Brader Ted. 2006. *Campaigning for Hearts and Minds: How Emotional Appeals in Political Ads Work*. Chicago: University of Chicago Press.

Brewster, Lee G. 1972. "Queens Liberation." *Drag: The Magazine about the Transvestite* 1 (6): 12. https://archive.org/stream/drag00leeg_0/drag00leeg_0_djvu.txt, p. 12.

———. 1973. "Angela Keyes Douglas." *Drag: The Magazine about the Transvestite* 3 (10): 28–33. https://archive.org/stream/drag310unse/drag310unse_djvu.txt.

Brown Boi Project. n.d. "About Brown Boi Project." Facebook, n.d. https://www.facebook.com/brownboiproject/about/?entry_point=page_nav_about_item&tab=page_info.

Browne, William P. 1988. *Private Interests, Public Policy, and American Agriculture*. Lawrence: University Press of Kansas.

———. 1990. "Organized Interests and Their Issue Niches: A Search for Pluralism in a Policy Domain." *Journal of Politics* 52 (2): 477–509.

Buechler, Steven M. 1995. "New Social Movement Theories." *Sociological Quarterly* 36 (3): 441–64.

Califia, Patrick. 2003. *Sex Changes: Transgender Politics*, San Francisco: Cleis.

Cameron, A. Colin, and Pravin K. Trivedi. 1986. "Econometric Models Based on Count Data: Comparisons and Applications of Some Estimators and Tests." *Journal of Applied Econometrics* 1 (1): 29–53.

Carmichael, Jason T., J. Craig Jenkins, and Robert J. Brulle. 2012. "Building Environmentalism: The Founding of Environmental Movement Organizations in the United States, 1900–2000." *Sociological Quarterly* 53 (3): 422–53.

Cigler, Allan J. 1991. "Interest Groups: A Subfield in Search of an Identity." In *Political Science: Looking to the Future*, vol. 4, edited by William Crotty, 99–135. Evanston, IL: Northwestern University Press.

Cigler, Allan J., and John Mark Hansen. 1983. "Group Formation through Protest: The American Agriculture Movement." In *Interest Group Politics*, edited by Allan J. Cigler and Burdett A. Loomis, 84–109. Washington, DC: Congressional Quarterly Press.

Clark, Peter B., and James Q. Wilson. 1961. "Incentive Systems: A Theory of Organizations." *Administrative Science Quarterly* 6 (2): 129–66.

Clemens, Elisabeth S. 1997. *The People's Lobby: Organizational Innovation and the Rise of Interest Group Politics in the United States, 1890–1925*. Chicago: University of Chicago Press.

Condon, Meghan, and Matthew Holleque. 2013. "Entering Politics: General Self-Efficacy and Voting Behavior among Young People." *Political Psychology* 34 (2): 167–81.

D'Emilio, John. 1983. *Sexual Politics, Sexual Communities: The Making of a Homosexual Minority in the United States, 1940–1970.* Chicago, IL: The University of Chicago Press.

D'Emilio, John, William B. Turner, and Urvashi Vaid, eds. 2000. *Creating Change: Public Policy and Civil Rights*. New York: St. Martins.

Dahir, Mubarak. 2002. "Transgender Breakthrough: People in the United States Have a Surprising Understanding and Acceptance of Transgendered Lives, a Major New Survey Shows." *The Advocate*, October 15, 2002.

Dahl, Robert A. 1956. *A Preface to Democratic Theory*. Chicago: University of Chicago Press.

———. 1961. *Who Governs? Democracy and Power in an American City*. New Haven, CT: Yale University Press.

Davies, James C. 1962. "Toward a Theory of Revolution." *American Sociological Review* 27 (1): 5–19.

Della Porta, Donatella, and Mario Diani. 2016. *Social Movements: An Introduction*, 2nd edition. Malden, MA: Blackwell.

Denny, Dallas. 1996. "Vision 2001: A Gender Odyssey—Part III." *AEGIS News*, August 1996. https://www.digitaltransgenderarchive.net/downloads/kk91fk54w.

———. 2001. "Consumer Relations: WPATH's Evolving Relations with Those It Serves." *DallasDenny.com*, November 3, 2001. http://dallasdenny.com/Chrysalis/2011/11/03/consumer-relations/.

———. 2006. "Transgender Communities of the United States in the Late Twentieth Centuries." In *Transgender Rights*, edited by Paisley Currah, Richard M. Juang, and Shannon P. Minter, 171–91. Minneapolis: University of Minnesota Press.

———. 2009. "Deceit and Betrayal at IFGE." *DallasDenny.com*, September 19, 2009. http://dallasdenny.com/Chrysalis/2011/09/19/deceit-and-betrayal-at-ifge/.

———. 2010. "Transgender Education through the Decades." *DallasDenny.com*, August 23, 2010. http://dallasdenny.com/Writing/2013/08/23/transgender-education-across-the-decades-keynote-speech-empire-conference-may-2010/.

———. 2013. "29 Linear Feet!" *DallasDenny.com*, October 12, 2013. http://dallasdenny.com/Chrysalis/2013/10/13/twenty-nine-linear-feet/.

———. 2016. "Transgender Alliance for Community." *DallasDenny.com*, January 1, 2016. http://dallasdenny.com/Writing/2016/01/06/transgender-alliance-for-community/.

Devor, Aaron, and Nicholas Matte. 2007. "Building a Better World for Transpeople: Reed Erickson and the Erickson Educational Foundation." *International Journal of Transgenderism* 10 (1): 47–68.

Devor, Aaron H. 2002. "Reed Erickson (1912–1992): How One Transsexed Man Supported ONE." In *Before Stonewall: Activists for Gay and Lesbian Rights in*

Historical Context, edited by Vern Bullough, 383–92. New York: Haworth Medical Press.

Diani, Mario, and Doug McAdam, eds. 2003. *Social Movements and Networks: Relational Approaches to Collective Action*. Oxford: Oxford University Press.

Dignan, Joe. 2006. "Recalling a San Francisco Stonewall." *Gay City News*, June 29–July 5, 2006. http://gaycitynews.nyc/gcn_526/recallingasanfrancisco.html.

Djupe, Paul A., and Andrew R. Lewis. 2015. "Solidarity and Discord of Pluralism: How the Social Context Affects Interest Group Learning and Belonging." *American Politics Research* 43 (3): 394–424.

Djupe, Paul A., and Christopher Gilbert. 2008. "Politics and Church: Byproduct or Central Mission?" *Journal for the Scientific Study of Religion* 47 (1): 45–62.

Downey, Dennis J., and Deana A. Rohlinger. 2008. "Linking Strategic Choice with Macro-Organizational Dynamics: Strategy and Social Movement Articulation." In *Research in Social Movements, Conflicts and Change*, edited by Patrick G. Coy. Bingley, UK: Emerald Group.

Duberman, Martin B. 1993. *Stonewall*. New York: Dutton Books.

Dusso, Aaron. 2010. "Legislation, Political Context, and Interest Group Behavior." *Political Research Quarterly* 63 (1): 55–67.

Edelman, Murray. 1964. *The Symbolic Uses of Politics*. Urbana: University of Illinois Press.

Ekins, Richard, and Dave King, eds. 2006. *Virginia Prince: Pioneer of Transgendering*. Binghamton, NY: Haworth Medical Press.

Faderman, Lillian, and Stuart Timmons. 2006. *Gay L.A.: A History of Sexual Outlaws, Power Politics, and Lipstick Lesbians*. New York: Basic Books.

Feinberg, Leslie. 1996. *Transgender Warriors: Making History from Joan of Arc to Dennis Rodman*. Boston: Beacon.

Finkel, Steve E. 1985. "Reciprocal Effects of Participation and Political Efficacy: A Panel Analysis." *American Journal of Political Science* 29 (4): 891–913.

Flavin, Patrick, and Michael T. Hartney. 2015. "When Government Subsidizes Its Own: Collective Bargaining Laws as Agents of Political Mobilization." *American Journal of Political Science* 59 (4): 896–911.

Fominaya, Cristina Flesher. 2010. "Collective Identity in Social Movements: Central Concepts and Debates." *Sociology Compass* 4 (6): 393–404.

FORGE. n.d. "Our Mission and Our History." Accessed May 1, 2017. http://forge-forward.org/about/our-mission-and-history/.

Fouratt, Jim. 2015. "Meet My Friend Sylvia Rivera aka Ray . . . in V Own Words." Facebook, October 7, 2015. https://www.facebook.com/notes/jim-fouratt/meet-my-friend-sylvia-riviera-aka-ray-in-v-own-words/10153166830991636/.

Frohlich, Norman, and Joe E. Oppenheimer. 1978. *Modern Political Economy*. Englewood Cliffs, NJ: Prentice-Hall.

Frye, Phyllis. 2001. "History of the International Conference on Transgender Law and Employment Policy, Inc." http://www.transgenderlegal.com/ictlephis1.htm.

Gale Cengage Research and Gale Research Inc. Various Years. *Encyclopedia of Associations.* Detroit: Gale/Cengage.

Gamson, Joshua. 1995. "Must Identity Movements Self-Destruct? A Queer Dilemma." *Social Problems* 42 (3): 390–407.

Gamson, William A. 1991. "Commitment and Agency in Social Movements." *Sociological Forum* 6 (1): 27–50.

Gamson, William A., and David S. Meyer. 1996. "Framing Political Opportunity." In *Comparative Perspectives on Social Movements: Political Opportunities, Mobilizing Structures, and Cultural Framings,* edited by Doug McAdam, John D. McCarthy, and Mayer N. Zald, 275–90. New York: Cambridge University Press.

Gamson, William A., Bruce Fireman, and Steven Rytina. 1982. *Encounters with Unjust Authorities.* Homewood, IL: Dorsey.

Ganz, Marshall. 2000. "Resources and Resourcefulness: Strategic Capacity in the Unionization of California Agriculture, 1959–1966." *American Journal of Sociology* 105 (4): 1003–62.

Gay and Lesbian Alliance against Defamation. n.d. "GLAAD Media Reference Guide—Transgender Issues." Accessed April 14, 2016. http://www.glaad.org/reference/transgender. Italics in original.

Gender Education and Advocacy. 1999. "Announcing GEA: Press Release." http://www.transgenderlegal.com/pb010600.htm.

Gender Education and Media. n.d. "GEM Mission Statement." Accessed March 15, 2016. http://www.genderedmedia.org/gem/mission.shtml.

GLAD. 2014. "Cases: Barreto-Neto v. Town of Hardwick Police Department." http://www.glad.org/work/cases/barreto-neto-v-town-of-hardwick-police-department/.

Godwin, Kenneth, and Robert Cameron Mitchell. 1982. "Rational Models, Collective Goods and Non-electoral Political Behavior." *Western Political Quarterly* 35 (2): 160–81.

Goldstein, Kenneth. 2002. "Getting in the Door: Sampling and Completing Elite Interviews." *PS: Political Science and Politics* 35 (4): 669–72.

Gray, Virginia, and David Lowery. 1993. "Stability and Change in State Interest Group Systems, 1975–1990." *State and Local Government Review* 25 (2): 87–96.

———. 1996a. "A Niche Theory of Interest Representation." *Journal of Politics* 58 (1): 91–111.

———. 1996b. *The Population Ecology of Interest Representation: Lobbying Communities in the American States.* Ann Arbor: University of Michigan Press.

———. 1997. "Life in a Niche: Mortality Anxiety among Organized Interests in the American States." *Political Research Quarterly* 50 (1): 25–47.

———. 1998. "To Lobby Alone or in a Flock: Foraging Behavior among Organized Interests." *American Politics Research* 26 (1): 5–34.

———. 2001. "The Expression of Density Dependence in State Communities of Organized Interests." *American Politics Research* 29 (4): 374–91.

Gray, Virginia, John Cluverius, Jeffrey Harden, Boris Shor, and David Lowery. 2015. "Party Competition, Party Polarization, and the Changing Demand for Lobbying in the American States." *American Politics Research* 43 (2): 175–204.

Green, Jamison. 2004. *Becoming a Visible Man.* Nashville: Vanderbilt University Press.

Gurr, Ted Robert. 1970. *Why Men Rebel.* Princeton: Princeton University Press.

Hadden, Jennifer. 2015. *Networks in Contention: The Divisive Politics of Climate Change.* New York: Cambridge University Press.

Halpin, Darren R. 2010. *Groups, Representation, and Democracy. Between Promise and Practice.* Manchester: Manchester University Press.

Halpin, Darren, and Carsten Daugbjerg. 2015. "Identity as Constraint and Resource in Interest Group Evolution: A Case of Radical Organizational Change." *British Journal of Politics and International Relations* 17 (1): 31–48.

Halpin, Darren, and Grant Jordan. 2009. "Interpreting Environments: Interest Group Response to Population Ecology Pressures." *British Journal of Political Science* 39 (2): 243–65.

Halpin, Darren R., and Herschel F. Thomas III. 2012. "Interest Group Survival: Explaining Sources of Mortality Anxiety." *Interest Groups and Advocacy* 1 (2): 215–38.

Hannan, Michael T., and Glenn R. Carroll. 1995. "Density-Dependent Evolution." In *Organizations in Industry: Strategy, Structure, and Selection*, edited by Glenn R. Carroll and Michael, 115–20. New York: Oxford University Press.

Hannan, Michael T., and John Freeman. 1987. "The Ecology of Organizational Founding: American Labor Unions, 1836–1985." *American Journal of Sociology* 92 (4): 910–43.

———. 1988. "The Ecology of Organizational Mortality: American Labor Unions, 1836–1985." *American Journal of Sociology* 94 (1): 25–52. Hansen, John Mark. 1985. "The Political Economy of Group Membership." *American Political Science Review* 79 (1): 79–96.

———. 1991. *Gaining Access: Congress and the Farm Lobby, 1919–1981.* Chicago: University of Chicago Press.

Hardin, Russell. 1982. *Collective Action.* Baltimore, MD: Resources for the Future.

Heaney, Michael T. 2004. "Outside the Issue Niche: The Multidimensionality of Interest Group Identity." *American Politics Research* 32 (6): 611–51.

———. 2007. "Identity Crisis: How Interest Groups Struggle to Define Themselves in Washington." In *Interest Group Politics*, 7th edition, edited by Allan J. Cigler and Burdett A. Loomis, 279–300. Washington, DC: CQ.

Heaney, Michael T., and James M. Strickland. 2018. "A Network Approach to Interest Group Politics." In *The Oxford Handbook of Political Networks*, edited by Jennifer Nicoll Victor, Alexander H. Montgomery, and Mark Lubell, 433–52. New York: Oxford University Press.

Hetherington, Kevin. 1998. *Expressions of Identity*: Space, Performance, Politics. London: Sage.

Highleyman, Liz. 2008. "Who Was Lou Sullivan?" *Seattle Gay News*, February 22, 2008. http://www.webcitation.org/6cnXAzlHG.

Hojnacki, Marie, David C. Kimball, Frank R. Baumgartner, Jeffrey M. Berry, and Beth L. Leech. 2012. "Studying Organizational Advocacy and Influence: Re-examining Interest Group Research." *Annual Review of Political Science* 15 (1): 379–99.

Holyoke, Thomas T. 2013. "A Dynamic Model of Member Participation in Interest Groups." *Interest Groups and Advocacy* 2 (3): 278–301.

Hunt, Scott A., and Robert D. Benford. 2004. "Collective Identity, Solidarity, and Commitment," In *The Blackwell Companion to Social Movements*, edited by David A. Snow, Sarah A. Soule, and Hanspeter Kriesi, 433–58. Malden, MA: Blackwell.

Intersex Society of North America. n.d. "Our Mission." Accessed January 15, 2016. http://www.isna.org/.

Jackson, Larry R., and William A. Johnson. 1974. *Protest by the Poor*. Lexington, MA: D. C. Heath.

Jenkins, J. Craig. 1983. "Resource Mobilization Theory and the Study of Social Movements." *Annual Review of Sociology* 9: 527–53.

Jenkins, J. Craig, and Charles Perrow. 1977. "Insurgency of the Powerless: Farm Worker Movements (1946–1972)." *American Sociological Review* 42 (2): 248–68.

Jian, Lu, and Chris King-Chi Chan. 2016. "Collective Identity, Framing and Mobilisation of Environmental Protests in Urban China: A Case Study of Qidong's Protest." *China: An International Journal* 14 (2): 102–22.

Johnson, Erik W., and Scott Frickel. 2011. "Ecological Threat and the Founding of U.S. National Environmental Movement Organizations, 1962–1998." *Social Problems* 58 (3): 305–29.

Johnson, Janet Buttolph, and Henry T. Reynolds. 2005. *Political Science Research Methods,* 5th edition. Washington, DC: CQ.

Jordan, Grant, and Darren Halpin. 2004. "Olson Triumphant? Recruitment Strategies and the Growth of a Small Business Organisation." *Political Studies* 52 (3): 431–49.

Jordan Grant, and William Maloney. 1998a. "Manipulating Membership: Supply Side Influences on Group Size." *British Journal of Political Science* 28 (2): 389–409.

———. 1998b. *The Protest Business? Mobilizing Campaign Groups*. Manchester: Manchester University Press.

———. 2006. "'Letting George Do It': Does Olson Explain Low Levels of Participation?" *Journal of Elections, Public Opinion and Parties* 16 (2): 115–39.

Kelly, Caroline, and Sara Breinlinger. 1995. "Identity and Injustice: Exploring Women's Participation in Collective Action." *Journal of Community and Applied Social Psychology* 5 (1): 41–57.

King, David C., and Jack L. Walker. 1992. "The Provision of Benefits by Interest Groups in the United States." *Journal of Politics* 54 (2): 394–426.

Kornhauser, William. 1959. *The Politics of Mass Society*. New York: Free.

Koyama, Emi. n.d. "Guide to Intersex & Trans Terminologies." Accessed November 10, 2016. http://www.survivorproject.org/basic.html.

Lee, Steve. 2016. "Michael Silverman to Step Down as TLDEF's Executive Director." *San Diego LGBT Weekly*, April 5, 2016. http://lgbtweekly.com/2016/04/05/michael-silverman-to-step-down-as-tldefs-executive-director/.

Lichbach, Mark Irving. 1998. *The Rebel's Dilemma*. Ann Arbor: University of Michigan Press.

Lilly, Christiana. 2016. "Kylar Broadus-Trans Advocate of Color." *South Florida Gay News*, March 28, 2016. http://southfloridagaynews.com/Lifestyle/kylar-broadus-trans-activist-of-color.html.

Lou Sullivan Society. n.d. "About Lou Sullivan." Accessed August 1, 2016. http://www.lousullivansociety.org/about-lou-sullivan.html.

Lowery, David, and Holly Brasher. 2004. *Organized Interests and American*. Boston, MA: McGraw-Hill.

Lowery, David, and Virginia Gray. 1995. "The Population Ecology of Gucci Gulch, or the Natural Regulation of Interest Group Numbers in the American States." *American Journal of Political Science* 39 (1): 1–29.

Lowery, David, Virginia Gray, Justin Kirkland, and Jeffrey J. Harden. 2012. "Generalist Interest Organizations and Interest System Density: A Test of the Competitive Exclusion Hypothesis." *Social Science Quarterly* 93 (1): 21–41.

Lowry, Robert C. 1999. "Foundation Patronage toward Citizen Groups and Think Tanks: Who Gets Grants?" *Journal of Politics* 61 (3): 758–76.

Marcus, George E., W. Russell Neuman, and Michael MacKuen. 2000. *Affective Intelligence and Political Judgment*. Chicago: University of Chicago Press.

Marsh, David. 1976. "On Joining Interest Groups: An Empirical Consideration of the Work of Mancur Olson Jr." *British Journal of Political Science* 6 (3): 257–71.

Marshall, Catherine, and Gretchen B. Rossman. 2006. *Designing Qualitative Research*, 4th edition. Thousand Oaks, CA: Sage.

Martin, Isaac William. 2013. *Rich People's Movements: Grassroots Campaigns to Untax the One Percent*. New York: Oxford University Press.

Martino, Mario, with Harriet. 1977. *Emergence: A Transsexual Autobiography*. New York: Crown.

McAdam, Doug. 1995. "'Initiator' and 'Spinoff' Movements: Diffusion Processes in Protest Cycles." In *Repertoires and Cycles of Collective Action*, edited by Mark Traugott, 217–39. Durham, NC: Duke University Press.

McCarthy, John D., and Mayer N. Zald. 1973. *The Trend of Social Movements in America: Professionalization and Resource Mobilization*. Morristown, NJ: General Learning Press.

———. 1977. "Resource Mobilization and Social Movements: A Partial Theory." *American Journal of Sociology* 82 (6): 1212–41.

McFarland, Andrew S. 1976. *Public Interest Lobbies: Decision Making on Energy*. Washington, DC: American Enterprise Institute for Public Policy Research.

———. 1984. *Common Cause: Lobbying in the Public Interest*. Chatham, NJ: Chatham House.

McLaughlin, Jessica. 2015. "Sexual Reassignment Surgery: The Path to Medicare Coverage." *Law Street*, April 18, 2015. http://lawstreetmedia.com/issues/health-science/sexual-reassignment-surgery-effects-medicares-lifted-ban/.

Melucci, Alberto. 1980. "The New Social Movements: A Theoretical Approach." *Social Science Information* 19 (2): 199–226.

———. 1988. "Getting Involved: Identity and Mobilization in Social Movements." *International Social Movement Research* 1: 329–48.

———. 1995. "The Process of Collective Identity." In *Social Movements and Culture*, edited by Hank Johnston and Bert Klandermans, 41–63. Minneapolis: University of Minnesota Press.

———. 1996. *Challenging Codes: Collective Action in the Information Age*. Cambridge: Cambridge University Press.

Meyer, David S., and Debra C. Minkoff. 2004. "Conceptualizing Political Opportunity." *Social Forces* 8 (4): 1457–92.

Meyer, David S., and Douglas R. Imig. 1993. "Political Opportunity and the Rise and Decline of Interest Group Sectors." *Social Science Journal* 30 (3): 253–70.

Meyer, David S., and Nancy Whittier. 1994. "Social Movement Spillover." *Social Problems* 41 (2): 277–98.

Meyerowitz, Joanne. 2002. *How Sex Changed*: A History of Transsexuality in the United States. Cambridge, MA: Harvard University Press.

Minkoff, Debra C. 1994. "From Service Provision to Institutional Advocacy: The Shifting Legitimacy of Organizational Forms." *Social Forces* 72 (4): 943–69.

———. 1995. Org*anizing for Equality: The Evolution of Women's and Racial-Ethnic Organizations in America, 1955–1985*. New Brunswick, NJ: Rutgers University Press.

———. 1997. "The Sequencing of Social Movements." *American Sociological Review* 62 (5): 779–99.

———. 2002. "Macro-Organizational Analysis." In *Methods of Social Movement Research*, edited by Bert Klandermans and Suzanne Staggenborg, 260–85. Minneapolis: University of Minnesota Press.

Minkowitz, Donna. 1994. "Love Hurts." *Village Voice*, April 19, 1994.

Moe, Terry M. 1980. *The Organization of Interests: Incentives and the Internal Dynamics of Political Interest Groups*. Chicago: University of Chicago Press.

Morgan, Robin. 1973. "Lesbianism and Feminism: Synonyms or Contradictions." *The Lesbian Tide* 2 (10/11): 30–34.

Ness, Immanuel. 2015. "Transgender Activism." In *Encyclopedia of American Social Movements*, edited by Immanuel Ness, 1379–82. New York: Routledge.

New York Daily News. 1952. "Ex-GI becomes Blonde Beauty: Operations Transform Bronx Youth." *New York Daily News*, December 1, 1952.

Nothing, Ehn. 1996. "Introduction: Queens against Society." In *Street Transvestite Action Revolutionaries: Survival, Revolt, and Queer Antagonist Struggle*, 3–11. https://untorellipress.noblogs.org/files/2011/12/STAR.pdf.

Nownes, Anthony J. 2004. "The Population Ecology of Interest Group Formation: Mobilizing for Gay and Lesbian Rights in the United States, 1950–98." *British Journal of Political Science* 34 (1): 49–67.

———. 2010. "Density Dependent Dynamics in the Population of Transgender Interest Groups in the United States, 1964–2005." *Social Science Quarterly* 91 (3): 689–703.

Nownes, Anthony J., and Grant Neeley. 1996. "Public Interest Group Entrepreneurship and Theories of Group Mobilization." *Political Research Quarterly* 49 (1): 119–46.

O'Brien, Jodi. 2009. "Transgender Studies." In *Encyclopedia of Gender and Society*, edited by Jodi O'Brien, 848–53. Thousand Oaks, CA: Sage.

Olson, Mancur. 1965. *The Logic of Collective Action: Public Goods and the Theory of Groups*. Cambridge, MA: Harvard University Press.

Online Archive of California. 2006. "Guide to the FTM International Records." http://www.oac.cdlib.org/findaid/ark:/13030/kt2z09q73q/entire_text/.

Pasulka, Nicole. 2015. "Ladies in the Streets: Before Stonewall, Transgender Uprising Changed Lives." *National Public Radio*, May 5, 2015. http://www.npr.org/sections/codeswitch/2015/05/05/404459634/ladies-in-the-streets-before-stonewall-transgender-uprising-changed-lives.

Peña, Susana. 2010. "Gender and Sexuality in Latina/o Miami: Documenting Latina Transsexual Activists." *Gender and History* 22 (3): 755–772.

Polletta, Francesca, and James M. Jasper. 2001. "Collective Identity and Social Movements." *Annual Review of Sociology* 27: 283–305.

Putnam, Robert D. 2001. *Bowling Alone: The Collapse and Revival of American Community*. New York: Simon and Schuster.

Raymond, Janice G. 1979. *The Transsexual Empire: The Making of the She-Male*. Boston: Beacon.

Reckhow, Sarah. 2013. *Follow the Money: How Foundation Dollars Change Public School Politics*. New York: Oxford University Press.

Renaissance Transgender Association. n.d. "Mission Statement." Accessed April 2, 2016. http://www.ren.org/.

Rimmerman, Craig A. 2015. *The Lesbian and Gay Movements: Assimilation or Liberation?* 2nd edition. Boulder, CO: Westview.

Roberts, JoAnn. 2012. "I'm JoAnn Roberts." http://www.cdspub.com/jar.html.

Rosenstone, Steven J., and John Mark Hansen. 1993. *Mobilization, Participation, and Democracy in America*. New York: Macmillan.

Rothenberg, Lawrence S. 1988. "Organizational Maintenance and the Retention Decision in Groups." *American Political Science Review* 82 (4): 1129–52.

Salamon, Lester M. 1995. *Partners in Public Service: Government-Nonprofit Relations in the Modern Welfare State*. Baltimore: Johns Hopkins University Press.

Salisbury, Robert H. 1969. "An Exchange Theory of Interest Groups," *Midwest Journal of Political Science* 13 (1): 1–32.

Schattschneider, E. E. 1960. *The Semisovereign People: A Realist's View of Democracy in America*. Fort Worth: Holt, Rinehart, and Winston.

Schlozman, Kay Lehman, Sidney Verba, and Henry E. Brady. 2012. *The Unheavenly Chorus: Unequal Political Voice and the Broken Promise of American Democracy*. Princeton, New Jersey: Princeton University Press.

Schoenfeld, A. Clay, Robert F. Meier, and Robert J. Griffin. 1979. "Constructing a Social Problem: The Press and the Environment." *Social Problems* 27 (1): 38–61.

Schrock, Douglas, Daphne Holden, and Lori Reid. 2004. "Creating Emotional Resonance: Interpersonal Emotion Work and Motivational Framing in a Transgender Community." *Social Problems* 51 (1): 61–81.

Seel, Benjamin, and Alex Plows. 2000. "Coming Live and Direct: Strategies of Earth First!" In *Direct Action in British Environmentalism*, edited by Benjamin Seel, Matthew Paterson, and Brian Doherty, 112–32. London: Routledge.

Shibuyama, Loni. 2011. "Finding Aid to the Reed L. Erickson Papers, Coll2010.001." *One National Gay and Lesbian Archives*, June 2. http://www.onearchives.org/uploads/collections/2010–001_erickson.pdf.

Simcock, Bradford L. 1979. "Developmental Aspects of Antipollution Protest in Japan." *Research in Social Movements, Conflicts, and Change* 2: 83–104.

Skocpol, Theda. 2004. *Diminished Democracy: From Membership to Management in American Civil Life*. Norman: University of Oklahoma Press.

Skocpol, Theda, and Vanessa Williamson. 2013. *The Tea Party and the Remaking of Republican Conservatism*. New York: Oxford University Press.

Smelser, Neil J. 1962. *Theory of Collective Behavior.* New York: Free.

Smith, Miriam. 2014. "Introduction: Theories of Group and Movement Organizing." In *Group Politics and Social Movements in Canada*, 2nd edition, edited by Miriam Smith, xi–xx. Toronto: University of Toronto Press.

Smith, Raymond A., and Donald Haider-Markel. 2002. *Gay and Lesbian Americans and Political Participation: A Reference Handbook*. Santa Barbara: ABC-CLIO.

Snow, David. 2001. "Collective Identity and Expressive Forms." University of California, Irvine eScholarship. http://repositories.cdlib.org/csd/01-07.

Soule, Sarah A. 2013. "Bringing Organizational Studies Back into Social Movement Scholarship." In *The Future of Social Movement Research: Dynamics, Mechanisms, and Processes*, edited by Jacquelien van Stekelenburg, Conny Roggeband, and Bert Klandermans, 107–24. Minneapolis: University of Minnesota Press.

Soule, Sarah A., and Brayden G. King. 2008. "Competition and Resource Partitioning in Three Social Movement Industries." *American Journal of Sociology* 113 (6): 1568–1610.

Spade, Dean. 2016. "About." http://www.deanspade.net/about/.

Spargo, Tamsin. 1999. *Foucault and Queer Theory*. New York: Totem Books.

Stretesky, Paul, Sheila Huss, Michael J. Lynch, Sammy Zahran, and Bob Childs. 2011. "The Founding of Environmental Justice Organizations Across US Counties during the 1990s and 2000s: Civil Rights and Environmental Cross-Movement Effects." *Social Problems* 58 (3): 330–60.

Strolovitch, Dara Z. 2007. *Affirmative Advocacy: Race, Class, and Gender in Interest Group Politics*. Chicago: University of Chicago Press.

Stryker, Susan. 2008. *Transgender History*. Berkeley: Seal.

———. n.d. "About Lou Sullivan." Lou Sullivan Society. https://www.lousullivan society.org/about-lou-sullivan.html.

Survivor Project. n.d. "Survivor Project." Accessed July 13, 2016. http://www.survivor project.org/.

Suzan. 2012. "The Transsexual Counseling Service and National Transsexual Counseling Unit's Purpose." Womenborntranssexual.com, August 28. https://womenborntranssexual.com/2012/08/29/the-transsexual-counseling-service-and-national-transsexual-counseling-units-purpose/.

Sylvia Rivera Law Project. n.d. "Trans 101." Accessed March 2, 2016. http://srlp.org/resources/trans-101/.

Taormino, Tristan. 2000. "Trouble in Utopia." *The Village Voice*, September 12. http://www.villagevoice.com/news/trouble-in-utopia-6417677.

Tarrow, Sidney G. 1988. "National Politics and Collective Action: Recent Theory and Research in Western Europe and the United States." *Annual Review of Sociology* 14: 421–40.

———. 1989. *Struggle, Politics, and Reform: Collective Action, Social Movements and Cycles of Protest*. Ithaca: Center for International Studies, Cornell University.

———. 2011. *Power in Movement: Social Movements and Contentious Politics*, revised and updated 3rd edition. New York: Cambridge University Press.

TAVA. n.d. "History." Accessed July 24, 2016. http://transveteran.org/about-us/history/.

Taylor, Jami K., and Daniel C. Lewis. 2014. "The Advocacy Coalition Framework and Transgender Inclusion in LGBT Rights Activism." In *Transgender Rights and Politics: Groups, Issue Framing, and Policy Adoption*, edited by Jami K. Taylor and Donald P. Haider-Markel, 108–32. Ann Arbor: University of Michigan Press.

Taylor, Jami K., and Donald P. Haider-Markel, eds. 2014. *Transgender Rights and Politics: Groups, Issue Framing, and Policy Adoption*. Ann Arbor: University of Michigan Press.

Taylor, Verta, and Nancy E. Whittier. 1992. "Collective Identity in Social Movement Communities: Lesbian Feminist Mobilization." In *Frontiers in Social Movement Theory*, edited by Aldon D. Morris and Carol McClurg Mueller, 104–29. New Haven, CT: Yale University Press.

Tilly, Charles, and Sidney Tarrow. 2015. *Contentious Politics*, 2nd edition. New York: Oxford University Press.

Transgender Community of Police and Sheriffs. n.d. "About TCOPS / TCOPS International: The Organization." Accessed November 13, 2015. http://www.tcops-international.org/.

Transgender Law and Policy Institute. n.d. "About TLPI." Accessed March 5, 2015. http://www.transgenderlaw.org/aboutTLPI.htm.

Transgender Law Center. n.d. "National Equality Map." Accessed July 17, 2016. http://transgenderlawcenter.org/equalitymap.

Transgender Legal Defense and Education Fund. n.d. "About TLDEF." Accessed July 21, 2016. http://transgenderlegal.org/page.php?id=2.

TransGriot. 2007. "Why the Transgender Community Hates HRC." TransGriot, October 8, 2007. http://transgriot.blogspot.com/2007/10/why-transgender-community-hates-hrc.html.

Trans People of Color Coalition. n.d. "Trans People of Color Coalition." Accessed April 15, 2016. http://transpoc.org/.

Transexual Menace. 1995. "National Gender Lobbying Day Takes Off." *In Your Face*, Fall 1995. https://www.digitaltransgenderarchive.net/downloads/9019s249g.

Trans Student Educational Resources. n.d. "TSER." Accessed June 13, 2016. http://www.transstudent.org/.

Trans United. n.d. "Mission." Accessed January 23, 2017. http://www.transunited-fund.org/about/#mission.

TransWomen of Color Collective. n.d. "Who We Are." Accessed June 14, 2016. http://www.twocc.us/about/.

TransYouth Family Allies. 2017. "About." *Facebook*, January 24, 2017. https://www.facebook.com/imatyfa/about/?ref=page_internal.

Tri-Ess. n.d. "What Is Tri-Ess?" Accessed March 28, 2016. http://www.tri-ess.org/docs/whatis.html.

TrueChild. n.d. "Who We Are, What We Do." Accessed July 17, 2016. http://truechild.org/whoweare.

Truman, David B. 1951. *The Governmental Process: Political Interests and Public Opinion*. New York: Alfred A. Knopf.

Valentine, David. 2007. *Imagining Transgender: An Ethnography of a Category*. Durham: Duke University Press.

Valentino, Nicholas, Ted Brader, Eric W. Groenendyk, Krysha Gregorowicz, and Vincent L. Hutchings. 2011. "Election Night's Alright for Fighting: The Role of Emotions in Political Participation." *Journal of Politics* 73 (1): 156–70.

Valentino, Nicholas A., Krysha Gregorowicz, and Eric W. Groenendyk. 2009. "Efficacy, Emotions, and the Habit of Participation." *Political Behavior* 31 (3): 307–30.

Verba, Sidney, Kay Lehman Schlozman, and Henry E. Brady. 1995. *Voice and Equality: Civic Voluntarism in American Politics*. Cambridge, MA: Harvard University Press.

Vogel, David. 1989. *Fluctuating Fortunes: The Political Power of Business in America.* New York: Basic Books.

Walker, Jack L. 1983. "The Origins and Maintenance of Interest Groups in America." *American Political Science Review* 77 (2): 390–406.

———. 1991. *Mobilizing Interest Groups in America: Patrons, Professions, and Social Movements.* Ann Arbor: University of Michigan Press.

Whittier, Nancy. 1995. *Feminist Generations: The Persistence of the Radical Women's Movement.* Philadelphia: Temple University Press.

Wilchins, Riki. 2014. "The Start of Trans Activism, 1994–1995." In *Trans Bodies Trans Selves: A Resource for the Transgender Community,* edited by Laura Erickson-Schroth, 525–27. New York: Oxford University Press.

Wilcox, Clyde. 2009. "Of Movements and Metaphors: The Co-Evolution of the Christian Right and the GOP." In *Evangelicals and Democracy in America,* vol. 2: *Religion and Politics*, edited by Steven Brint and Jean Reith Schroedel, 331–56. New York: Russell Sage Foundation.

Williamson, Vanessa, Theda Skocpol, and John Coggin. 2011. "The Tea Party and the Remaking of Republican Conservatism." *Perspectives on Politics* 9 (1): 25–44.

Wilson, James Q. 1974. *Political Organizations.* New York: Basic Books.

Witko, Christopher. 2009. "The Ecology of Party-Organized Interest Relationships." *Polity* 41 (2): 211–34.

———. 2015. "Case Study Approaches to Studying Organization Survival and Adaptation." In *The Organization Ecology of Interest Communities*, edited by David Lowery, Darren Halpin, and Virginia Gray, 117–35. New York: Palgrave MacMillan.

Xavier, Jessica. 1996. "So You Wanna Be in Politics? A Realistic Assessment of Transgender Political Involvement." *AEGIS News* 4 (7): 1–6. https://www.digitaltransgenderarchive.net/downloads/9z902z89q.

Yang, Guobin. 2000. "Achieving Emotions in Collective Action: Emotional Processes and Movement Mobilization in the 1989 Chinese Student Movement." *The Sociological Quarterly* 41 (4): 593–614.

Young, McGee. 2008a. "From Conservation to Environment: The Sierra Club and the Organizational Politics of Change." *Studies in American Political Development* 22: 183–203.

———. 2008b. "The Political Roots of Small Business Identity." *Polity* 40 (4): 436–63.

———. 2010. *Developing Interests: Organizational Change and the Politics of Advocacy.* Lawrence: University Press of Kansas.

Index

Note: Page numbers in italics indicate figures; those with a *t* indicate tables.